FIRST-CENTURY PALESTINIAN JUDAISM

AN ANNOTATED GUIDE TO WORKS IN ENGLISH

Second Edition, Revised and Expanded

by

David Ray Bourquin

Edited by Michael Burgess

THE BORGO PRESS
An Imprint of Wildside Press

MMVII

Studies in Judaica and the Holocaust
ISSN 0884-6952

Number Six

Library of Congress Cataloging in Publication Data:

Bourquin, David Ray, 1941-
    First-century palestinian Judaism : an annotated guide to works in English /
by David Ray Bourqin ; edited by Michael Burgess. – 2nd ed., rev. and expanded
    p. cm. — (Studies in Judaica and the Holocaust, ISSN 0884-6952 ; no. 6)
    Includes indexes.
    ISBN 0-8095-0401-4. — ISBN 0-8095-1401-X (pbk.)
    1.   Judaism—History—Post-exilic   period,   586   B.C.-210   A.D.—
Bibliography. I. Burgess, Michael, 1948- . II. Series. III. Title.
Z6370.B68 2007   95-5121
016.296/0933—DC20   CIP

Published in the United States of America by
The Borgo Press, an imprint of Wildside Press.

SECOND EDITION

CONTENTS

DEDICATION

To my Mother and Father,
with love and appreciation
for their years of love and sacrifice

and

To the memory of Samuel Sandmel

PREFACE TO THE SECOND EDITION

This presentation of my bibliography is now an annotated and revised edition. The annotations are descriptive rather than evaluative. In each annotation I have given an overview of the contents of the book or periodical article. In many of the book annotations, I have also included some crucial quotations which show the author's point of view or highlight some of his or her conclusions. In addition, I have included a number of additional periodical articles in an attempt to be even more inclusive.

The order of presentation of the material has also been changed. Book and periodical materials have been arranged in separate sections under various subject categories. It seemed important to me to assist the reader with a comparative approach to each subject so that the scholarship of each writer can be evaluated in the light of other scholarly work on the subject. Under each subject category the material is arranged alphabetically by author.

One of the amazing things which became clear to me as I read the material was the enormous amount of scholarly publication concerning a few primary documents. These primary documents are the works of Josephus and Philo, the Bible (including what Christians call the New Testament), the Apocrapha and Pseudepigrapha (especially I and II Maccabees), the Dead Sea Scrolls, the Nag Hammadi texts, the Mishnah and Talmud.

There are several essential things to watch for when evaluating the writings of the scholars on these topics. First, notice the material the author selects and the weight he or she gives to certain parts of the material in terms of its accuracy and importance for deciding the issue under investigation. Next, ask whether the conclusions drawn by the author are really supported by the evidence which has been cited. Does the author build on ideas which have not been proved but which the author is now treating as established fact? Has the author demonstrated the inaccuracy of a certain conclusion or has he just assumed that it must be false? If an author says "it can be assumed," has he shown why this should be the case. These are some examples of the kinds of questions the reader should be continually asking as the books and periodical articles are read.

I want to thank the faculty and administration of the Pfau Library and the California State University, San Bernardino for the Sabbatical which provided the time for me to do the research for this project. I also want to thank the staff of the School of Theology Library at Claremont, the Honnold Library of the Claremont Colleges and especially the Interlibrary Loan staff of the Pfau library for their generous assistance in locating and obtaining for my use many of the materials presented here.

It is my sincere hope that in investigating this topic Jews and Christians will be ever more faithful to their traditions and will be able to grow in understanding, wisdom and appreciation for their own traditions and for the tradition of each other.

—David Ray Bourquin

PREFACE TO THE FIRST EDITION

This book is intended to serve as an introduction to sources for the study of first-century Palestinian Judaism. Contemporary Rabbis will already be familiar with most, if not all, of the Jewish scholars represented here, but may be less familiar with Christian authors on this subject. It has been my experience, however, that many persons engaged in professional Christian ministry are very unfamiliar with this topic, and I hope they will find the book espe-cially useful. I am pleased to note that many Christian seminaries are doing a much better job of educating their students in this area than was the case a few years ago. In addition, I hope that students and informed laymen, both Christian and Jewish, will find this book useful for beginning their exploration of this topic.

Because I have Master's Degrees in religion and in librarian-ship, I have brought my education, interest, and perspective in both fields to this work. The reader should take special note of the in-dexes at the back of the volume. I would especially note the "Index of Periodicals and Serials." This index will allow the user to investi-gate whether any particular library she or he is using contains the journals listed in this index since most librarians arrange their peri-odicals or serials list alphabetically by title.

I have confined the entries in this bibliography to works available in English because of my intention to have the work used by those who wish to be introduced to the subject and are not trained scholars in this field. The reader should also be aware of what might be considered, at first glance, as a serious gap or short coming of the work. There is very little material about the Dead Sea Scrolls or the Qumran community. I have included a few of the basic works on these topics and some bibliographic material for those who wish to study this particular aspect further. The importance of the Scrolls for constructing a picture of the Judaism of this time is, of course, cru-cial. However, because the Scrolls and their importance for this time period have received so much publicity and attention, and because the Essene community was only one group within the Judaism of the time, I felt it was important to emphasize the vast scholarship which deals with Judaism, other than the Essene community, during the first-century in Palestine. There are many sources available to lead the interested person to further study of the Dead Sea Scrolls and I would urge those interested to study this area. I trust this work will lead them to study other areas beyond the Scrolls and the New Testament which they might otherwise neglect.

Finally, I wish to thank the faculty and administration of the California State University, San Bernardino for the Faculty Professional Development Grant given in support of this project. I also wish to thank the administration of the John M. Pfau Library and my colleagues on the Library Retention, Promotion and Tenure Committee for recommending the Library Grant given in support of this project. I also wish to thank the administration of the Pfau Library and my colleagues on the Library Retention, Promotion and Tenure Committee for recommending to the Library Administration that I be granted release time to work on this project.

INTRODUCTION

Jesus was a Jew.

This simple statement would be acknowledged by Christians as true, but there are more things they would want to say about the importance of Jesus for their faith. The problem, as I see it, is that Christian belief does not begin with this simple fact. For example, if you asked most Christians what Jesus said in response to being asked what was the first commandment, they would probably answer that you should love God with all your heart and mind and your neighbor as yourself. This response ignores the fact that in the Markan version, specifically in Mark 12:29, Jesus begins his answer with some of the most important words in Judaism, even in the Judaism of his time. Jesus quotes Deuteronomy 6:4, the Shema, which begins, "Hear, O Israel: the Lord our God, the Lord is One." Jesus indicates that as a first-century Palestinian Jew, these words are so important to him that he points them out as the beginning of his answer concerning which commandment is first.

This is one small example of the ways in which Christians overlook the Jewishness of Jesus and, in the process, lose elements which I believe could lead to a richer and more accurate picture of the message, mission, and person of Jesus.

Given the fact that Jesus was a Jew, what were the religious concepts he learned, accepted, and perhaps adapted, as a first-century Palestinian Jew? This question is a mine field of problems. First, there is great skepticism among many New Testament scholars that we can ever have an accurate picture of the historical Jesus and his teaching. The Gospels were not written with biographical intention, were ultimately compiled by those who held a post-resurrection view of Jesus, and were arranged and collected to serve the purposes of the emerging early Christian church. While some "softening" of this position has occured in recent scholarship, serious questions remain.

The accuracy and completeness of our knowledge of first-century Palestinian Judaism is also being debated, especially when we ask about pre-70 A.D. Judaism, prior to the destruction of the Second Temple. While the Dead Sea Scrolls have added an exceedingly important piece of the puzzle, much of our knowledge of pre-70 A.D. Judaism is based on conclusions drawn from material available in the Mishnah and the Babylonian and Palestinian Talmuds as well as Apocrypha and Pseudepigrapha which were not written during the time under question. The problem becomes even more complex when we ask about the Judaism of areas away from Jerusalem, such as Galilee. Can we really know the nature of what Samuel Sandmel called "Synagogue Judaism" (see Sandmel's *Judaism and Christian Beginnings*, p. 5.). Our knowledge of the historical Jesus and of first-century Palestinian Judaism is not as complete as we would like, though I seem to find less skepticism about our knowledge of the latter.

While there is skepticism, I believe that a study of the sources listed here will bring the reader much rich detail about the Judaism of this period. I am especially interested in having the reader gain not only a knowledge of the period, but an appreciation for elements within Judaism which may have been understood by Christians previously only in a limited and pejorative sense because knowledge of them was based exclusively on the New Testament. I have in mind two areas which need to be reexamined in the thinking of many Christians; namely, the Pharisees and the Law or Torah. I do not pretend to comprehend these areas with the depth of understanding and feeling Jews may have, but these two areas illustrate why Christians need go beyond the New Testament for a fuller understanding of the Judaism of this time.

It may surprise many Christians to know the gratitude with which modern Judaism points to the Pharisees as those who began what has evolved into rabbinic Judaism. (I still must learn how Orthodox, Conservative, Reform, and Reconstructionist Judaism bring their own perspective to this topic.) The Pharisees attempted to apply the holiness of life in the Temple to life outside the Temple. Their interest was in living all life before God and in having holiness brought into every aspect of daily life. With the destruction of the Second Temple in 70 A.D., Judaism was faced with a question of survival and the need to decide in what form it would survive. It was the Pharisees who gave direction and leadership so that the rabbinic traditions were gathered in the Mishnah. The Torah, its study and interrpretation, became the center of Judaism.

The second area to consider is the Law. Much Christian understanding of the Law is based on a Pauline view of the Law or at least a modern caricature of Paul's view. This view leads to understanding the Law as a burden, as the basis for what Christians have viewed as a dry legalism and as the basis for a "works righteous-ness." As the reader works through the sources in this bibliography, I hope he will begin to perceive the Law as understood within Juda-ism; namely, as a great gift from God who has shown what he de-sires from mankind and has given his Law to instruct mankind in holy and joyful living. I do not share the view that Paul is the foun-der of Christianity in opposition to the beliefs of Jesus, but when we take seriously the idea of Jesus as a Jew, I think the Christian's view of the Law will be supplemented and a broader view may be real-ized than the one Paul came to in the midst of a crisis situation wherein the survival of Christianity was at stake.

I have given special attention to Jewish scholarship about this period because I believe it is important for Christians to know the content and the points of view offered through Jewish scholar-ship. The diversity of opinion among Jewish scholars may be both a surprise and a cause for renewed study among Christians who take up this important study. Christian-Jewish relations have often been marked by persecution, animosity, fear and prejudice. It is my pro-found hope that through the study of resources such as those pre-sented here, my fellow Christians will not only know more of first-century Palestinian Judaism, thereby coming to an even greater un-derstanding and appreciation for Jesus, but that they will have a more profound respect and appreciation for Judaism in our time. I hope that a dialogue based on mutual understanding and respect will allow both Jew and Christian to grow in knowledge, appreciation and faithfulness to their respective traditions.

—David Ray Bourquin
Redlands, California

ABOUT THE AUTHOR

DAVID RAY BOURQUIN graduated from Wheaton College in 1963 with a B.A. in Literature. He earned a Master of Divinity degree from United Theological Seminary, Dayton, Ohio, in 1966. In 1967 he received a Master of Theology degree from Princeton Theological Seminary. His Master's in Library Science was earned at the University of Southern California in 1971. He served as a librarian at the University of Redlands for eleven years, and at California State University, San Bernardino for nearly twenty-two years. He retired from academe in 2004, but has continued to do extensive reading and research.

A.

PRIMARY SOURCES

A1. *The Apocrypha and Pseudepigrapha of the Old Testament in English, with introductions and critical and explanatory notes to the several books*, ed. by R. H. Charles. Oxford: Clarendon Press, 1964 (c1913), 2 v.

Though now superseded by the work of James Charlesworth, the *Apocrypha* is still important, if for no other reason than to understand scholarly opinion on this body of literature during the early part of the twentieth century. In his Preface Charles writes: "For students of both the Old and New Testaments the value of the non-Canonical Jewish literature from 200 B.C. to A.D. 100 is practically recognized on every side alike by Jewish and Christian scholars. But hitherto no attempt has been made to issue an edition of this literature as a whole in English. Indeed, such an undertaking would have been all but impossible at an earlier date, seeing that critical editions of some of the Apocrypha and Pseudepigrapha have not been published till within the last few years"—p. iii, Vol. 1. Volume 1 covers the Apocrypha, including fifteen items from 1 Esdras to Additions to Esther. Charles organizes them under the headings, "Historical Books," "Quasi-Historical Books Written with a Moral Purpose," "Wisdom Literature," and "Additions to and Completions of the Canonical Books." Volume 2 covers the Pseudepigrapha from the Book of Jubilees through Fragments of a Zadokite Work. Seventeen items are included in this volume, organized under the headings, "Primitive History Rewritten from the Standpoint of the Law," "Sacred Legends," "Apocalypses," "Psalms," "Ethics and Wisdom Literature," and "History."

A2. *The Apocrypha of the Old Testament. Expanded Edition Containing the Third and Fourth Books of the Maccabees and Psalm 151, Revised Standard Version*, ed. by Bruce Metzger. New York: Oxford University Press, 1977, 340 p.

Recent discoveries and research mean that even this volume has now become somewhat dated. The materials gathered here show us the religious and intellectual environment of the intertestamental period, and set the stage for the period of Judaism covered in the later New Testament.

A3. *The Babylonian Talmud*. Translated into English with notes, glossary and indices, and ed. by Isidore Epstein. London: Soncino Press, 1935-48, 36 v.

Though superseded in our time by the translation of Jacob Neusner, this set is still very important for its additional material. In addition to providing the basic text of the *Talmud*, Epstein has added indices of Biblical references and subjects at the end of each Tractate. "The Foreword and the introductions to the Orders and Tractates deal adequately with the structure of the Talmud, its contents, its redaction, its study and its identification with the life and fate of the people of Israel"—p. xiv, Vol. 1. "Bible, Midrash and Talmud have formed the three main basic categories of Torah discipline"—p. xiv, vol. 1. "The Sacred Scriptures as well as Rabbinic literature in Talmud and Midrash embody a civilization whose influence pervades and explains many of the phenomena of Jewish existence"—p. xv, vol. 1. There are helpful introductions and notes sprinkled throughout the volumes.

A4. *The Dead Sea Scrolls in English*, ed. by Geza Vermes. 3rd ed. Baltimore: Penguin Books, 1987, 320 p.

The third edition contains introductory essays by Vermes which discuss "The Community," "The History of the Community," and "The Religious Ideas of the Community." The documents themselves, forty-two in all, are organized into four categories: "The Rules," "Hymns, Liturgies and Wisdom Poetry," "Bible Interpretation," and "Miscellanea." The book is also enhanced by an interesting bibliography of the "Major Editions of Qumran Manuscripts," and a "General Bibliography." The major, up-to-date English translation of the Qumran non-Biblical material.

A5. *Everyman's Talmud*, ed. by Abraham Cohen. New York: Schocken Books, 1975 (c1949), 403 p.

"The Talmud is a work wherein is deposited the bulk of the literary labors of numerous Jewish scholars over a period of some 700 years, roughly speaking, between 200 BCE and 500 CE. The Talmud is extant in two recensions. What is known as the Palestinian Talmud was composed shortly after 400 CE, whereas the Babylonian Talmud, always referred to as the Talmud, was put into shape about 500 CE. From the point of view of literary form and structure, the Talmud may be described as a commentary upon the Mishnah of R. Judah, the Patriarch, composed about 220 CE. The Mishnah is an epitome of the religious and civil law of the Jews, as it was interpreted, formulated and developed in Palestine up to the beginning of the third century"—p. iii.

"Since the prime purpose of the redactors of the Talmud was to preserve the ancient discussions of the Mishnah, the body of the Talmud assumed the form of a dialogue of the Amoraim, the offical expositors of the law who flourished between 200-500 CE. Interspersed in the commentary are numerous digressions, large and small—ostensibly justified by the principle of the association of ideas—containing copious fragments from a genre of literature known as the Haggada, in contradistinction to the Halakah. The latter embraces two areas of prescribed conduct, one relating to the rules of ritual and religion, the other pertaining to the rights and obligations of men in civil society." "As for the Haggada, it embraces whatever is excluded from the Halakah"—p. iii-iv.

"While there is now no lack of books which regale the English reader with selections from the Talmud, tales from the Talmud, and wise sayings of the Rabbis, there is no work which attempts a comprehensive survey of the doctrine of this important branch of Jewish literature. To supply that want is the task undertaken in the present volume. Its aim is to provide a summary of the teachings of the Talmud on Religion, Ethics, Folk-lore, and Jurisprudence"—p. vii. Materials are organized under such topical headings as: "The Doctrine of God," "God and the Universe," "The Doctrine of Man," "Revelation," "Social Life," "Folk-Lore," and "Jurisprudence."

A6. ***Josephus***, translated and ed. by H. St. J. Thackery, R. Marcus, and Louis H. Feldman. Cambridge: Harvard University Press, 1963-81, 10 v.

Part of the Loeb Classical Library, this set features the Greek original on the left-hand page and the English translation of the text on the right, plus helpful introductions and extensive notes.

A7. ***The Mishnah***, translated by Herbert Danby. London: Oxford University Press, 1938, 844 p.

For years the standard translation, *The Mishnah* will no doubt be replaced by Neusner's translation, but is still of interest. In addition to providing the text itself and many footnotes, Danby provides an introduction on the purpose and character of the Mishnah, its origin and development, its arrangement, its method and language, and something on the history of its interpretation and the various texts and editions of the *Mishnah* up to that date. Of special interest are the appendices, which provide a list of Rabbinical teachers quoted or referred to in the text of the *Mishnah*, and the rules of uncleanness as summarized by Elijah, the Gaon of Wilna.

Danby states: "*The Mishnah* may be defined as a deposit of four centuries of Jewish religious and cultural activity in Palestine, beginning at some uncertain date (possibly during the earlier half of the second century B.C.) and ending with the close of the second century A.D."—p. xiv.

A8. ***The Mishnah: A New Tanslation***, by Jacob Neusner. New Haven: Yale University Press, 1988, 1162 p.

In his Preface Neusner writes: "The purpose of this translantion is to present the *Mishnah* in as close to a literal rendition of the Hebrew as is possible in American English. Since most of the *Mishnah* is expressed in highly patterned and formalized language, this fresh translation will make possible an understanding of the forms and formal character of the first document of Rabbinic Judaism. My students and former students have translated the first of the six divisions, piece by piece. These translations were part of their dissertations or honors theses, read line by line in my seminar at Brown University. I have done the rest"—p. ix.

"I call attention to my translation of the *Mishnah*'s first and closest companion, *Tosefta*, a work of sayings supplementary to the *Mishnah* produced over the two hundred years following A.D. 200, at the time the *Mishnah* appeared. The *Tosefta* is the first commentary to the *Mishnah*, and some of its materials (though not a large proportion) may even go back to the time in which the *Mishnah* itself was taking shape"—p. xi.

A9. ***The Nag Hammadi Library in English***, general editor, James Robinson. Third, completely revised ed. New York: Harper & Row, 1988, 549 p.

In addition providing to a useful introduction by James Robinson and an afterword by Richard Smith on the modern relevance of Gnosticism, this volume also contains the translation of forty-seven items, including: The Gospel of Thomas, The Gospel of Philip, The Prayer of the Apostle Paul, The Gospel of the Egyptians, and the Thought of Norea. Each document also has a helpful introduction, and Robinson has also included a "Table of Tractates in the Coptic Gnostic Library." Though there is a great variety of material here, some translated from Greek and Coptic, the material is still helpful for understanding Gnostic thought. An important background volume for understanding part of the New Testament.

A10. ***Old Testament Pseudepigrapha***, ed. by James H. Charlesworth. Garden City, NY: Doubleday & Co., 1983-85, 2 v.

Volume 1 includes texts of nineteen Apocalypses and eight Testaments. Volume 2 includes Expansions of the "Old Testament" and Legends (thirteen items), Wisdom and Philosophical Literature (five items), Prayers, Psalms and Odes (seven items), and a Supplement with Fragments of Lost Judeo—Hellenistic Works (seven items) and History (six items). Charlesworth provides discerning introductions to each section which provide commentary on the original languages of the documents, dates of composition, the places where each item was composed, the historical significance of the materials, their theological importance, their relation to canonical books, their relation to other Apocryphal works, and their cultural importance.

A11. ***Philo***, with an English translation by Francis H. Colson and G. H. Whitaker. Cambridge: Harvard University Press, 1962 (c1929), 10 v. plus 2 supplements.

Part of the Loeb Classical Library, as with the Josephus volumes the Greek original and English translation are displayed on facing pages. Introductions to each volume and extensive notes in the text help explain each work. Extensive indices are also very useful. Philo's work is essential in the assessment of the views of Hellenistic Jews in the Diaspora.

A12. *The Talmud of Babylonia: An American Translation.* Chico, CA: Scholars Press, 1984- , 36 v.

Jacob Neusner calls his translation of Berakhot in volume one of the set, a conversational translation, and he comments on that type of translation in the following words. "The single significant trait in what follows is the extensive use of square brackets to add to the flow of discourse those sources alluded to but not cited. The translation is richly augmented by understanding not made explicit and by rhetorical shifts and turns in no way indicated in the original Aramaic. To state the theory of translation of this document as simply as I can: Here I propose to talk my way through an account of what the document says—not stated in square brackets but translated into fairly fluent American English—and of what the document means. That is, both what we need to know to make sense of it, and also what we are supposed to conclude on the basis of what the document says and the facts added by me, are supplied"— p. 7. "For the reader who does not know Hebrew or Aramaic at all, we add an enormous quantity of explanatory language, included in square brackets in the text, to make the text readable and accessible in its own terms"—p. 26. When the rabbis from the various schools in Babylonia commented on the laws of the Mishnah, these comments were recorded, and the Babylonian Talmud became more important than the Palestinian or Jerusalem Talmud.

A13. *The Talmud of the Land of Israel*, translated by Jacob Neusner. Chicago: University of Chicago Press, 1982- , 35 v.

Vol. 1 of this set is a translation of Berakhot by Tzvee Zahavy, who has subtitled his volume: "a preliminary translation and explanation." He writes in his preface: "This book makes available the first English translation in the past one hundered years of Berakhot, the opening tractate of the Talmud of the Land of Israel (Yerushalmi, Palestinian Talmud), composed in the Land of Israel at the beginning of the fifth century C.E. I call this translation preliminary because the state of scholarship on Yerushalmi texts is still at an early stage"—p. ix. One of the important contributions of this set can be seen in Zahavy's explanation of his work. "I have added my own brief commentary to my translation of Yerushalmi Berakhot. At the end of each section of Talmud, before turning to the next Mishnah selection, I review and summarize the redactional flow of the material just covered and specify the relationship of the preceding Talmudic units of discourse to the concerns of the relevant Mishnah passage"—p. x-xi. "The theory of the present translation follows that of the series as a whole. I strive to adhere closely to the text so that the reader has a sense of the structure and balance of the original. Yet at the same time I try to convey the flow of the legal arguments and debates, the dramatic unfolding of events in stories, and the sensitivities to words and language in the exegetical texts"—p. xii.

B.

BOOKS

THE DEAD SEA SCROLLS AND QUMRAN

B1.   **Baumgarten, Joseph M.** *Studies in Qumran Law.* Leiden: E. J. Brill, 1977, 209 p.

Section titles include: "Rabbinic Methodology and Qumran," "Purity and the Temple," "The Calendar," and "Jurisprudence." The thirteen papers which make up the volume were written over a twenty-five year period beginning with 1952. Baumgarten says the laws within the scrolls cannot be confined within the framework of Pharisaic-rabbinic *halakha.* "Yet it is more apparent than ever that without careful evaluation against the norms of the halakha as distilled in rabbinic sources, the religious regimen which governed the Essene community will never be fully comprehensible"—p. ix. Baumgarten writes that the Essenes followed the solar calendar present in the Book of Jubilees.

B2.   **Black, Matthew.** *The Scrolls and Christian Origins.* Chico, CA: Scholars Press, 1983 (c1961), 206 p.

In Part One entitled "Historical," Black covers the Essenes, the reports of Greek historians, patristic accounts of Jewish sects, and what he calls sectarian Judaism and the primitive Church. In Part Two, "Religious and Theological," he covers the Qumran community baptismal rites and sacred meal, their concept of the Law, Prophetism, apocalyptic, and their conception of the Messiah. In a last brief section of conclusions, Black compares and contrasts the beliefs of the Essenes with those of Christianity, particlularly in regard to Messiah and salvation. Because so much has happened in Scroll research since the book was published in 1961, this research must be judged in the light more recent findings and research.

B3.   **Black, Matthew, ed.** *The Scrolls and Christianity*. London: Society for Promoting Christian Knowledge, 1969, 132 p.

This edited work contains chapters by such famous scholars as W. F. Albright, R. K. Harrison, F. F. Bruce, and Black himself, and covers such topics as: Qumran and the Essenes, the rites and customs of the Qumaran sect, the teacher of righteousness and the Messiahs, eschatology in the Dead Sea Scrolls, Jesus and the Gospels in the light of the Dead Sea Scrolls, and a final chapter by Black on the Dead Sea Scrolls and Chrisitian origins. In his chapter on Jesus and the Gospels in the light of the Scrolls, F. F. Bruce covers topics having to do with the fulfillment of prophecy, interpretation of the Law, fellowship meal, and Jesus and the teacher of righteousness. Bruce thinks that, although the conceptions of the Servant of Yahweh and the Son of Man do not appear explicitly in the Scrolls, their influence can be discerned in the thought and language of the Qumran community.

B4.   **Bruce, Frederick F.** *Biblical Exegesis in the Qumran Texts*. Grand Rapids: Eerdmans, 1959, 82 p.

Bruce covers the Qumran community, the Zadokite work, Messianic interpretation, Servant of the Lord and Son of Man, the interpretation of Daniel, and Biblical exegesis in the Qumran texts and the New Testament. He lists the commentaries found at Qumran up to 1959 and writes: "...the commentary on the first two chapters of the Book of Habakkuk found in Cave I is succinctly referred to as 1 Q p Hab. From Cave I we also have fragmentary commentaries on Micah, Zephaniah and the Psalms; and from the other caves (especially from cave IV) several more commentaries, of which one on the Psalms, one on Nahum and a few on Isaiah are particularly interesting"—p. 7. In an especially interesting passage, Bruce notes that, "Just as the Qumran commentators at times chose that form of the biblical text which lent itself best to their interpretation, so in the New Testament we note the same sort of thing time after time. For example, the LXX text of Ps. 40:6, 'a body hast thou prepared for me,' lends itself better to the thought of our Lord's incarnation in Heb. 10:5*ff.* than the MT 'ears hast thou dug for me' would have done..."—p. 70.

B5.   **Charlesworth, James H., ed.** *John and Qumran*. London: Geoffrey Chapman Publishers, 1972, 231 p.

Among the most relevant chapters in this anthology are: "The Dead Sea Scrolls and the New Testament" by Raymond Brown, "The Calendar of Qumran and the Passion Narrative in John" by A. Jaubert, and "Qumran, John and Jewish Christianity" by Gilles Quispel. Quispel notes: "All this material must have evolved in part or totally from an independent, Palestinian tradition of the sayings of Jesus, transmitted by Jewish Christians. It is therefore important of ask to what extent the author of the Fourth Gospel used a special tradition of sayings of Jesus, not taken from Mark or other canonical Gospels, but ultimately derived from a Palestinian source..."—p. 139.

B6.   **Cross, Frank M.** *The Ancient Library of Qumran and Modern Biblical studies*. Rev. ed. Garden City, NY: Anchor Books, 1961, 260 p.

Originally the Haskell Lectures of 1956-1957, *The Ancient Library* talks about the original discovery, the Essenes, the Righteous Teacher, the Old Testament at Qumran, and "The Essenes and the Primitive Church." In a Postscript, Cross discusses the Essene faith and the early Christians and their Gospel. In writing about the similarities between the two groups that he thinks he finds, Cross talks about similar language, doctrines, and institutions. He writes: "Both were apocalyptic communities which in their common life attempted to bridge the gap between the Old Age and the New Age. There are, however, distinctions to be made between Essene apocalypticism and New Testament eschatology"—p. 181. Cross notes that one of the major differences in this area is the priestly flavor of Essene apocalypticism.

B7.   **Danielou, Jean.** *The Dead Sea Scrolls and Primitive Christianity*. Baltimore: Helicon Press, 1958, 128 p.

Danielou organizes his book around three areas: namely, 1) what he calls the religious community of Qumran and the evangelical milieu, by which he means a focus on John the Baptist and Jesus and the Zadok priests; 2) Christ and the Teacher of Righteousness; and 3) Early Developments of the Church and the Community of Qumran. In the third section he discusses the Hellenists, the origin of Gnosticism, the fourth Gospel and Qumran, and Ebionism and Essenism. Danielou believes that the early Christians did have contact with the community at Qumran, and he analyzes the similarities and differences between the Christians and the Essenes.

B8. **Driver, Godfrey R.** *The Judean Scrolls: The Problem and a Solution.* New York: Schocken Books, 1966 (c.1965), 624 p.

The problem Driver has in mind is the fact that when the Scrolls were first discovered, they were dated anywhere from the Exile to the Crusades. After looking at the evidence, he concludes, "...the Scrolls will be seen to be closely related to the Jewish Revolt against Rome in A.D. 66-73, and that they are therefore more or less contemporary with the New Testament. Consequently, they are documents of prime importance for the understanding of the New Testament and present a challenge which Christian scholars will neglect at their peril"—p. 6. Among the topics discussed by Driver are: ancient and modern discoveries of ancient manuscripts, the various parties in Judaism in the first century C.E., historical allusions in the Scrolls, the sons of Zadok, the revolt, the history of the scrolls, and the relevance of other ideas in Jewish scriptures.

B9. **Fitzmyer, Joseph A.** *The Dead Sea Scrolls: Major Publications and Tools for Study, with an Addendum.* Missoula, MT: Scholars Press, 1977, 171 p.

This book includes a list of abbreviations used for the Dead Sea Scrolls, a list of the major Scrolls published, a bibliography of various bibliographies of the Scrolls, lists of the Scrolls and fragments, lists of outlines of the Scrolls, and a select bibliography on some topics covered by the Scrolls. There are also lists of writings on such topics as the Qumran Scrolls and the New Testament. A very useful resource for the study of the Scrolls.

B10. **Forkman, Goeran.** *The Limits of the Religious Community: Expulsion from the Religious Community Within the Qumran Sect; Within Rabbinic Judaism, and Within Primitive Christi-anity.* Lund: CWK Gleerup, 1972, 257 p.

Forkman begins with a study of some of the Old Testament conditions which provide important background for this topic, such as the death penalty and the theological motifs connected with expulsion. Under the sections on Qumran, Rabbinic Judaism, and Christianity he examines which deviations led to expulsion, how

23

expulsion was carried out, and the theological motifs which were connected with expulsion. In the section on Christianity he also examines some important texts from the New Testament related to this topic.

B11.   Garnet, Paul. *Salvation and Atonement in the Qumran Scrolls*. Tübingen: Mohr, 1977, 152 p.

Garnet first covers the soteriology of what he calls the emerging Qumran community by examining pre-Essene literature and then the writings of the founder of the community. He then turns to a study of salvation in the "leader and member hymns," and a review of atonement in 1QS, the Damascus Docment, 1QM, and 1QpHAB. Garnet finds a concern for the land of Israel in the Qumran community, and says this is related to the view of atonement. Garnet writes, "Returning to the question with which this study opened, we may now say that our first-hand source for sectarian Judaism of the time of Christ does not seem to provide for the way the gospels have presented the significance of the sufferings of Jesus"—p. 119. He presents one of three conclusions stemming from this idea when he writes: "The thinking of Jesus on the atoning value of suffering and death represents his own original interpretation of the fourth Servant Song"—p. 120.

B12.   Gartner, Bertil. *The Temple and the Community in Qumran and the New Testament: A Comparative Study in the Temple Symbolism of the Qumran Texts and the New Testament*. Cambridge: Cambridge University Press, 1965, 164 p.

After reviewing the Priesthood and the Jerusalem Temple, Gartner studies the temple priests and Qumran. He then looks at the idea of the new temple in several of the Scrolls, and reviews the temple symbolism in the New Testament by reviewing some of Paul's writings, I Peter 2, and Hebrews 12, as well as the Gospels and the idea of the Temple of Christ. A good bibliography is attached. Gartner writes, concerning the understanding of the new temple in the Qumran community: "In a number of the texts we have quoted, the community is represented as the new temple, with two rooms, the 'Holy place,' and the 'Holy of holies'; but this is not all: the life of the community in perfect obedience to the Law is represented as the true sacrifice offered in the new temple"—p. 44.

B13. **Gaster, Theodor H.** *The Dead Sea Scriptures in English Translation, with Introduction and Notes.* 3rd rev. ed. Garden City, NY: Anchor/Doubleday, 1976, 578 p.

In this edition of his translation, Gaster uses the following categories to arrange the Scrolls: the service of God, the praise of God, the mercy of God, glory to God in the highest, the word of God, the triumph of God, virtue, vice, visions and testaments, and destiny. Each section has its own introduction. An appendix has a translation of the copper scroll and the "Prayer of Nabonidus." Each introduction is brief but helpful, and there is an overall Introduction which begins the book. Each chapter introduction is followed by a section of notes which the reader can use for further study. For this third edition, Gaster added "all of the coherent texts published since 1964."

B14. **La Sor, William S.** *Bibliography of the Dead Sea Scrolls, 1948-1957.* Pasadena, CA: The Library, Fuller Theological Seminary, 1958, 92 p.

La Sor organizes the 2,982 entries in this work in three sections. Part One is "General Works," and includes items such as books which offer an overview of Qumran, the date and authenticity of the Scrolls, or the archaeology of Qumran. Part 2, "The Text of Qumran," includes works on the editing of the Scrolls, concordances, and items on the actual Scrolls. Part 3, "Interpretation of the Qumran Literature," includes items on the name and location of Qumran, the history of Qumran, Qumran and the Essenes, and many other items. Materials in several languages are included, and there is an index of authors. Most items mentioned are periodical articles.

B15. **La Sor, William S.** *The Dead Sea Scrolls and the New Testament.* Grand Rapids, MI: William B. Eerdmans Publishing Co., 1972, 281 p.

La Sor discusses his topic in twenty chapters. He begins with a description of some of the sensationalistic claims which have been made about the Scrolls, and then reviews the discovery of the Scrolls, as well as looking at the content of each Scroll translated at that time. Some of the familiar topics covered include: ideas about the Qumran conception of the community of God, the idea of the end time and Messiah, as well as the Teacher of Righteousness. Two topics not often covered in other works on the Scrolls are: "Possible Non-Qumran Sources Concerning Qumran," and "The Epistle to the Hebrews and the Qumran Writings." Of course, comparisons are made concerning Jesus and various conceptions in the Scrolls. In his first appendix section, La Sor discusses the impact or lack thereof of research on the Scrolls as related to the text of the New Testament. He also discusses the difficulty of comparing the ideas of the New Testament and the Scrolls, particularly the miraculous element in the New Testament as La Sor understands it. Among La Sor's conclusions are these: "First, the two bodies of material are essentially different in historical perspectives. Second, the two bodies of material are essentially similar in religious perspectives. Third, it seems reasonable to conclude that the two movements were independent beyond the initial origins in Judaism. Fourth, the Dead Sea Scrolls furnish valuable material for the study of sectarian Judaism"—p. 254.

B16.   Pfeiffer, Charles. *The Dead Sea Scrolls and the Bible.* Grand Rapids, MI: Baker Book House, 1969, 152 p.

In addition to providing the usual information on where the Scrolls were found and something about the community which produced them, Pfeiffer covers the Scrolls in relation to the text of the Old Testament, Biblical interpretation at Qumran, the idea of the Messiah at Qumran, and the relation of Gnosticism to Qumranic literature.

B17.   Rabin, Chaim. *Qumran Studies.* Oxford: Oxford University Press, 1957, 135 p.

Even though an enormous amount of scholarly activity has been accomplished in relation to the Dead Sea Scrolls since 1957, Rabin's book is an example of scholarly writing which attempted to show that the Scrolls did not come from the Essenes but from some other group, in this instance, the Pharisees. He writes: "The broad outline of the theory advanced is that the Qumran community continues the haburah of the first century B.C., an organization within which people could trust each other in matters of tithing of produce, ritual purity of food and other halakhic matters affecting everyday contact between individuals."—p. viii. He ends the book with an unusual chapter on "Islam and the Qumran Sect."

B18. **Ringgren, Helmer.** *The Faith of Qumran: Theology of the Dead Sea Scrolls.* Philadelphia: Fortress Press, 1963, 310 p.

The theological doctrines summarized by Ringgren include God, dualism, angels and demons, man, sin, ethical ideas, and the messiah, among others. A second part of the book covers the organization of the community and cult, and the final section deals with the place of Qumran within the history of religion. The main items available to Ringgren at this time were: The Manual of Discipline, the Damascus Document, several Biblical commentaries, the Genesis Apocryphon, the Thanksgiving Psalms, and the War Scroll. In a final section he reviews the scholarly opinions of the time concerning possible influences on Qumran from groups like the Gnostics or the Samaritans.

B19. **Roth, Cecil.** *The Historical Background of the Dead Sea Scrolls.* New York: Philosophical Library, 1958, 87 p.

Roth first gives a general summary of the religious and political events of the first century CE, and then summarizes the Qumran documents known in 1958, showing how an understanding of the historical background of the time can help the student place these documents in perspective. He depends a great deal on Josephus for his history. He also offers a chronological chart of the history of the Zealots and the Qumran sect.

B20. **Stendahl, Krister, ed.** *The Scrolls and the New Testament.* New York: Harper & Bros., 1957, 308 p.

This edited work contains chapters by very prominent scholars in the field of New Testament studies. Oscar Cullman, W. F. Brownlee, Joseph Fitzmeyer, Nathan Glatzer, and Stendahl himself are some of the contributors. The light the Scrolls may shed on topics such as John the Baptist, the Lord's Supper, the Sermon on the Mount, Paul, and Hillel is explored. The extensive notes at the end of the volume provide further clarification. The sense of excitement at the discovery of the Scrolls was fresh in 1957, and is evident in each essay. The kind of claims made about the Scrolls at the time have subsequently been altered, but the book provides a good look at how the world of scholarship first began to deal with the Scrolls. Stendhal's point that the Pharisees and Sadducees were parties, while the Essenes saw themselves as an eschatological community is still interesting.

B21. Vermes, Geza. *The Dead Sea Scrolls: Qumran in Perspective.* Rev. ed. Philadelphia: Fortress Press, 1981 (c.1977), 240 p.

Vermes covers the authenticity and dating of the Scrolls, the library of Qumran, life and institutions at Qumran, the identity of the community, their history, the religious ideas of the community, and the relation of Qumran to Biblical studies. He points out, "The first essays in the 1950's on the religious outlook of the Qumran sect all suffered from a serious defect in that scholars in those days tended to envisage the Scrolls as self-contained and entitled to independent treatment. Today, with the hindsight of decades of research and a considerably increased, though still incomplete, documentation, it is easier to conceive of the theology of the Community as part of the general doctrinal evolution of ancient Judaism."—p. 163. "Since the key to any understanding of Judaism must be the notion of the Covenant, it may safely be taken as an introduction to Essene religious thought"—p. 163-164.

EARLY CHRISTIANITY

B22. Bagatti, Bellarmino. *The Church From the Circumcision: History and Archaeology of the Judaeo-Christians.* Jerusalem: Franciscan Press, 1971, 398 p.

Bagatti begins by discussing what he calls the Judaeo-Christian churches, including the church of Jerusalem. He then moves to Judaeo-Christian sects and their organization. Other chapter topics include: "The Question of the Law," "Proselytism Among the Jews," and "Christian Synagogues and Sacred Grottos." He then begins a lengthy discourse on what he calls "signs," which express ideas, rather than being visible simply as images. Among these signs are the sign of the cross. Bagatti discusses the archaeological evidence for various signs, including signs relative to the Messiah, signs relative to Christ as "creature," and signs of Jesus as "Saviour." He ends the book with chapters on "The Initiation of the Judaeo-Christians," "The Return of the Sinner," and "Funeral Rites." Bagatti relates the archaeological material to doctrinal texts throughout his work.

B23. Bauer, Walter. *Orthodoxy and Hersey in Earliest Christianity.* Philadelphia: Fortress Press, 1971, 326 p.

The original German edition of this work was published in 1934. Though events and issues after the first century are discussed, there are some items of special interest, namely: "The Old Testament, the Lord, and the Apostles," and Appendix 1 by Georg Strecker, entitled "On the Problem of Jewish Christianity." Strecker writes, "Walter Bauer's opinion that "the Judaists soon became a heresy, rejected with conviction by the gentile Christians," and that the Jewish Christians were "repulsed" by gentile Christianity, needs to be corrected. Not only is there "significant diversity" within the gentile Christian situation, but the same holds true for Jewish Christianity."—p. 285.

B24. Conzelmann, Hans. *A History of Primitive Christianity.* Nashville, TN: Abingdon Press, 1973, 190 p.

Conzelmann focuses on the primitive Christian community and the influence of Paul's thought. He first examines the sources for his study both within and outside the New Testament, and includes a chapter on "Hellenisitic Christianity Before Paul." Throughout his work Conzelmann gives attention to the Jewish Christianity.

B25. Davies, William D. *Christian Origins and Judaism.* Philadelphia: Westminster Press, 1962, 261 p.

This book consists largely of reprints of periodical articles by Davies. He calls for a new quest of the historical Jesus, looks at the Dead Sea Scrolls in relation to Christian origins, examines a passage in Matthew, and compares the Scrolls with Paul's view of flesh and spirit, in addition to other topics. Of special interest is an essay on "Apocalyptic and Pharisaism," where he writes: "In short, the background of Jesus is the rich complex of a Judaism which was liable to a dynamic irruption of the Prophetic tradition, but in which also Apocalyptic and Pharisaic elements were constantly coming to terms and mutually modifying one another." "Fully to appreciate the Jewish background of Jesus is to recognize that the 'Jesus' of Harnack and the 'Christ' of Schweitzer need not be mutually irreconcilable, but can be one and the same Person. It is no accident that the Gospel of 'Christian Rabbinism,' Matthew, is the most eschatological of the Gospels"—p. 30.

B26.   Elliott-Binns, Leonard E. *Galilean Christianity*. London: SCM Press, 1956, 80 p.

The chapter titles in this volume include, among others, "Galilee in the Time of Jesus," "The Galilean Ministry," "The New Centre at Jerusalem," and "The Later History of the Galilean Christians." In describing Galilee at the time of Jesus, Elliott-Binns reviews the land (by which he means fishing and agriculture), the poplulation, and the languages of the area. He lists the beliefs of the Galilean Christians as "a) an emphasis on the teaching of Jesus; b) an undeveloped Christiology; c) an absence of any doctrine of redemption; and d) a desire to maintain close links with Judaism"— p. 48.

B27.   Enslin, Morton S. *Christian Beginnings: Parts I and II*. New York: Harper Torchbooks, 1956 (c.1938), 200 p.

Writing in 1938, Enslin did not have access to discoveries such as the Dead Sea Scrolls, but his understanding of the idea that Christianity was a development from Judaism was an important basis for further scholarly development. In addition to customary topics such as the Maccabean revolt, Greek thought, and John the Baptist, he also includes a chapter entitled, "The Genius of Judaism: Its Literature."

B28.   Foakes-Jackson, Frederick J., and Kirsopp Lake, eds. *The Beginnings of Christianity*. London: Macmillan, 1920-33, 5 v.

The approach of this set is to deal with an examination of the book of Acts, but the first volume is the most relevant for our purposes. There is a discussion of the spirit of Judaism by C. G. Montefiore, and of the varieties of thought and practice in Judaism by the editors. Although somewhat dated, the book is still useful for studying what sources were used by the authors at this time to reconstruct a picture of Judaism in the first century as they understood it.

B29.   Frend, W. H. C. *The Rise of Christianity*. Philadelphia: Fortress Press, 1984, 1042 p.

Of special interest in this volume is Chapter 1, which gives the Jewish background of Christianity, and Chapter 4, which is entitled, "The Christian Synagogue, 70-135." Frend also writes of the pagan background of Christianity, which he says came to Christianity through Hellenistic Judaism.

B30. **Gager, John G.** *Kingdom and Community: The Social World of Early Christianity.* Englewood Cliffs, NJ: Prentice-Hall, 1975, 160 p.

Gager applies sociological and anthropological methods to the study of early Christianity. For example, he uses cognitive dissonance theories to explore missionary activity. While he values the exegetical and theological approaches of previous scholars, he thinks this has presented an incomplete picture. He also covers such subjects as the view of earliest Christianity as a millennarian movement, Christian missions, myth, the canon, orthodoxy and heresy, Roman social order, and the competitors of Christianity. He further explores how Christianity "...was critically determined by the experience of Judaism" (p. 136), and thinks that Christianity's understanding of community favored it over other "cults" of the time.

B31. **Hoffmann, R. Joseph, ed.** *The Origins of Christianity: A Critical Introduction.* Buffalo, NY: Promethus Books, 1985, 326 p.

Rather than write his own introduction to this subject, Hoffmann has selected material from a number of different authors and arranged them for this volume. He has chosen a variety of viewpoints from scholarship that was often groundbreaking and which has remained important. The material is arranged in four parts: "The Religious and Cultural Background," "Intellectual Currents and Themes," "The Gospels," and "The Jesus Tradition: History, Myth, and Legend." Hoffmann includes Jewish writers as well; for example, a piece by Leo Baeck on the Son of Man. Other topics include: the Messiah, the resurrection of the dead, the Pharisees, and many others. The items chosen originally appeared as chapters in books by the various authors. Hoffmann gives information on the position and education of each author and a brief list of some of their publications. An unusual but very interesting approach to its subject.

B32.   Rowland, Christopher. *Christian Origins: An Account of the Setting and Character of the Most Important Messianic Sect of Judaism*. London: SPCK, 1985, 428 p.

Rowland covers Jewish life and thought at the beginning of the Christian era, and the emergence of a Messianic sect. In the Messianic section he covers Jesus and Paul, ending with a section titled "From Messianic Sect to Christian Religion." In examining the controversial issue of whether Jesus claimed to be the Messiah, Rowland writes, "It is inconceivable, in the light of the eschatological character of Jesus' message, that the messianic issue would not have come up either for Jesus or his contemporaries. At the very least, we must say that Jesus' claim to be the agent of the coming of the kingdom of God placed him on the same level as the Messiah of Jewish hope, whose task it was to be the agent of God's reign of righteousness"—p. 182. He also states: "When early Christians wanted to explore the relationship between God and Christ they used two streams, one of which has been explored in some detail in New Testament scholarship, the Wisdom tradition of Judaism, and the other, about which little has been written, the angelmorphic ideas developing in ancient Judaism"—p. 251.

B33.   Russell, David S. *From Early Judaism to Early Church*. Philadelpaia: Fortress Press, 1986, 150 p.

According to Russell, the early church drew from several areas to make the transition from early Judaism; namely, the effect of Hellenism, the fluid nature of what was accepted as Scripture, the development and meaning of Torah, concepts about prayer, angels, the Logos, the Jewish apocalypse, and the ideas surrounding the Messiah and resurrection.

B34.   Theissen, Gerd. *Sociology of Early Palestinian Christianity*. Philadelphia: Fortress Press, 1978, 144 p.

The introduction of self-conscious sociological methods of study to the subject of early Christianity has been one of the more fruitful approaches to this subject in recent times. Theissen analyzes roles, factors, and functions. In terms of roles, he looks at wandering charismatics, sympathizers in local communities, and the Son of Man. The factors he examines are socio-economic, socio-political, socio-cultural, and socio-ecological. Finally, he also constructs a functional outline of the Jesus movement. He analyzes why the Jesus movement failed as a renewal of Judaism within Palestine, and why it succeeded with a different approach outside of Palestine.

B35. Toynbee, Arnold, ed. *The Crucible of Christianity: Judaism, Hellenism, and the Historical Background to the Christian Faith.* New York: World Publishing Company, 1969, 368 p.

Though the information and many of the scholarly judgments in this book are significantly dated, the chapters represent some of the finest scholarship available in 1969. Contributors include David Flusser, Robert Grant, and Cardinal Danielou. A chronological approach is used, with each chapter focusing on a special theme. Toynbee himself begins the book with a section on Palestine under the Seleucids and Romans. Other topics include: Jewish religious parties and sects, Hellenism in Palestine and Syria, the historical context of Jesus and his message, the conflict of the church with the Roman Empire, Greek philosophy and pagan religions as part of the context for the rise of Christianity, and Christianity's eventual break with Judaism. There is a wonderful level of scholarship evident here, making this volume still worthy of consultation.

THE HERODS

B36. Hoehner, Harold W. *Herod Antipas.* Cambridge: Cambridge University Press, 1972, 436 p.

Hoehner looks at Antipas's youth, background, and realm, including geography, population, and economics. He then examines the monarch's reign, and includes sections on Antipas and John the Baptist, as well as the relationship of Antipas and Jesus, using much of the text of Mark for this latter reconstruction.

B37. Jones, Arnold H. *The Herods of Judaea.* Oxford: The Clarendon Press, 1938, 271 p.

Writing in 1938, Jones covers the time from the rise of Herod the Great through the rebellion against Agrippa II. He writes in his introduction, "But the very interest we feel in the origins of Christianity tends to distort our view, and we are prone to assign to the early Christian movement, because of its later importance, a prominence which it did not possess at the time. It has been my deliberate object in writing this book to counteract this very natural propensity and to present the course of events in what is to be best of my judgment its true contemporary perspective"—p. xix.

B38. Minkin, Jacob. *Herod: A Biography.* New York: Macmillan, 1936, 277 p.

Minkin acknowledges dependence on the following sources: the works of Josephus; Ernest Renan's *History of the People of Israel*; A. Hausrath's *History of the New Testament Times*; Emil Schurer's *A History of the Jewish People in the Times of Jesus Christ*; George Adam Smith's *Jerusalem*; F. W. Farrar's *The Herods*; John Vickers's *The History of Herod*; Ludwig Friedlander's *Roman Life and Manners*; Walter Otto's *Herodes*; and Hugo Willrich's *Das Haus des Herodes*. Clearly, this list of sources would need updating for a study of Herod in the 1990's. One must also wonder whether a modern author would regard the available evidence for a life of Herod as sufficient to permit this kind of comment from Minkin: "Herod was the engineer of his life. Every step of his career was planned. There were no surprises. Everything went as though by precise mathematical calculation"—p. 5. His closing comments on Herod contain this remark: "Hero or demon, during his long reign, he was the mastering brain, the grappling will and dominant hand which gave his country an era of uninterrupted peace and prosperity such as it had not known since the days of King Solomon"—p. 263.

B39. Perowne, Stewart. *The Later Herods: The Political Background of the New Testament.* New York: Abingdon Press, 1958, 216 p.

Perowne states that he used Josephus, Tacitus, Suetonius, and Dio Cassius as primary sources for the background information on historical events. The survey runs from Archelaus through the last of the Herods. Chapter 8 is of special interest and is entitled, "John and Jesus—Antipas the Fox." Perowne emphasizes the struggle of the Jews with the foreign powers which sought to dominate them. He writes about the failure of the Herods: "...it is the story of the lives of them and their people, and of Jewish policy, leaning now to Rome, now to nationalism, never reconciling the two irreconcilables, and of the final and inevitable outcome that this book will try to tell"—p. xvi.

B40.   Perowne, Stewart. *The Life and Times of Herod the Great.* New York: Abingdon Press, 1959, 186 p.

This volume devotes a great deal of attention to Herod's involvement with the international politics of his time. Chapter titles include: "Julius Caesar and the Jews," "Herod the King," "Women at War," "Herod and Octavian," "Herod and Mariamme," and several others. Two chapters are given to a discussion of the Temple. A number of photos enhance the text. The authors' assessment (and bias) can be demonstrated with the following remarks: "But the real cause of Herod's failure must be sought in himself. With all his brilliance, all his energy, all his wealth, Herod was ignorant. He was ignorant because he was insensitive. He was blasted with the defect that the Greeks called anaesthesia, lack of perception. He did not realize the spiritual world in which he lived. Herod could hardly have been expected to recognize in the birth of Christ the beginning of a new era, because this, the most important event of his whole life and reign, occurred only a few months before his death"—p. 179-180.

JERUSALEM

B41.   Avigad, Naham. *Discovering Jerusalem.* Nashville, TN: Thomas Nelson, 1983, 270 p.

This book covers the period of the first Temple, the time after its destruction, the period of the second Temple, and the time following *its* destruction, including Byzantine Jerusalem and the Middle Ages. Avigad recounts the results of his archaeological work from 1970-81. The difficulties and challenges of excavating a city so frequently destroyed and rebuilt are recounted. He combines a description of passages in literary sources such as Josephus with a description of how various archaeological digs proceeded and the results they produced. He gives special attention to the Jewish quarter of the city.

B42.   Ben-Dou, M. *In the Shadow of the Temple: The Discovery of Ancient Jerusalem.* New York: Harper & Row, 1985 (c.1982), 384 p.

Ben-Dou describes an archaeological dig at the very foot of the Temple Mount, in an excellent blend of the story of the excavation itself and its results, which proved so important for understanding the history of Jerusalem. The chapter titles show the breadth of the information uncovered: "Remains from the Kingdom of Judah," "The Walls of the Temple Mount," "Daily Life in the Second Temple Period," "Jerusalem Under Christian Rule." The time period covered extends from the Kingdom of Judah through about the 17th century. The many plates and drawings give a marvelous visual sense to the text, and the power of the writing and the breadth of the coverage make this a very useful book for this area of the study of Judaism.

B43.   Brandon, Samuel G. F. *The Fall of Jerusalem and the Christian Church: A Study of the Effects of the Jewish Overthrow of A.D. 70 on Christianity.* 2nd ed. London: S.P.C.K., 1957, 294 p.

In twelve chapters, Brandon covers such topics as: the church in Palestine according to the Synoptic Gospels and other Palestinian sources, Christianity according to the Jerusalem church, the Palestinian church, and the Markan reaction to AD 70. Among the points made by Brandon is the idea that the Jerusalem church had organized successful missionary work among Gentiles outside Palestine, the Jerusalem Christians were devoted to the Temple, the Synoptic Gospels show that some Christian communities in Galilee and Samaria accepted the supremacy of the Jerusalem church, and the primitive Christian movement in Palestine was closely concerned with the cause of Jewish nationalism. Brandon also thinks that Mark's defamatory account of Jesus's family shows he wanted to separate Jesus from his Jewish milieu. The place of origin of the Gospel of Matthew was Alexandria, in Brandon's view. He also concludes that missionary efforts by Jerusalem Christians made the Christian community in Alexandria a stronghold of Jewish Christian teaching, but the destruction of the Temple in 70 CE smashed this Jewish Christian source, and left only Alexandria as the effective representative of the Jewish Christian position. The destruction of the Temple was crucial for Christianity, because it emancipated it from its Jewish cradle, and made it possible for it to become a world religion.

B44.   Gaston, Lloyd. *No Stone on Another: Studies in the Significance of the Fall of Jerusalem in the Synoptic Gospels.* Leiden: E. J. Brill, 1970, 537 p.

Gaston offers an analysis of Mark 13, and then looks at the topics of Jesus and the Temple, including a section on the community as Temple in Qumran. He also discusses "The Fall of Jerusalem as a Political Event in Luke-Acts," and examines the fall of Jerusalem and eschatology. In his last paragraph, Gaston writes, "In conclusion, then, we can see where two tragic mistakes were made in connection with the eschatological expectation of the early church. The first occurred when the threat of judgment on Israel became, under the pressure of persecution, a prediction or even a hope for vengence. The second occurred when Mark expected the end to come in connection with the fall of Jerusalem and this expectation was seen to be fulfilled by Matthew as a judgment against Israel. Very much against his own intention, then, Matthew became one of the principle sources of the persecution of Israel, which has haunted the history of the church down to our own day"—p. 487.

B45. **Jeremias, Joachim.** *Jerusalem in the Time of Jesus.* Philadelphia: Fortress Press, 1975 (c.1969), 434 p.

The first two parts of Jeremias's four-part work deal with the economic conditions of Jerusalem, including industry, commerce, and foreign visitors. Part 3 covers social status, including the clergy (*i.e.*, priests), lay nobiblity, scribes, and Pharisees. The last Part covers "Racial Purity," and deals with Jewish ancestry, Jewish slaves, Gentile slaves, Samaritans, and the social position of women. Jeremias's extensive work is greatly detailed and heavily footnoted for the scholar.

B46. **Kenyon, Kathleen M.** *Digging Up Jerusalem.* London: Ernest Benn, 1974, 288 p.

Kenyon first surveys the first hundred years of archaeological activity in Jerusalem, and then deals with the topography and history of Jerusalem. Having covered the excavation methods used by archeologists and the results gathered from their excavations, she then takes a chronological approach to the history of Jerusalem, beginning with the pre-Israelite settlement, moving to David's Jerusalem, Jerusalem at the time of Solomon, and on through Jerusalem in the time of Herod the Great and in the first century CE. She closes with a chapter on "Byzantine, Moslem, and Crusader Jerusalem." The many plates and drawings make the book exceptionally useful to the scholar and student. Kenyon is one of the premier archeologists in this field, and her theories have always been stimulating in relation to other scholarship.

B47. **Mazar, Benjamin.** *The Mountain of the Lord.* Garden City, NY: Doubleday & Co., 1975, 304 p.

Mazar summarizes in great detail what we know of the history of Jerusalem, especially of the Temple mount and of the First and Second Temples. The text is copiously illustrated with many plates detailing the archaeological investigations of the site. Mazar also looks at the evidence given in the Bible about the Temple, and examines various Hellenistic sources, Josephus, the Temple Scroll from Qumran, and the Mishnah and Talmud. He further delineates the apocalyptic mystique about Jerusalem, and traces the history of that city from the earliest times through the twentieth century.

B48. **Wilkinson, John D.** *Jerusalem as Jesus Knew It: Archaeology as Evidence.* London: Thames and Hudson, 1978, 208 p.

Wilkinson writes, "The aim of the present book is to explore Jesus' relationship with the Jerusalem of his day"—p. 8. He then explores what we can actually know about Jesus's life, and what Jerusalem was like during the first century of the Christian era. At the end of his introduction, he concludes: "Jesus, as an itinerant preacher and healer, is hardly likely to have set up inscriptions or erected monuments. Thus, archaeology is unlikely to provide much which has a direct relationship to him as an individual. But it can shed a good deal of light on the world in which he lived"—p. 12. Wilkinson then provides background information on day-to-day life in early Jerusalem. He writes about Jesus and the Temple, and focuses on events in the last week of Jesus's life. He closes with general comments on the idea of "Holy Places" in Jerusalem. His approach throughout the work is to review the events of Jesus's life in light of what modern-day archaeology can provide about the sites in Jerusalem where these things actually happened.

B49. **Yadin, Yigael, ed.** *Jerusalem Revealed: Archaeology in the Holy City, 1968-1974.* New Haven, CT: Yale University Press, 1976, 139 p.

In this engaging series of essays by many scholars, the ancient city is described in sections discussing the modern excavations, the city's tombs, and its water supply. The medieval city is delineated in essays on the Islamic architecture of Jerusalem, specifically in the area south of Temple mount, as well as the other Muslim sites. The last section focuses on modern Jerusalem, with essays on the reconstruction of the Jewish quarter in the old city, on the four Sephardic synagogues in the old city, and others. Numerous line drawings and photos, mostly in black and white, illustrate the text.

JESUS

B50.   Aulen, Gustaf. *Jesus in Contemporary Historical Research.* Philadelphia: Fortress Press, 1976 (c.1973), 167 p.

Aulen surveys publications issued after 1960, with special attention to the work of C. H. Dodd, Herbert Braun, and Joachim Jeremias. He covers such topics as: Jesus's continuity or discontinuity with Judaism, Jesus's lifestyle, the Kingdom of God, and the earthly Jesus versus faith in Christ. He affirms the validity of research into the historical Jesus, but also says that the researcher must remember "...its picture of Jesus is not and cannot become a total picture, that the church's faith in Christ builds on presuppositions which were not available during Jesus' lifetime, and that these viewpoints must be considered in every encounter between the Jesus depicted in research and the Christ who is the subject of the church's faith"—p. 161.

B51.   Bammel, Ernst, and Charles F. D. Moule, eds. *Jesus and the Politics of His Day.* Cambridge: Cambridge University Press, 1984, 511 p.

Was Jesus a revolutionary? What were his relationships with the political and religious establishments of his day? What was the nature of his trial? What can we gain from the New Testament materials which might be relevant to these questions? Seventeen international scholars review these issues and the relevant New Testament passages to see what answers might be suggested.

B52.   Barrett, Charles K. *Jesus and the Gospel Tradition.* London: S.P.C.K., 1967, 116 p.

Barrett approaches his subject under the three headings of The Tradition, Christ Crucified, and Christ to Come. He states that when a student of the New Testament asks about Jesus, the question involves both history and theology. Consequently, Barrett seeks to answer several questions in his book: "First, what do we really know, as historians, about Jesus? Did he really say this? Did he really do that? And secondly, if our historical knowledge of Jesus is in any way limited or uncertain, how is our theological estimate of him affected?"—p. ix. In a Postscript the author writes: "What did Jesus teach about God? It is an elementary but important starting-point that he knew and accepted the Old Testament conception of God: God was the Lord—one, holy, mighty, and loving. This conception was given new content and force both by Jesus' ethical teaching and by his eschatological teaching"—p. 104.

B53. Braun, Herbert. *Jesus of Nazareth: The Man and His Time.* Philadelphia: Fortress Press, 1979, 142 p.

Braun states that his book is not designed for the specialist. He covers such subjects as: the religious background, the sources, Jesus's life, Jesus's view of the end time, Jesus's authority, cultic matters, religious law, and others. In an Epilogue, he writes: "...from the insight that the Jesus tradition intends to teach a person to understand himself as totally a recipient to the recognition that Jesus does not want to be acknowledged as an external authority in advance; he wins authority through what he has to say as he commands and frees a person. But God is not the basis for this authority of Jesus; he is the expression for the way a person can go in obedience and humility"—p. 137.

B54. Bruce, Frederick F. *Jesus and Christian Origins Outside the New Testament.* Grand Rapids, MI: William B. Eerdmans Publishing Co., 1974, 215 p.

To find out what can be known about Jesus from areas outside the New Testament, Bruce examines Qumran, as well as Jewish, pagan, apocraphal, Islamic, and Gnostic documents. He explains where many of the documents were found, and then delineates their content, even to the level of individual sayings. Using this method, the author shows what new pictures of Jesus would emerge.

B55.   Bultmann, Rudolf. *Jesus and the Word.* New York: Charles Scribner's Sons, 1958 (c1934), 226 p.

Of special interest in Bultmann's work is his section on the historical background of the ministry of Jesus, where he discusses the Jewish religion and the Messianic movements. Also of importance is a chapter on "Jesus as Rabbi."

B56.   Carmignac, Jean. *Christ and the Teacher of Righteousness.* Baltimore, MD: Helicon Press, 1962, 168 p.

In his first chapter, Carmignac asks if Jesus imitated the Teacher of Righteousness. The next two chapters compare Jesus and the Teacher in terms of their person, and then their works and doctrine. The fourth and final chapter is entitled, "The Teacher of Righteousness Self-Revealed." Carmignac chastises those writers who wrote sensationalist articles soon after the discovery of the Scrolls about the supposed similarities between the Essenes and Christianity. Carmignac then begins a careful sorting of the evidence to show the differences between these two groups, as, for example, the differences in the way in which the term Messiah was used. The author's Roman Catholic persuasion can be seen in such statements as: "We have noted that among these parallel practices it is the organization of the two communities, Christian and Essene, which provides the chief similarities. Therefore, it can no longer be considered unlikely that Christ intended to found a visible and hierarchical society"—p. 128.

B57.   Charlesworth, James H. *Jesus Within Judaism.* New York: Doubleday, 1988.

This volume offers an excellent summary of modern-day on research on Jesus. The six chapters include: "Research on the Historical Jesus in the Eighties," "Jesus and the Old Testament Pseudepigrapha," "Jesus and the Dead Sea Scrolls," "Jesus, the Nag Hammadi Codicies, and Josephus," "The Jesus of History and the Archaeology of Palestine," and "Jesus's Concept of God and His Self-Understanding." There are several appendicies which list the documents in the Old Testament Pseudepigrapha, the Apocrypha and Pseudepigrapha in the New Testament, the Nag Hammadi Codices, and the Dead Sea Scrolls. A final appendix lists the results of Jesus research from 1980-1985, and provides a selected and annotated bibliography that offers material for further study.

Charlesworth shows the major shift which has occured in modern scholarship with the new interest in the historical Jesus. In his introduction he contrasts some recent work against the conclusions of Bultmann. For example, he quotes from E. P. Sanders's *Jesus and Judaism*: "The dominant view today seems to be that we can pretty well know what Jesus was out to accomplish, that we can know a lot about what he said, and that those two things make sense within the world of first-century Judaism."

B58.   Cullmann, Oscar. *Jesus and the Revolutionaries.* New York: Harper and Row, 1970, 84 p.

Cullmann examines the revolutionary movements of Jesus's day under headings dealing with the worship, society, and politics of the day. In a concluding section, he writes, "Jesus' attitude to the three problems discussed above demonstrates a remarkable uniformity. It is governed by an eschatological radicalism. This leads on the one side to an unreserved criticism of the existing order, but on the other side also to a rejection of resistance movements, since these divert one's attention from the kingdom of God with their goals, and violate by their use of violence the command to absolute justice and absolute love"—p. 51-52.

B59.   Davies, William D. *The Setting of the Sermon on the Mount.* Atlanta, GA: Scholars Press, 1989 (c1964), 546 p.

A reprint of one of the most thorough studies of this subject. Following a general introduction, Davies discusses the Sermon on the Mount as presented in Matthew's Gospel, examining Pentateuchal motifs, the idea of a new Exodus and a New Moses, and how the Mosaic categories are transcended. The setting of Jesus's sermon is placed in the context of the Jewish Messianic expectation, as seen in the Old Testament, the Apocrypha, the Pseudipigrapha, the Dead Sea Scrolls, and the Rabbinic writings. In the period of what he calls "Contemporary Judaism," he covers Gnosticism, the Qumran community, and the events at Jamnia. Davies also discusses Paul's comments on this tradition, and examines the antecedents behind Matthew's Gospel, including the speculative source books which modern scholars have termed "Q" and "M." He further shows how Jesus's words were transmitted, and talks about the idea of Jesus as a teacher, eschatological preacher, and rabbi. He concludes that: 1. The Sermon on the Mount (which he calls "SM") in the Gospel tradition "preserves only the whisper of the voice of Jesus" (p. 436); 2. Jesus's sayings and the "law of Christ" and his commandments "...played a more significant part in the New Testament as a whole than is often recognized" (p. 437); 3. "Thus it is that our effort to set the SM historically in its place finally sets us in our place. And the place in which it sets us is the Last Judgment, before the infinite succour and the infinite demand of Christ" (p. 440).

B60.   Edersheim, Alfred. *The Life and Times of Jesus the Messiah.* New American ed. Grand Rapids, MI: Wm. B. Eerdmans Publishing Co., 1943 (c1897), 2 v.

Edersheim takes a chronological approach to his subject, and his Christian bias is evident even in his selection of words to describe such topics as "The Preparation for the Gospel: The Jewish World in the Days of Christ," or "The Old Faith preparing for the New." He does look at Hellenism and examines some Rabbinic material, but is heavily dependent on the Mishnah and the Talmuds for his perspective on Judaism at the time of Jesus. His bias against the Judaism of the time as he conceives it is shown in the following statement: "It is sadly characteristic, that practically, the main body of Jewish dogmatic and moral theology is really only Haggadah, and hence of no absolute authority. The Halakhah indicated with the most minute and painful punctiliousness every legal ordinance as to outward observances, and it explained every bearing of the Law of Moses. But beyond this it left the inner man, the spring of actions, untouched"—Vol. 1., p. 105. This book and several others of its kind have been included herein to give the reader a sense of how much modern scholarship has progressed, at least in terms of the resources it now has available to reconstruct life in the first century of the Christian era, and how a greater appreciation of Judaism and its contribution to early Christianity is presently being shown by current researchers.

B61.   Flusser, David G. *Jesus.* New York: Herder & Herder, 1969, 159 p.

Flusser writes: "In order to understand Jesus, we have to know about contemporary Judaism. The Jewish material is important, therefore, not just because it allows us to place Jesus in his own time, but because it allows us to interpret his sayings aright"—p. 10. Flusser takes a topical approach with such subjects as The Law, The Son of

Man, Jerusalem, Love, etc. In the chapter on the Law he writes, "Few people seem to realize that in the synoptic gospels, Jesus is never shown in conflict with current practice of the law—with the single exception of the plucking of ears of corn on the sabbath....The general opinion was that on the sabbath it was permissible to pick up fallen ears of grain, and rub them between the fingers; but according to Rabbi Jehuda, also a Galilean, it was also permissible to rub them in one's hand. Some of the Pharisees, therefore, found fault with Jesus' disciples for behaving in accordance with their Galilean tradition"—p. 46.

B62. Goldstein, Morris. *Jesus in the Jewish Tradition.* New York: Macmillan, 1950, 319 p.

Goldstein attempts to present a book "which tells with continuity through the centuries, from the first century of the Christian Era until modern times, the story of what is known regarding Jesus in Jewish life and literature...." He assembled all of the original Hebrew and Aramaic source material, "with all the variant readings of manuscripts and early printed editions which had escaped censorship," and translated, interpreted, and evaluated these texts— p. vii. Goldstein covers both the Tannaitic and Amoraic periods, delineating authentic references in Jewish literature to Jesus, as well as references which are incorrectly identified with Jesus, and indirect allusions to Jesus. In a section on post-Talmudic times he covers disputations and polemics in the Middle Ages, and Jesus in relation to the totality of Jewish life. The earliest authentic references were found in the Talmud and Midrash. The author concludes that the Jews did not accept Jesus as the Messiah because the Jewish religious leaders did not believe the required conditions for the appearance of a Messiah had actually been met (p. 233).

B63. Hagner, Donald A. *The Jewish Reclamation of Jesus: An Analysis and Critique of the Modern Jewish Study of Jesus.* Grand Rapids, MI: Zondervan Publishing House, 1984, 341 p.

After a brief opening chapter in which he offers his assessment of Jewish study of Jesus, Hagner reviews the history of such scholarship. He organizes his research into such categories as: the authority of Jesus, eschatology and ethics, the religious teaching of Jesus, and the person and mission of Jesus. He closes by saying that some of the questions still open include: the use of rabbinic literature for the study of first-century Judaism, and whether an accurate assessment of Jesus can be made just by studying his teachings. The selected bibliography in this book is very useful for further study.

B64. Hengel, Martin. *Was Jesus a Revolutionist?* Philadelphia: Fortress Press, 1971, 46 p.

In this brief guide Hengel examines: "Portraits of Jesus as a Revolutionist," "The Zealot Movement," "Jesus and the Zealot Movement," and "Jesus' Actions and Message." He concludes that Jesus was not a revolutionist if we mean that he desired to do violence to any person or state. However, he was certainly not content with the *status quo*: "He broke with the proud self-assurance of the ideology about 'election' of this people, in that he promised the Gentiles participation in the Kingdom of God....Nor can one educe the incident of the tribute money at Mark 12:12-17 to prove that Jesus held a conservative attitude of faithfulness to the state. When Jesus demands and receives the tribute coin, the Roman silver denarius, from his opponents—which no real Zealot would touch because it bore the image of Caesar—he only desires to call the attention of his opponents to the consequence which comes from their use of Caesar's money"—p. 33.

B65. Klausner, Joseph. *From Jesus to Paul.* New York: Beacon Press, 1961 (c1939), 624 p.

In addition to looking at the life and thought of Paul, Klausner examines what he calls Judaism outside of Palestine at the time of the rise of Christianity, as well as contemporaneous pagan religious thought. After reviewing Hellenistic Jewish thought, Klausner discusses Jewish Christianity, Gentile Christianity, and the unique case of Paul. Klausner reviews the part Paul played in taking what was a completely Jewish, prophetic, and Pharisaic teaching as represented in the teachings of Jesus, and forming from it a new religion. He believes that Jesus's overemphasis on the idea of God as his father also negated much of Jesus's Jewish origins. He traces the pagan, non-Jewish influences upon Paul which led him to the creation of this new religion.

B66. **Klausner, Joseph.** *Jesus of Nazareth: His Life, Times, and Teaching.* New York: Macmillan Company, 1949 (c1925), 434 p.

Though Klausner's scholarhip is somewhat dated, his book still remains one of the classic Jewish interpretations of Jesus. Drawing on such sources as the Talmud and Midrash, Joesphus and Tacitus, the early Church Fathers, the apocrypha and the Gospels, KIausner describes the political, economic, and religious conditions of the time. He then reviews Jesus's life and teachings. For Klausner, Jesus is "a great teacher of morality and parable"—p. 414. He understands that Jesus is a Jew who "became" a Christian because his history and teaching were separated from the history of Israel.

B67. **Maccoby, Hyam.** *Revolution in Judea: Jesus and the Jewish Resistance.* New York: Taplinger Publishing Company, 1980 (c1973), 256 p.

Maccoby sees Jesus as part of the Jewish resistance movement trying to overthrow Rome: "Jesus was a good man who fell among Gentiles. That is to say, he fell among those who did not understand that to turn him into a god was to diminish him. He tried to bring about the kingdom of God on earth, and he failed; but the meaning of his life is in the attempt, not in the failure. As a Jew, he fought not against some metaphysical evil but against Rome. Yet the movement which denied his life by deifying him misrepresented him as being opposed to the people whom he most loved and on whose behalf he fought. It was an entirely fitting outcome that this movement, Gentile-Christianity, made a successful accommodation with Rome and became the official religion of the Empire which crucified Jesus"—p. 195.

B68. **Montefiore, Claude J.** *Some Elements of the Religious Teaching of Jesus According to the Synoptic Gospels.* New York: Arno Press, 1973 (c1910), 171 p.

Montefiore's work is an example of classic Jewish scholarship on the person of Jesus and his teachings. His material was originally presented in six parts as the Jowett lectures of 1910. He deals with the issues of Jesus as a prophet, Jesus and the law, the kingdom of God, the nature of God and his relation to man, the views of Jesus about himself and his mission, and "Expansions and Modifications of the Authentic Teaching of Jesus which are found in the Synoptic Gospels." In his first chapter, he talks about the difficulties of a Jewish scholar coping with the subject of Jesus. His perspective brings new light to such topics as the prophets and the law, as well as on Jesus himself. Though some of his scholarship is dated, his book remains a stimulating piece of work. Montefiore finds some curious contradictions in the teaching of Jesus, and does an interesting job of showing how the Gospel authors expanded on Jesus's teachings.

B69. Pelikan, Jaroslav. *Jesus Through the Centuries.* New Haven, CT: Yale University Press, 1985, 288 p.

Pelikan's work takes us from the first century of the Christian era, where Jesus is treated under the heading "The Rabbi," to our own time, where the author discusses (in Chapter 18) "The Man Who Belongs to the World." In "The Rabbi," Pelikan delineates the differences between the normal rabbinic approach to scripture and what Jesus accomplished, when he writes about Jesus's reading of Isaiah in the synagogue: "But instead of doing what a rabbi was normally expected to do, which was to provide an exposition of the text that compared and contrasted earlier interpretations and then applied the text to the hearers, he proceeded to declare: 'Today this scripture has been fulfilled in your hearing'"—p. 12.

B70. Riches, John K. *Jesus and the Transformation of Judaism.* New York: Seabury Press, 1982 (c1980), 254 p.

Riches believes that the essential question in any study of Jesus is the one originally put by Reimarus: *i.e.*, what was Christ's purpose? Riches covers the synoptic tradition about Jesus and the developments in Judaism up to the time of Jesus. He then looks at Jesus's preaching of the Kingdom, Jesus and the Law of Purity, Jesus's theism and its role in tranforming first-century Palestinian Judaism. Riches writes: "I have argued first that Pharisaism, Essenism and Zealotism all presented fairly detailed programmes of resistance, and, in part at least, aggression towards Hellenism and its agents and also towards Jewish groups with different strategies. Jesus in his preaching and call to discipleship attacked the basis of current Jewish strategies by challenging the beliefs about God on which they rested, notably the belief that God's justice required that he should destroy the wicked, notably the oppressors of Israel"—p. 168.

B71. Rivkin, Ellis. *What Crucified Jesus?* Nashville, TN: Abingdon Press, 1984, 124 p.

In his title Rivkin asks not *who* crucified Jesus, but *what*. He blames the Roman imperial system, which allowed the appointment of Jewish high priests, even though no biblical or oral Law sanctioned this practice. He further writes: "And insofar as the bet din (boule) of the Pharisees was concerned, it exercised jurisdiction only over those who freely chose to follow the teachings of the Scribes-Pharisees; over the conduct of public worship; and over the liturgical calendar. Not only was the bet din a boule, not a sanhedrin, but it was presided over by a nasi, not the high priest and it consisted exclusively of teachers of the twofold Law. Had there been no Roman imperial system, Jesus would have faced the buffetings of strong words, the batterings of skillfully aimed proof texts, and the ridicule of both Sadducees and Scribes-Pharisees, but he would have stood no trial, been affixed to no cross"—p. 118.

B72. Rosenberg, Roy A. *Who Was Jesus?* Lanham, MD: University Press of America, 1986, 132 p.

Rosenberg studies the idea of the Messiah, Jesus, and his relation to Judaism, the Sermon on the Mount, the Last Supper, and Jesus's trial and crucifixion. He shows that Jesus did not himself claim to be the Messiah, but was a teacher who sought to prepare his followers for the kingdom of God: "His teaching that a heavenly being would be the ruler during the new age he derived from sectarian Judaism"—p. 91. The author says that Jesus identified this heavenly being with the Son of Man. He further writes about Jesus's teaching: "While denying the validity of many of the ritual strictures imposed by the 'oral law' of the Pharisees, he developed his own 'oral law' governing human relationships, a set of requirements that went beyond anything mandated by the Torah"—p. 91.

B73. Sanders, E. P. *Jesus and Judaism.* Philadelphia: Fortress Press, 1985, 354 p.

Sanders discusses two primary questions: what was Jesus's intention in his ministry?; what was Jesus's relation with his contemporaries? He then investigates whether Jesus actually desired to overthrow Judaism, and whether the split between Christianity and Judaism occured during Jesus's lifetime—or afterward. Explaining why he rejects the "sayings" approach of understanding Jesus, Sanders delineates what he says are the known facts about Jesus. For the author, Jewish eschatology is the principle context in which to examine Jesus's work. Jesus was an eschatological prophet who enacted a destruction of the Temple in order to draw attention to the imminent arrival of the Kingdom of God. Israel would then be restored and God himself would rebuild the Temple.

B74. **Sigal, Phillip.** *The Halakhah of Jesus of Nazareth According to the Gospel of Matthew.* Lanham, MD: University Press of America, 1986, 269 p.

This book was based upon the author's doctoral dissertation. Sigal states in his preface: "Having specialized in rabbinic-talmudic studies and engaged in a work on the origin of the halakhah, I perceived that the halakhah of the New Testament is an integral part of the sequence from the Old Testament to the Mishnah"—p. iii. After examining earlier scholarship on this subject, the author looks at the stages in the formation of rabbinic halakhah, including what he calls "proto-Rabbinic" halakhic activity. He then discusses the figure of Jesus as portrayed in Matthew and the halakhah of divorce, and then at the Matthean Jesus and the sabbath halakhah. He concludes: "1. The Matthean Jesus was not in controversy with the men who were the immediate predecessors of the rabbis of Yabneh, a scholar group that I call 'proto-rabbis.' The Pharisaioi of the New Testament constitute a variety of pietistic and separatist extremists in the Jewish community, who adhered to a Sabbath and divorce halakhah best exemplified by the Book of Jubilees and the writings of Qumran; 2. On the subject of divorce the Matthean Jesus has a wholly independent viewpoint which stands alone in the first century. His halakhah against polygamy became the Christian norm, albeit often breached, but did not gain a position of authority in Judaism until the Middle Ages...; 3. On the subject of the Sabbath the Matthean Jesus stands out as an articulate dissenter from the Ezraic-Nehemiahan quiescent Sabbath which turned into a day on which the stringencies often defeated the healing purpose of a Sabbath. In effect Jesus' healing on the Sabbath, as a sign that *hoste exestin tois sabbasin kalos poiein*, 'it is permitted to act beneficially on the Sabbath,' proclaimed the very purpose of the Sabbath as a redemptive-healing day; 4. During his brief ministry Jesus was a proto-rabbi whose views influenced his contemporaries and possibly entered tannatic literature as the views of others"—p. 157-159.

B75. **Sloyan, Gerard S.** *Jesus in Focus: A Life in Its Setting.* Mystic, CT: Twenty Third Publications, 1983, 207 p.

A presentation of the life and teachings of Jesus with emphasis on the Jewish context of Jesus, *Jesus in Focus* employs a format which could make it useful as a supplemental college text. Sloyan writes in a "popular" style, *sans* footnotes, and his book is obviously intended for a very general audience.

B76. **Swetnam, James**. *Jesus and Isaac: A Study of the Epistle to the Hebrews in the Light of the Aqedah.* Rome: Biblical Institute Press, 1981, 243 p.

The Aqedah is the Jewish term for the story of the near sacrifice of Isaac by the patriarch Abraham. Swetnam believes that many of the difficulties in understanding various passages in the Book of Hebrews can be clarified if we recognize that the author is writing against the background of the story of the Aqedah. He reviews a century of research on the Aqedah, and then looks at the story itself as presented in the Old Testament, early Judaism, and the New Testament. Several passages in Hebrews are discussed to show how they are illuminated by his theory. Swetnam also studies the idea of the Son of Man in Hebrews as a title for Jesus. Originally the author's doctoral dissertation, *Jesus and Isaac* also contains an extensive and useful bibliography.

B77. **Trocme, Etienne.** *Jesus as Seen by His Contemporaries.* Philadelphia: Westminster Press, 1973, 134 p.

The "contemporaries" discussed by Trocme include: "Dominical Sayings," by which he means "isolated sayings, and groups of sayings of Jesus, which neither include nor accompany a narrative" (p. 27); "Apophthegms," by which he means the term used by Bultmann to describe "brief anecdotes in the synoptic tradition which centre upon a saying of Jesus, and in which the narrative has no other purpose than to provide a framework for this saying" (p. 48); and "Biographical Narratives," including the Jesus of the parables and miracle stories, as well as what is actually known of Jesus as a public figure. In order to make Jesus comprehensible, "A comparison must be made between the attitudes taken by Jesus to the various ideas people had of his person"—p. 123.

B78.   Vermes, Geza. *Jesus and the World of Judaism*. London: SCM Press, 1983, 224 p.

For Vermes, reading the Gospels as a historian means placing Jesus in the context of the Judaism of his time. He finds the idea of the Kingdom of God central to Jesus's message. The meaning of the phrase "Son of Man" is also explored, along with the impact of the Dead Sea Scrolls on present-day Jewish and New Testament studies. The themes of eschatology, the true Israel, and attitudes toward the Bible are also examined, especially as these occur in the Dead Sea Scrolls and in the New Testament.

B79.   Vermes, Geza. *Jesus the Jew: A Historian's Reading of the Gospels*. New York: Macmillan, 1974 (c1973), 288 p.

In the first part of this work, Vermes examines the setting of Jesus's life in Galilee and within charismatic Judaism. In the second section he discusses the titles of Jesus, including prophet, lord, Messiah, Son of Man, and Son of God. Vermes believes that Jesus is perfectly recognizable within the framework of Judaism as a zaddik or just man, and as a healer, leader, and teacher whose background is first-century Galilean charismatic religion.

B80.   Weiss-Rosmarin, Trude, ed. *Jewish Expressions on Jesus: An Anthology*. New York: Ktav Publishing House, 1976, 421 p.

Many of the greatest modern Jewish scholars are represented here, including: Martin Buber, Walter Kaufmann, Joseph Klausner, Samuel Sandmel, and Solomon Zeitlin. The thirteen essays focus on a rediscovery of the historical Jesus, with emphasis on his trial and death. The picture which emerges is of a Jew in the Second Jewish Commonwealth who preached rebellion against Rome, and was sentenced and executed for treason. Chapter topics include: Jesus in the Talmud, the historical Jesus, Jesus and the Pharisees, the Crucifixion, and Jesus: Jew or Christian?

B81.   Westerholm, Stephen. *Jesus and Scribal Authority*. Lund: CWK Gleerup, 1978, 178 p.

Westerholm brings a thorough knowledge of his subject to this revision of his doctoral thesis. He first delineates what he calls "The Makers of Halakhah" by describing the Pharisees and their law, the nature of scribal authority and the "scribes of the Pharisees," and halakhic assemblies and the sages of the halakhah. He then turns to Jesus's view of scribal authority, and examines such issues as tithing, ritual purity, the Sabbath, oaths, and divorce. He concludes that Jesus was not a Pharisee, and that he did not have a statutory understanding of the law. Jesus's compliance with the law came from the heart, but there was in fact compliance.

B82.   Yoder, John H. *The Politics of Jesus*. Grand Rapids, MI: Wm. B. Eerdmans Publishing Co., 1972, 260 p.

The importance of the idea of revolution in the time of Jesus can be seen from some of Yoder's chapter titles: "The Implications of the Jubilee," "God Will Fight for Us," "The Possibility of Nonviolent Resistance," and "Christ and Power." Yoder believes that apocalyptic thought was very important to the religious philosophers of the first century C.E. "In the world view of that time the gap between the present and the promise was not fundamental. What we are doing now is what leads to where we are going. Since the 'this-worldly' and the 'other-worldly' were not perceived in radical dichotomy, to be 'marching through Emmanuel's ground' today is to be on the way to Zion"—p. 249. "So when Jesus formulated the celebrated commandment, 'Sell what you possess and give it as alms' (a better translation would be, 'sell what you possess and put in practice compassion'), this was not a 'counsel of perfection' but neither was it a constitutional law to found a utopian state of Israel. It was a jubilee ordinance which was to be put into practice here and now, once, in A.D. 26, as a 'refreshment' prefiguring the 'reestablishment of all things'"—p. 76.

B83.   Zeitlin, Solomon. *Who Crucified Jesus?* 5th ed. New York: Bloch Publishing Company, 1975 (c1964), 250 p.

After reviewing the movement of the first-century Jewish nation from theocracy to commonwealth and from commonwealth to Roman province, Zeitlin reviews the social classes of the time of Jesus, and presents his case about the two Sanhedrins, one political and one religious. In the chapter on "The Trial and the Crucifixion," Zeitlin writes, "We have thus proved that the crucifixion of Jesus was committed by Pilate, the Roman procurator, not by the Jews. True, the high priest delivered Jesus to Pilate for trial but that was not done by the will of the Jewish people. Political conditions which prevailed at the time in Judea forced some of the leaders to fight against their own brethren, and to help the Romans to destroy the real Jewish patriots. The Jewish people did not crucify Jesus"—p. 179. In his Preface, Zeitlin makes these comments concerning the availability of writings on this period by Jews: "The reader may notice that in the bibliography dealing with the life of the Jews and the sects during the Second Commonwealth, I did not refer to any Jewish works. It is with chagrin that I note that there is no literature written by Jews to which the reader may be referred. It is indeed rather strange that we should not have any literature written by Jews on this most important period in Jewish history, a period when Judaism was cemented, and had the greatest influence not only on the Jewish people but on civilization as well. We do not have many books on this period written by Christian scholars. However, they have given preference to one set of sources—The New Testament and Josephus—while they have ignored or misunderstood the Tannaitic literature"—p. vi. Thankfully, these remarks are no longer true.

JEWISH HISTORY

B84. Alon, Gedalia. *Jews in Their Land in the Talmudic Age, 70-640 C.E.* Jerusalem: Magnes Press, 1980, 2 v.

In order to lay the foundation for the discussion of the time period just after the destruction of the Temple in 70 C.E., Alon discusses some of the events and institutions which were important to the Jews in Jesus's time. His early chapters in volume one are also important for the depth of their coverage of the time which resulted in the Talmud. The threads of thought and influence which stretch from Jesus's time to that of the Talmud are important to consider, and the early chapters of this work help with that approach. Alon's sensitivity to the social and political factors important in shaping the early Christian era make this work especially valuable for the student and researcher alike.

B85. Alon, Gedalia. *Jews, Judaism and the Classical World: Studies in Jewish History in the Times of the Second Temple and Talmud.* Jerusalem: Magnes Press, 1977, 499 p.

Alon covers sixteen different topics, including: "Did the Jewish People and its Sages Cause the Hasmoneans to Be Forgotten?,"

"The Attitude of the Pharisees to Roman Rule and the House of Herod," "The Burning of the Temple," and "The Origin of the Samaritans in the Halakhic Tradition." What Alon brings to this study is his mastery of Torah and his extensive knowledge of classical literature and history. He is therefore able to provide a very broad and inclusive perspective in his work. His remarks on the socio-politcal forms of the Jewish community have anticipated much of the sociological approach to Biblical times that is now *au courant* in Biblical scholarship.

B86. **Avi-Yonah, Michael.** *The Jews Under Roman and Byzantine Rule: A Political History of Palestine from the Bar Kokhba War to the Arab Conquest.* Jerusalem: Magnes Press, 1984, 286 p.

Though this work includes much material covering historical events after the time of Jesus, it remains an important guide to the understanding of what happened just after the time of Jesus. Some of the same political tensions which existed in Jesus time remained relevant for generations, and thus Avi-Yonah's discussion of the tensions between the Romans and the Jews are illuminating. In his early chapters, Avi-Yonah covers such topics as: "Roman Rule in Jewish Eyes," "The Jews and Greek Culture," and the demographic and economic situation of the area just after the time of Jesus. The original book was published in 1946, and revisions were made by other hands at later dates.

B87. **Avi-Yonah, Michael, and Zvi Baras, eds**. *The World History of the Jewish People: Society and Religion in the Second Temple Period.* Jerusalem: Massada Publishing Ltd., 1977, Vol. 8.

This one volume of a large standard set covers the Jewish religion of the first century C.E., the development of oral law, the synagogue and its worship, the Sadducees and Pharisees, the Qumran sect and the Scrolls, the messianic idea in apocryphal literature, the rise of Christianity, and the Sicarii and Zealots. Each section has been written by a major Jewish scholar; *e.g.*, J. Klausner writes on the rise of Christianity. Interestingly, Klausner states: "Certainly no absolute historicity can be claimed for the story of Jesus's life even in the form presented here, in which certain improbable events have been omitted along with material found in only one source. Yet it contains nothing that is impossible, and is in complete accordance with the general situation of the Jews and Judaism at that time. It is also a faithful psychological portrayal of an extraordinary, mystically religious man, whom a worldwide religious movement found it possible to regard as its *fons et origo*. Certainly, too, the present account may be seen to contain deeds, sentiments and thoughts that are based on tendentious reports necessary for the development of the new religious movement"—p. 248.

B88.   Baron, Salo W., ed. *Judaism: Postbiblical and Talmudic Period.* New York: Liberal Arts Press, 1954, 245 p.

Baron's anthology collects the literature of the time, beginning with such Apocryphal materials as the Maccabean books and Tobit, and moving on to Hellenistic materials (*i.e.*, Philo and Josephus), then to such sectarian movements as the Samaritans and Essenes, to such Tannaitic collections as the Mishnah and Halakhic Midrash, and finally to Amoraic collections, whch are examined through a thematic approach where subjects like atonement, future life, and prayer are reviewed.

B89.   Baron, Salo W. *A Social and Religious History of the Jews.* 2nd rev. and enl. ed. New York: Columbia University Press, 1952-1973, 18 v. in 9.

Each volume of this set is topically arranged; Volume One of the nine-volume edition covers to the beginning of the Christian Era. Volume Two is subtitled, "Chrsitian Era: The First Five Centuries," and it is Chapter 10 in this volume which is the most relevant to this bibliography. This section covers such topics as: "Messianic Expectations"; "Rise of Christianity"; "Jesus the Messiah"; "Judeo-Christian Following"; "Pauline Schism"; "Formation of the Church"; and "Triumph of Disruptive Forces." The final volume of the set contains the indexes to all of the earlier volumes.

B90.   Ben-Sasson, Haim H., ed. *A History of the Jewish People.* Cambridge, MA: Harvard University Press, 1976 (c.1969), 1170 p.

The major sections of this work include: "Origins and the Formative Period," "The Period of the First Temple, the Babylonian Exile and the Restoration," "The Period of the Second Temple," "The Era of the Mishnah and Talmud (70-640)," "The Middle Ages," and "The

Modern Period." A great amount of detail is included in this work, as well as an extensive and detailed bibliography. M. Stern, author of the chapter on the Second Temple period, comments: "The rule of Torah in the Second Temple era cannot be comprehended without an understanding of the development of the halakhah. The halakhah—'the path wherein Israel walks'—formed the main part of the oral tradition and encompassed all aspects of the Jew's personal and communal conduct"—p. 283. "Among the messianic movements at the end of the Second Temple era was one that was to play a role of the greatest importance in the history of the entire human race: Christianity, whose origins are linked to the personality of Jesus of Nazareth....Most of Jesus' Jewish followers in Palestine remained within the Jewish faith. Those of the first generation, such as Jesus' brother James, continued to observe the Jewish commandments, even though they differed from other Jews by believing in Jesus"—p. 287.

B91. **Bickerman, Elias J.** *From Ezra to the Last of the Maccabees: Foundations of Postbiblical Judaism.* New York: Schocken Books, 1962, 186 p.

After describing the return of the Jews from Babylonian Exile, Bickerman delineates the Judaism of Ezra and of Elephantine. He then looks at the influence of the Greeks, assesses the impact of Hellenism, and examines the Greek version of the Torah. Part Two of the book is a lengthy look at the circumstances which led to the development and outcome of the Maccabean revolt. Bickerman shows how the revolt was successful against Hellenism on one level, while on another, the Jews were able to adapt Hellenistic views "after their poison had been drawn"—p. 181. They simply fitted the ideas into the Torah so they would serve the God of their fathers.

B92. **Buchler, Adolf.** *Types of Jewish Palestinian Piety from 70 B.C.E. to 70 C.E.* New York: Ktav Publishing House, 1968 (c.1922), 264 p.

Buchler studies Hillel, the ancient pious men, the pious men of the Psalms of Solomon, and Honi the Hasid. He disagrees with the work of Bousset, stating that Bousset's failure to present his subject matter correctly was due in large part to his "...insufficient knowledge of the rabbinic literature..."—p. 5. Buchler studies the piety of these men as demonstrated in their prayer life, devotion to

Torah, and acts of loving kindness. He also analyzes the idea of sacrifice as it was understood by these rabbis. Commenting on Honi, he writes, "...he represented a perculiar type of Hasid; but neither he nor the other pious men were Essenes, but strict Pharisees attached to God with all their heart, and serving their fellow-men with all their soul"—p. 264.

B93. Buehler, William W. *The Pre-Herodian Civil War and Social Debate: Jewish Society in the Period 76-40 B.C. and the Social Factors Contributing to the Rise of the Pharisees and the Sadducees.* Basel: Komm. Friedrich Reinhardt, 1974, 128 p.

Buehler first examines the social conditions existing in Rome from 76-40 B.C., and then the classes of society according to Josephus. Chapter 3 delineates the social climate in Palestine between 76-40 B.C. The final two chapters concern the historical background of Jewish society during this period, and present some of the views of the Pharisees and the Sadducees. In his "Conclusions" section, Buehler says that the most important of the social factors affecting the development of the Pharisees and Sadducees was the "struggle between the forces of monarch and oligarchy; between the commercial aristocracy of the dynastoi and the old patrician families. It was this political development which forged the Pharisees and the oligarchy into a common front opposing the Hasmoneans and their supporters"—p. 117. He also points out that there were two different groups of aristocrats; thus, simply to equate the Sadducees with the priesthood is too simple a solution.

B94. Cohon, Beryl D. *Men at the Crossroads; Between Jerusalem and Rome; Synagogue and Church: The Lives, Times, and Doctrines of the Founders of Talmudic Judaism and New Testament Christianity.* South Brunswick, NJ: Thomas Yoseloff, 1970, 270 p.

With such a long subtitle, we need only list those whom Cohon included: under the heading "Rome and Jerusalem," we find Herod, Hillel and Shammai; under "Birthpangs of the Messiah," the Sadducees and Pharisees, the Essenes, Zealots, Apocalyptists and Messiahs, and Pontius Pilate; under "The Birth of Christianity," John the Baptist, Jesus, and Paul; under "Disaster Breaks," Josephus, Yohanan Ben Zakkai; and under "Talmudic Masters and Apostolic Fathers," Akiba and various other apostles and martyrs.

Yohanan Ben Zakkai was a well-known teacher of the law, and is credited with beginning the movement which evolved into rabbinical Judaism. Akiba is supposed to have had a hand in completing the Old Testament canon and in developing the Synagogue calendar.

B95. Collins, John J. *Between Athens and Jerusalem: Jewish Identity in the Hellenistic Diaspora*. New York: Crossroad, 1983, 258 p.

Collins covers the religion and politics of Ptolemaic Egypt and of Rome, plus what he calls the common ethic, philosophical Judaism, and the mysteries of God, in which are found such writings as the Prayer of Joseph and the Testament of Job. He concludes that "some strands of Hellenistic Judaism attempted to relate the Jewish law to the surrounding culture by playing down its most distinctive elements, and others by seeking a common ground in Greek philosophy"—p. 195. "The pattern of 'covenantal nomism' which E. P. Sanders had posited as the dominant construction of Judaism was certainly represented in the Diaspora, in such diverse works as the chronicle of Demetrius, fourth Maccabees, and the books of Adam and Eve. Yet it was not the only, or even the dominant, factor in the religion of Hellenistic Judaism. The Jewish tradition could also be construed as the story of a glorious past which fostered ethnic pride with little regard for religious laws or for anything that could be called nomism, as we found conspicuously in Artapanus"—p. 244. "The common thread of Jewish identity, however, comes from the reliance, in whatever form, on the Jewish tradition. The author of 3 Baruch still uses the pseudonym of a Hebrew prophet"—p. 245.

B96. Davies, Moshe, ed. *Israel: Its Role in Civilization*. New York: Harper & Bros., 1956, 338 p.

Of the four sections which make up this book; namely, 1) "The Role of Israel in the Modern World"; 2) "What History Teaches"; 3) "The New State"; and 4) "America and Israel," it is Part Two which proves of most interest to this bibliography, especially H. Louis Ginsberg's section on "The Dead Sea Manuscript Finds," and Morton Smith's article on "Palestinian Judaism in the First Century." Smith believes that Palestinian Judaism was heavily influenced by Hellenism, and he examines Josephus to see how the Pharisees became such a dominant group.

B97. Davies, William D., and Louis Finkelstein, eds. *The Cambridge History of Judaism.* New York: Cambridge University Press, 1984- , 4+ v.

Volume 1 of this standard set contains the general introduction, and covers the Persian period, while Volume 2 describes the Hellenistic Age. In the latter book is an essay of special interest entitled, "The Pharisaic Leadership After the Great Synagogue," by Louis Finkelstein. What makes this set so important is not only the articles themselves, but the copious, well-documented footnotes and the separate bibliography, both which can lead the student to further sources. A major work for any scholar of Judaism.

B98. Drazin, Nathan. *The History of Jewish Education from 515 B.C.E. to 220 C.E.: During the Periods of the Second Commonwealth and the Tannaim.* Baltimore: The Johns Hopkins Press, 1940, 103 p.

Drazin states that by the time of the Second Commonwealth the Jewish school was already developed and tested. He studies the Jewish philosophy of education during this era, as well as the evolution of the school system, its administration, the content of the education, the pedagogical methods, and the education of girls and women. His survey covers elementary, secondary and higher education. At the elementary level, he states, Jewish schools concentrated on the reading of the Scriptures. Drazin says that "colleges" were founded first, then secondary education, then elementary. The emphasis was on ethical living, not on learning a specific body of knowledge.

B99. Ebner, Eliezer. *Elementary Education in Ancient Israel During the Tannaitic Period (10-220 C.E.).* New York: Bloch Publishing Company, 1956, 128 p.

Ebner first points out the differences in the way Jewish boys and girls were educated during the early Christian era. He reviews the origin and development of the elementary school system and their teachers. There are also chapters on school organization, curriculum, and methods of instruction. A helpful bibliography completes the book. Ebner is particularly helpful in showing the developments in the Jewish educational system from the time when it was the responsibility of each father to educate his children to the period when the actual teaching was done by a teacher in a formal school setting.

B100. Eddy, Samuel K. *The King Is Dead: Studies in the Near Eastern Resistance to Hellenism, 334-31 B.C.* Lincoln: University of Nebraska Press, 1961, 390 p.

Eddy studies the Persians, other Iranians, the Western Asians, and the Jews to 166 B.C. Of special importance is the chapter on "The Jews Under the Hasmoneans." The last chapter contains the author's general conclusions: "Here [in Judah] the resistance was not always the work of aristocrats. While Judas, a Hasmonean of priestly rank, rebelled, so did the Hasidim, who had scarcely any rank at all. The sources of opposition in Judah were therefore unique"—p. 325.

B101. Ellison, Henry L. *From Babylon to Bethlehem: The People of God from Exile to Messiah.* Atlanta: John Knox Press, 1979 (c.1976), 136 p.

Beginning with a section on the importance of the intertestamental period, Ellison continues with an examination of the Babylonian exile and the work accomplished by prophets such as Nehemiah and Ezra. He then examines Judea during the late Persian dispersion, including the coming and influence of the Greeks and the Romans. He finishes with an examination of the reign of Herod the Great.

B102. Fairweather, William. *The Background of the Gospels; or, Judaism in the Period Between the Old and New Testaments.* Edinburgh: T. & T. Clark, 1908, 455 p.

For literary sources Fairweather uses such canonical literature as Chronicles, Ezra, Esther, Ecclesiastes, Zechariah, and the book of Daniel. He also used the Apocrypha and Pseudepigrapha available to him at the time, Josephus, Greek and Roman writers, known inscriptions on monuments and coins, and the Mishnah and Talmud. He examines the fundamental characteristics of Judaism, pre and post Maccabaean rulers, apocalyptic literature, and Hellenism. Surprisingly, he also includes a section on the Essenes. The reader will find this older work of scholarship curious, but still valid in parts.

B103. Finegan, Jack. *Light from the Ancient Past: The Archaeological Background of Judaism and Christianity.* Princeton, NJ: Princeton University Press, 1959.

Though this work was written in 1959, it remains a classic which is still cited in many bibliographies dealing with the archaeology of the ancient world of the Middle East. Finegan begins with Mesopotamia, and then moves on to Egypt, ancient Palestine, the empires of Western Asia (such as Assyria), "The Holy Land in the Time of Jesus," and the travels of Paul. He also reviews the ancient manuscripts relating to this region as they were known in 1959, shows the relevance of the catacombs and sarcophagi, and concludes with a survey of ancient churches. The volume includes 204 well-reproduced illustrations and plates which significantly enhance the book.

B104. Finkelstein, Louis. *The Jews: Their History, Culture and Religion.* 4th ed. New York: Schocken Books, 1970-71, 3 v.

Many different authors are represented in this standard set. The two chapters most relevant to this bibliography can be found in Volume One: "The Historical Foundations of Postbiblical Judaism," by Elias Bickerman; and "The Period of the Talmud (135 B.C.E.-1035 C.E.)," by Judah Goldin.

B105. Foerster, Werner. *From Exile to Christ; A Historical Introduction to Palestinian Judaism.* Philadelphia: Fortress Press, 1981 (c.1964), 264 p.

In Part 1, "The Historical Situation," Foerster covers the Babylonian Exile, Syrian Rule, the Maccabean War, various Jewish groups such as the Essenes, the Hasmoneans, and the fall of Jerusalem. Part 2 delineates the political, social, cultural, and economic background of Jesus's time. Part 3, "The Religious Situation," mentions factors common to all Jews, including instruction in the Scriptures, and such groups as the Sadducees and Pharisees. A closing chapter views Jesus in the context of everything Foerster has previously been discussing. The author emphasizes Jesus's discontinuity with historical Judaism.

B106. Freyne, Sean. *Galilee from Alexander the Great to Hadrian, 323 B.C.E. to 135 C.E.: A Study of Second Temple Judaism.* Wilmington, DE: Michael Glazier, 1980, 491 p.

The topics covered in this book include: the geography and population of Galilee, the rise of Hellenism and the Jewish response, Galilee under the Romans, the cities of Galilee, the economic and social conditions of this region, and how the Galileeans related to the idea of revolution. Additional topics include: the Temple, Halakhah, and the presence of Christianity in Galilee. In a retrospective, Freyne writes, "While hellenism, especially in terms of land-ownership and control over the produce of the land, made its full impact in Galilee as well as elsewhere in the Ptolemaic and Seleucid period, a considerable number of Galilean peasants would appear to have maintained some tenuous links with the land....Galilean political attitudes were not at all so radical or sharply defined as has often been suggested....As long as the temple survived, the 'other way' of the halakhah had little attraction for the country people, and there were few Pharisaic scribes active in the province though occasional attempts to extend their influence to the region can be seen from the ministry of Jesus and the mission of Johanan ben Zakkai"—p. 392-393.

B107. Glatzer, Nahum N. *Hillel the Elder: The Emergence of Classical Judaism.* New York: B'nai B'rith Hillel Foundations, 1956, 100 p.

Glatzer begins by looking at the historical and cultural background of the time of Hillel. He then examines the beginnings and ascent of Hillel, the ways and beliefs of the Hasid, Hillel's relations with the common man, the place of "learning" in his views, the two rival schools of Hillel and Shammai, and his proselytes and death. In his introduction, Glatzer writes, "A study of Hillel the Elder is essential for an understanding of the first pre-Christian century and the period preceding the destruction of the Temple in 70 C.E., an era of decisive importance in Jewish history. The study is based on talmudic and midrashic sources (some legendary) and on background information found in the Apocrypha and the Dead Sea sectarian writings"—p. 13. Glatzer also talks about Hillel's relations with the poor, and the tradition that poverty and avoidance of injustice went together: "Hillel accepted this tradition and the emphasis put on it by the sectarian groups. He made the poor and the broken a loving concern of his private life and represented the cause of the poor in his academy as against the advocates of the older, conservative, Pharisaism and its spokesman, Shammai"—p. 44.

B108. Grant, Michael. *The History of Ancient Israel.* New York: Charles Scribner's Sons, 1984.

This history begins even before the Jews enter Canaan and before the Patriarchs. However, it is the last two chapters of the book which are of special interest for this bibliography, because there Grant discusses the Maccabean revolt, Herod the Great, and the eventual rebellion against the Romans. Well-known classical historian Grant has a marvelous way of simplifiying, but not distorting, very complex historical and social issues. His writing style is easy to follow and his scholarship remarkably thorough.

B109. Grant, Michael. *The Jews in the Roman World.* New York: Charles Scribner's Sons, 1973, 347 p.

Grant actually begins his history in the age of the Maccabees. He then focuses on Jewish life under Herod and his successors, and reviews the threats to the Jewish state of the Romans, Greeks, and Christians. His last sections focus on the wars against the Romans and the life of the Jews in the later empire. Grant sees one threat coming from "Paul's Bid to Change the Jews"; in that chapter he writes: "Paul's conversion to belief in Jesus as the Messiah had occurred in A.D. 36-7. But within the following decade, as some of the earliest passages of the New Testament show, the youthful Jewish movement which accepted his Messiahship had already become dramatically split, between those who wished to keep it within the Judaism of Judea, and those who sought to extend it to the great outer world of Gentile Greeks"—p. 147. Grant includes many interesting details in his account: "...a Galilean pilgrim was murdered by the Samaritans as he was on his way to Jerusalem, and some said that more that one were killed. The angry Jews, engaging as their commander a certain Eleazar ben Dinai—who had been terrorizing the country for nearly twenty years and was described in the Mishnah as the Son of a Murderer—poured northwards out of the capital bent on vengence. Cumanus sent Sebastian cavalry to kill or arrest these Jewish marchers, and fighting between Jews and Samaritans now broke out in many areas"—p. 149.

B110. Green, William S., ed. *Approaches to Ancient Judaism.* Chico, CA: Scholars Press, 1978- , v.

This series had reached six volumes by 1989. Each one is part of the Brown Judaic Studies series. Volume 2 has no individual title, but the titles of the others are: Volume 1: Theory and Practice; Volume 3: Text as Context in Early Rabbinic Literature; Volume 4: Studies in Liturgy, Exegesis, and Talmudic Narrative; Volume 5: Studies in Judaism and Its Greco-Roman Context; Volume 6: Studies in the Ethnography and Literature of Judaism. The series includes a mixture of original essays and reprints, but is still very useful for the subject of this bibilography. The focus of many of the essays is on the use of Rabbinic literature for the study of first-century Judaism. There are also articles on the various Dead Sea Scrolls.

B111. Guignebert, Charles A. *The Jewish World in the Time of Jesus.* New York: E. P. Dutton, 1951 (c.1939), 288 p.

The four main areas covered in this work are: "The Political and Religious Condition of Palestine," "Innovations and Foreign Influences," "The Real Nature of Jewish Religious Life in Palestine," and "Hellenistic Judaism." In the section on sources, Guignebert mentions the books of Maccabees, Josephus, the books of Daniel and Ecclesiates, the Targums and Talmud, the Midrashim and Mishnah. In his "Conclusion," Guignebert states that both the eras of King David and the Maccabees were overly glorified by subsequent writers. He also emphasizes the influences coming to Israel from other areas of the Middle East, and says that the impetus for upheaval at the time of Jesus was the hope of a Messiah. He writes, "As for the Gospel, it was in origin the book in which a sect, originally issuing out of Israel, had laid down the first principles of its hope and faith, but it was born outside of Israel, and the writers who have given us the three oldest versions of it, viz. the Gospel according to Mark, Matthew, and Luke, and still more to the author and redactor of John, were already completely outside Judaism." Although now somewhat dated, his commentary retains some validity even today.

B112. Hamerton-Kelly, Robert, and Robin Scroggs, eds. *Jews, Greeks and Christians: Religious Cultures in Late Antiquity; Essays in Honor of William David Davies.* Leiden: E. J. Brill, 1976, 320 p.

In addition to the useful bibliography of the writings of William David Davies which is included in this book, there are also chapters by E. P. Sanders on "The Covenant as a Soteriological Category and the Nature of Salvation in Palestinian and Hellenistic Judaism," by Jacob Neusner on "Method and Substance in the History of Judaic Ideas: An Exercise," and one by Birger Gerhardsson on "The Hermeneutic Program in Matthew 22:37-40."

B112. Hengel, Martin. *Judaism and Hellenism; Studies in Their Encounter in Palestine During the Early Hellenistic Period.* Philadelphia: Fortress Press, 1974, 2 v.

Volume 1 covers Hellenism as a political, economic, and cultural force in Palestine, and demonstrates its influence on the Jews. Hengel delineates the encounter and conflict between Palestinian Judaism and the spirit of the Hellenistic Age, and what he calls "The 'Interpretatio Graeca' of Judaism and the Hellenistic Reform Attempt in Jerusalem." In his concluding section, the author writes: "It is not possible to say that Palestinian Judaism, leaving aside the interlude under Antiochus IV, which was speedily remedied, maintained a straight course through the Hellenistic period untouched by the alien civilization and completely faithful to the Old Testament tradition. Still less can it be claimed that it was completely permeated by the Hellenistic spirit and fell victim to syncretism, betraying its original task. The truth lies between the extremes"—p. 310. Further, "With Jesus' prophetic and eschatological message of the imminence of the kingdom of God, and the kerygma of the primitive community which took that message further—its revolutionary consequences were recognized above all by the group of 'Hellenists' in Jerusalem who were familiar with the self-contradictory nature of the Jewish mission— the protective attitude of Judaism over against its environment, which had been developed in the controversy with Hellenism and was most strongly expressed by the absolutized place of the Torah, was shattered in pieces"—p. 313-314. The second volume of this set consists entirely notes for the first volume, plus an extensive bibliography.

B114. Herford, Robert T. *Judaism in the New Testament Period.* London: The Lindsey Press, 1928, 256 p.

Herford examines Judaism before the period of the New Testament, including the sects and parties operating within Judaism at the time of the New Testament, and presents the teaching of the Pharisees and non-Pharisaic Judaism. He also views the impact of Christianity on Judaism. Herford spends a great deal of time talking about the common ground of beliefs that Jesus and the Pharisees shared, and wonders at this curious philosophical conjuction, since they apparently did not borrow much directly from one another.

B115. Hoenig, Sidney B. *The Great Sanhedrin: A Study of the Origin, Development, Composition and Functions of the Bet Din ha-Gadol During the Second Jewish Commonwealth.* New York: Bloch Publishing Company, 1953, 310 p.

Hoenig first examines the name "Synedrion" in classical literature, the papyri, Jewish-Greek sources, and Tannaitic texts. He then explores the nature of the Great Sanhedrin, and looks at Biblical sources and the Zadokite fragment to understand its origins. Next he reviews the emergence of the Bet Din ha-Gadol during Hasmonean times. He examines the institution itself, with chapters on its membership, number, meeting places, and functions. Among the latter he lists its religious authority, place of last appeal, supervision of officials, the special trials it conducted, and its supervision of the calendar and the Temple.

B116. Jagersma, Henk. *A History of Israel from Alexander the Great to Bar Kochba.* Philadelphia: Fortress Press, 1986, 256 p.

In this sequel to his *A History of Israel in the Old Testament Period*, Jagersma covers Israel's history from 330 B.C. to 135 A.D. His primary objective is to show the variety of scholarly opinions held about this time period by indicating "divergent and alternative perspectives"—p. 1. He emphasizes the cultural, literary, social and economic aspects of the period, and also focuses on the political rulers and wars of the time.

B117. Kraft, Robert, and George Nickelsburg, eds. *Early Judaism and Its Modern Interpreters.* Philadelphia: Fortress Press, 1984, 544 p.

The introductory section of this interesting anthology focuses on the modern study of early Judaism. Part One, dealing with early Judaism in its historical setting, contains essays on the political and social history of the Jews in the Greco-Roman times, the diversity in post-biblical Judaism, the Samaritans, and Judaism as seen by "outsiders." The second part covers the Dead Sea Scrolls, other manuscript finds, and the nonliterary discoveries of archaeologists. Part Three delineates the Septuagint, the Testament of Job, Apocalyptic and Wisdom literature, and other appropriate texts. This book is particularly important for providing a general survey of current scholarly opinion in the field. The variety of essays provides for various personal perspectives, and the bibliographies at the end of each chapter give further helpful material for the student and researcher. Highly recommended.

B118. Lieberman, Saul. *Hellenism in Jewish Palestine: Studies in the Literary Transmission, Beliefs, and Manners of Palestine in the I Century B.C.E.—IV Century C.E.* 2nd ed. New York: Ktav, 1962, 231 p.

The interesting topics covered in this volume include: the texts of Scripture in the early Rabbinic period, corrections of the Soferim, critical marks in the Hebrew Bible, the Rabbinic interpretation of Scripture, hermeneutic rules of the Aggadah, and Rabbinic polemics against idolatry, among many others. In order to keep the reader's attention focused on the main topic, Lieberman avoids detailed Halakhic discussions. "For this reason," he writes, "I have not, in my discussion of the literary transmission, concerned myself with investigations of the credibility of certain historic traditions in rabbinic literature. In these chapters our interest was fixed on literary activity, not on historic truth. In examining what the Rabbis report concerning by-gone times what was important to us was not the historic fact, but the view which the Rabbis held and their reaction to it....I have always worked on the assumption that actual contact (in the times under discussion) between Jew and Gentile exerted greater influence on the former than literary works"—p. xv. Lieberman demonstrates his own point of view in the last paragraph of his introduction: "Rabbinic literature is replete with valuable information about the life, manners and customs of the ancients. Many passages in it can be properly understood only in the general frame of its environment. The Jews of Palestine were by no means isolated from the ancient Mediterranean civilized world. They shared many of its general beliefs, conceptions and patterns of behavior"—p. 19. Concerning Biblical interpretation he writes, "The Rabbinic sages sought to understand the meaning of the difficult and rare words in Scripture not only through parallels in the Bible itself where the sense of expression is clear. They also sometimes explained them with the aid of other languages..."—p. 51.

B119. McCullough, William S. *The History and Literature of the Palestinian Jews from Cyrus to Herod: 500 B.C. to 4 B.C.* Toronto: University of Toronto Press, 1975, 252 p.

McCullough begins with a discussion of the late Babylonian and Persian periods of Jewish history, and then moves to a discussion of Judah around 550 B.C. He continues through the fifth and sixth centuries, the rebuilding of the Temple, and then examines Jewish history in the time of Nehemiah and Ezra. In Part Two, he covers the beginning of the Hellenistic age, and emphasizes the political setting of Judea just before and during Roman rule. Part Three contains his survey of the literature of the period. He examines the scholarly and pietistic traditions of scriptural exegesis, excluding the Dead Sea Scrolls, surveys and analyzes briefly the Apocalyptic and historical writings, and then looks at the Dead Sea Scrolls and the completion of the Canon of the Hebrew Scriptures. McCullough writes, "Not only were the Scriptures assembled, but Jewish values and customs, including the acceptable expressions of piety, were firmly established, and upon this foundation all subsequent Judaism was to be built. Since the Christian Church was initially the child of the Synagogue, it too stands in debt to these centuries, for much of Israel's legacy was appropriated by the early Christians and became in fact basic for the Christianity of the New Testament"—p. ix.

B120. Margolis, Max L., and Alexander Marx. *History of the Jewish People.* Philadelphia: Jewish Publication Society, 1944, 823 p.

Margolis and Marx cover an immense period of time and a large number of topics, beginning with Abraham and his age, which they place at 2000 B.C.E., and ending at the United States of America in 1925. Along the way they focus on the usual loci of early Jewish history, such as Moses, the conquest of Canaan, the kingdom of David, the time of Isaiah, Herod the Great, the time of Roman rule, the war with Rome ending in 67 C.E., and Moses Maimonides (1135-1204 C.E.), and further cover the history of the Jews in

Europe, including England, Germany, and Spain, as well as the United States.

B121. Miller, J. Maxwell, and John H. Hayes. *A History of Ancient Israel and Judah.* Philadelphia: Westminster Press, 1986, 524 p.

The authors place the rise of Israel in the setting of ancient New Eastern history. They then review the history of the Jews chronologically, closing with Judah during the Persian period and the activities of Ezra and Nehemiah. They indicate near the end of their book that "We know practically nothing about the history of the Jewish community between Ezra-Nehemiah and the conquest of Alexander the Great. What effect the Persian-Egyptian wars, the revolt of the satraps, the Phoenician rebellion initiated by Tennes, and the Persian reconquest of Egypt may have had on the Jerusalem community remains unknown"—p. 474.

B122. Mor, Menahem, and Uriel Rappaport, eds. *Bibliography of Works on Jewish History in the Hellenistic and Roman Periods, 1976-1980.* Jerusalem: Zalman Shazar Center, 1982, 95 p.

The authors refer to two earlier works which listed bibliographical material on this subject from 1946-1970 and from 1971-1975. Included in this guide are books, periodical articles, and festschriften, in many different languages. Materials are organized alphabetically by author under each subject heading. Typical categories include: "Judaism in the Period of the Second Temple," "The Pharisees," "The Essenes," "The Jews in Egypt," "The Jews in Italy," "1 Maccabees," "Roads," and others.

B123. Neusner, Jacob. *Ancient Judaism and Modern Category Formation: Judaism, Midrash, Messianism, and Canon in the Past Quarter Century.* Lanhan, MD: University Press of America, 1986, 138 p.

In the introduction Neusner describes how categories take shape and why they matter, examining them from a social constructionist point of view as well as circumstantially. He then applies these insights to the categories listed above in the subtitle. Neusner states that the word "Judaism" is usually used by the general public to refer to the Jewish religion (p. 20). In his last section he writes: "One route to the interpretation of a system is to specify the sorts of issues it chooses to regard as problems, the matters it chooses for its close and continuing exegesis....It is out of concern with this range of issues, and not some other, that the canon of Judaism in late antiquity defines its principal areas for discussion"—p. 119.

B124. Neusner, Jacob. *Ancient Judaism: Debates and Disputes.* Chico, CA: Scholars Press, 1984, 283 p.

Neusner writes: "In this book I propose to explain my work by systematically reviewing books of others, both of my own day and in times past." These include: Salo Baron's *History and Historians,* Ellis Rivkin's *The Shaping of Jewish History* and Rivkin's *A Hidden Revolution,* and Geza Vermes's *Jesus the Jew.* Neusner also comments on eighteen other items and three bibliographical essays. The scholars represented and the books chosen are some of the most important monographs published on the subjects Neusner has selected. He divides his guide into the following categories: 1) "Jewish History" in Theory; 2) "Jewish History" in Practice; 3) Describing "Judaism"; 4) Interpreting "Judaism"; 5) The Pharisees, Jesus Paul; and 6) Three Bibliographical Essays.

B125. Neusner, Jacob. *First Century Judaism in Crisis: Yohanan ben Zakkai and the Renaissance of Torah.* New York: Abingdon Press, 1970, 235 p.

This book is a popularized version of Neusner's *A Life of Yohanan ben Zakkai.* Yohanan is credited by the author with laying the foundation for present-day Judaism after the destruction of the Temple in 70 C.E. Neusner writes that he is only third in importance behind Moses and Jeremiah in shaping the Jewish religion. "We know for certain only this, that when everyone else had given up hope, Yohanan found a reason to persevere"—p. 11. In Part One, "Chaos & Routine," Neusner covers the Temple, Herod, the father of Yohanan (Zakkai), the economic life of the time, and Jewish education. He then discusses such topics as Shammai and Hillel and the Jerusalem Pharisees. In Part Two, "Society & Scripture," Neusner writes of the study of the Torah as a way of life, and delineates the various kinds of exegesis of the Torah. Part Three, "Death & Rebirth," covers Rome and the Pharisees, the theological challenge to Yohanan's philosophy and the latter's response to that challenge, and the shape of postwar Palestine, along with a discussion of various sects present at that time.

B126. Neusner, Jacob. *From Politics to Piety: The Emergence of Pharisaic Judaism.* Englewood Cliffs, NJ: Prentice-Hall, 1973, 168 p.

The eight chapters which make up this book include: The Problem of the Historical Pharisees, Hillel, Josephus's Pharisees: "The Real Administrators of the State," The Gospels' Pharisees: "Brood of Vipers," The Rabbinical Traditions about the Pharisees, Traditions of Yavneh (70-125 A.D.), Traditions of Usha (140-170 A.D.), and The Pharisees in History. In the section on the Pharisees in the Gospels, Neusner writes: "The Pharisees persecute the prophets, wise men, and scribes; they drive the messengers of God out of the synagogue. Surely the competition between the Pharisees and the Christian missionaries for the loyalty of the mass of Jews lies at the foundation of these sayings"—p. 77. In closing he says, "The Pharisees helped the Jews to reconcile themselves to their new situation, to accept what could not be changed, and to see significance in what could yet be decided. They invested powerlessness with such meaning that ordinary folk, living everyday lives, might still regard themselves as a kingdom of priests and a holy people"—p. 153-154.

B127. Neusner, Jacob. *History of the Jews in Babylonia.* Leiden: E. J. Brill, 1964-1970, 5 v.

The subtitles the five volumes are: "The Parthian Period," "The Early Sasanian Period," "From Shapur I to Shapur II," "The Age of Shapur II," and "Later Sasanian Times." Neusner says that because the sources for this period are not well known, other than ubiquitous Josephus, or if well known are often not historically interpreted, he has quoted extensively from the Talmudic sources. Neusner states: "While I shall try to show that certain limited parts of Talmudic literature originated in Babylonian Jewry during this period, I have otherwise been unable to find any Talmudic sayings, stories, or the like, introduced into Jewish tradition in Babylonia during the Tannaitic period"—Vol.1, p.xi. In volume 5 the author writes: "Since my effort has been to study the history of Babylonian Jewry and Judaism in the context of Iranian history, a more natural conclusion comes with the death of Yazdagird III in the middle of the seventh century A.D."—Vol. 5, p. xv. Volume 1 contains material from the first century C.E.; in a section on Hillel, Neusner writes: "Hillel came to Jerusalem from Babylonia at some point in Herod's reign and quickly achieved prominence in the Pharisaic party. Two questions concerning Hillel interest us here; first, that of his pre-Palestinian training, if any, and second, that of his relationships with Herod and, tangentially, Herod's relationships with the Pharisees"—Vol. 1, p. 36.

B128. Neusner, Jacob. *A Life of Rabban Yohanan Ben Zakkai: ca. 1-80 C.E.* Leiden: E. J. Brill, 1962, 200 p.

Neusner begins: "In the first century, men generally regarded religion as an irreducible historical reality. They did not, for the most part, try to explain it as a consequence of economic, social, or psychological causes. For Jews, Scripture embodied the record of man's genuine religious experience. They therefore looked into its ancient literature to find paradigmatic instruction on the nature of religion. They did so through the medium of disciplined exegesis, called midrash (from darash, to search)"—p. 1. Revered as the rabbi who would lay the first foundation to move Judaism from Temple to study of Torah in the broadest sense, Yohanan is described by Neusner in the following terms: "If Israel might enjoy better fortune by faithfulness to God's will then Yohanan ben Zakkai's task at Yavneh was to show how to do his will with neither sanctuary, nor holy city, nor (at the outset) national tribunal. The most pressing problems were liturgical, for the observance of holy days and festivals were commemorated in the sacrifical cult. Yohanan therefore decreed a series of specific modifications of law necessitated by the disaster. Somewhat later, he and his successors came to define the authority of the academy which issued these ordinances"—p. 147.

B129. Neusner, Jacob. *Major Trends in Formative Judaism.* Chico, CA: Scholars Press, 1983- , 3 v.+.

Volume 1 in this series, "Society and Symbol in Political Crisis," covers such topics as: Mishnah and Messiah, and Beyond Myth, After Apocalypse: the Mishnaic Conception of History. Volume 2, "Texts, Contents, and Contexts," includes chapters on: The Humanistic Study of Formative Judaism, Judaism and Scripture: The Case of Leviticus Rabbah," and American Study of Judaism: The Academic Setting. Volume 3, "The Three Stages in the

Formation of Judaism," includes five parts chronologically arranged from the first through fourth centuries, and then skips to the twentieth century. Part One of this volume, entitled "The First Century: The Pharisaic Stage in the Formation of Judaism," has a chapter entitled "Covenantal Nomism: The Piety of Judaism in the First Century."

B130. Oesterley, William O. *The Jews and Judaism During the Greek Period: The Background of Christianity.* Port Washington, NY: Kennikat Press, 1970 (c1941), 307 p.

Written in 1941, Oesterley's book first examines the historical background of the period beginning with the conquest of Perisa, and then looks at Jewish history from the third century B.C. to Roman domination. The author then takes a thematic approach, first looking at the sources, including the Scriptures, the Law, Apocalyptic writings and the influence of Persian thought. He studies the theology of Judaism by examining its belief in monotheism, the kingdom of Heaven, the Messiah, and other themes. He also delineates Jewish worship through an examination of the Temple and synagogue, and highlights the importance of teachers through the practices of the Pharisees and the Essenes. He concludes with a look at angels and demonology in Judaism.

B131. Oppenheimer, Aharon. *The Am Ha-aretz: A Study in the Social History of the Jewish People in the Hellenistic-Roman Period.* Leiden: E. J. Brill, 1977, 261 p.

Oppenheimer opens by examining the idea of tithes and ritual purity, and the relation of the 'Am Ha-Aretz to these ideas and to the Torah. He then looks at the relevance of the 'Ammei Ha-Aretz to the Pharisees and the Haverim, who were also strict in their observation of the purity laws. A final section discusses the relation of the Christians and Samaritans to the 'Am Ha-Aretz. "A synoptic glance at these sources reveals at the outset only this—that to apply to an individual or a group the term 'am ha-aretz is to criticize or disparage that individual or group"—p. 1. "In the sources the 'ammei ha-aretz are defined as such because they did not scrupulously observe certain commandments and because of their ignorance of the Torah"—p. 22.

B132. Rhoads, David. *Israel in Revolution, 6-74 C.E.: A Political History Based on the Writings of Josephus*. Philadelphia: Fortress Press, 1976, 199 p.

Rhoads covers the life of Josephus, comments on Josephus as a historian, and then examines the sources Josephus used as a basis for his work. He then moves to the historical background and covers the major Jewish sects. Writing about the resistance of the Jews towards Rome, he discusses Judas the Galilean and the Jewish revolt of 6 C.E., focusing on the dissension prevalent in both the Jewish countryside and in Jerusalem itself. The revolutionary Zealots and Sicarri constantly fomented violent resistance leading to war. Rhoads reaches several conclusions: "Our study has shown that there is little evidence for the presence or activity of a Jewish revolutionary sect in the prewar history of 6-44 C.E. We have seen that the faction of the Sicarii, led by the descendants of Judas of Galilee, may have been active in the two decades before the war; however, they did not organize or control other revolutionaries"—p. 174. According to Rhoads, a cross-section of the entire Jewish populace was responsible for the general unrest during this period.

B133. Riggs, James S. *A History of the Jewish People During the Maccabean and Roman Periods, Including New Testament Times*. New York: Charles Scribner's Sons, 1917 (c1900), 320 p.

Riggs uses 1 and 2 Maccabees, Josephus, Daniel, Enoch, and the Sibylline Oracles for his primary sources. He takes a chronological approach to his subject, focusing on the political atmosphere of the time. In a statement typical of the scholarship of his day, he states that we must know the period in which Jesus and his apostles lived in order to understand Jesus's progress, adding: "Conversely, their spirit and attitude interpret for us with unmistakable clearness the misconceptions of Judaism and the disastrous blindness of heathenism. The simple, graphic pictures of the gospels are true to fact in geography, customs, life, and national hope"—p. 145. Although Riggs's attitudes are somewhat *passé*, his book still includes some material of interest to the present-day scholar.

B134. Russell, David S. *The Jews from Alexander to Herod*. London: Oxford University Press, 1972 (c1967), 329 p.

Russell first covers the history of the period, with emphasis on the contemporary political leaders beginning with Alexander the Great, and continuing through the great rebellion of 166 B.C. to life under the Romans and the Dispersion. A second section on religion covers the foundations of Judaism, including the Torah, Temple and Synagogue, and such religious ideas as messianic hope. Russell then reviews the factions within Judaism, such as the Pharisees. The final section on the literature begins with both canonical and extra-canonical books, focusing specifically on prophecy. Zechariah 9-14 is reviewed, along with a section on apocalyptic and one on Wisdom literature. Concerning the Pharisees' differences with the Sadducees, he writes: "Both parties accepted the Torah as authoritative, but the Pharisees alone accepted the Prophets and the Writings also as authoritative sacred Scripture, whose teachings they used in their interpretation of the Torah itself"—p. 161.

B135. Safrai, Shemuel, and Menahem Stern, eds. *The Jewish People in the First Century: Historical Geography, Political History, Social, Cultural and Religious Life and Institutions.* 2 v. Assen: Van Gorcum, 1974-76.

Although all of the information in this two-volume anthology is useful, special attention should be given to the second book, where Safrai comments on religion in everyday life, the Temple and synagogue, and education and study of the Torah. In speaking of the religious life of the Jews, Safrai writes: "The most striking characteristic of the Jewish people in the period of the Second Temple was the observance of the Law of the one God, as revealed in the written Torah and the oral tradition. That the whole life of the Jewish people, from hour to hour of its working days as well as on the solemn moments of sabbath and feast-day, was dominated by the Law is evident from talmudic tradition, Josephus and the New Testament, especially the writings of Paul"—p. 793.

B136. Sanders, E. P., A. I. Baumgarten, and Alan Mendelson, eds. *Jewish and Christian Self Definition: Volume 2, Aspects of Judaism in the Graeco-Roman Period.* Philadelphia: Fortress Press, 1981, 450 p.

The twelve essays in this anthology have each been written by a different author who is also a major scholar in the area he covers. Of special interest are the following chapters: "Interpretation and the Tendency to Sectarianism: An Aspect of Second Temple History," by Joseph Blenkinsopp; "Christian and Jewish Self-Definition in the Light of Christian Additions to the Apocryphal Writings," by James H. Charlesworth; and "Jewish Acceptance and Rejection of Hellenism," by Jonathan Goldstein.

In his essay Charlesworth writes: "Although early Christians used and transmitted the Old Testament and Old Testament Apocrypha with little, if any, modification, they obviously felt compelled to rewrite and expand the Old Testament Pseudepigrapha"—p. 27. Jamesworth affirms: "Most prominent, especially in the interpolations in the Hellenistic Synagogal Prayers and the Testaments of the Twelve Patriarchs, are additions that can be classified as an example of teleological determinism; their interest was not only primarily doctrinal or historical, but to specify the only proper means of interpreting the fulfilment of prophecy. It is clear that early Christians read ancient prayers and narratives in the light of the life of Jesus of Nazareth, whom they claimed to be the Christ"—p. 54. He also asserts: "The complexity of traditions, both within the Christian additions to Jewish apocryphal writings and within the "canonical" New Testament, indicates that for hundreds of years (at least) there were numerous normative self-definitions within Christianity"—p. 55.

B137. Shurer, Emil. *The History of the Jewish People in the Age of Jesus Christ.* Edinburgh: T. & T. Clark, 1924, 5 v. New English Version revised and ed. by Geza Vermes and Fergus Millar. Edinburgh: T. & T. Clark, 1973-79, 4 v.

This massive work has been brought up to date by editors Vermes and Millar. The introduction to volume one elucidates the sources for the study of the subject. Part One of this volume presents the history of the period from the Maccabaean rising in 175 B.C. through the Roman-Herodian Age ending in 135 A.D. Volume Two takes a topical approach to cover the cultural setting and political institutions of the Jewish state, including such topics as the Priesthood and Temple worship and the Pharisees and Sadducees, and Messianism. Volume Three, Part One covers Judaism in the Diaspora, Jewish literature composed in Hebrew or Aramaic (such as religious poetry), Wisdom literature, Biblical Midrash, the writings of the Qumran community, and Jewish literature composed in Greek (for example, the work of Philo). The second part of Volume Three includes more material on the Biblical Midrash and an extensive section on the writings of Philo, plus a comprehensive index for all the volumes. *The History* has extensive bibliographies in several languages scattered throughout the volumes.

B138. Shunami, Shlomo. *Bibliography of Jewish Bibliographies.* Jerusalem: Magnes Press, 1969, 997 p.

This comprehensive source arranges its material under such topics as: "Bible," "Talmudic and Midrashic Literature," "Sects," "History," and others. Items under each subject category are arranged alphabetically by author, and there is an extensive index of names and subjects. A supplement or new edition is clearly needed.

B139. Shulvass, Moses A. *The History of the Jewish People, Volume 1: The Antiquity.* Chicago: Regnery Gateway, 1982, 250 p.

"Antiquity" in this case means coverage from the origins of the Jewish people in the ancient Near East to the time of the Jews living in Europe in the sixth century C.E. Topics of importance include: Judea under Persia, including information on the Samaritans; the encounter with Hellenism; and the religious life of the Jews under the Romans. Jesus is treated in a section on "Messianic Expectations and the Emergence of Christianity."

B140. Sigal, Phillip. *The Emergence of Contemporary Judaism, Volume 1: The Foundations of Judaism.* 2 v. Pittsburgh: Pickwick Press, 1977-80.

The subtitles of the two parts are: Part One: From the Origins to the Separation of Christianity; Part Two: Rabbinic Judaism. In part one Sigal discusses the foundations of Judaism in chapters on the religion of Israel, renewal, Hellenism's challenge and Judaism's response, and the variety of religious experience within Judaism. He then delineates the rise and separation of Christianity. In part two he examines Rabbinic-Talmudic Judaism and its theology, and then looks at what he calls the "media" of Judaism: namely, the synagogue and the primary sources, including the Bible, the Mishnah, Tosefta, and Talmud.

B141. Smallwood, E. Mary. *The Jews Under Roman Rule: From Pompey to Diocletian.* Leiden: E. J. Brill, 1976, 595 p.

Of special interest is Smallwood's description of Herod's rise to power, the chapter on the province of Judea from A.D. 6-41, and the section on Philip Antipas and Herod Agrippa I. In her Conclusion, she writes: "Judaism as a cult fulfilled the Roman criteria for permitted survival: it was morally unobjectionable and, at least among the Diaspora with whom alone Rome had direct and continuous dealings as subjects when formulating her Jewish policy in the first century B.C., politically innocuous"—p. 539. "In Palestine the Jewish religion was not a harmless racial eccentricity but a politically subversive force from the viewpoint of Rome as the occupying and governing power, because it was inextricably bound up with the nationalist aspirations which sprang from militant Jewish nationalism"—p. 541.

B142. Stone, Michael. *Scriptures, Sects and Visions: A Profile of Judaism from Ezra to the Jewish Revolts.* Philadelphia: Fortress Press, 1980, 160 p.

Among the eleven chapters these are of special interest: "New Light on the Third Century," "Enoch and Apocalyptic Origins," "Sects, Temples and the Occult," and "Gnosticism and Judaism." Stone comments: "By way of reminder: if we were dependent on the rabbinic sources alone, we would know very little about the Maccabean revolt and very little about the war against the Romans in 68-70 C.E. A good deal is known about the former because of two books which are preserved in Greek—one a translation from Hebrew—these are the two Books of Maccabees. A great deal is known about the details and the course of the war against the Romans because the writing of the Jewish historian, Flavius Josephus, survived in Christian hands"—p. 51. "The Pharisees and Sadducees play a major role in Josephus' narrative of the events in Judea. The Pharisees are characterized, above all, as exegetes of the scriptures, marked out by skill in this activity and by the authority with which they regard their own exegesis"—p. 74. "The body of evidence indicates that we must maintain a more complex view of the character of Judaism than might otherwise have been thought necessary. Even the temple, which was clearly the central common institution around whose sanctity the vast majority of the Jewish people united, was in fact subject to differing attitudes"—p. 81-82.

B143. Surburg, Raymond F. *Introduction to the Intertestamental Period.* St. Louis: Concordia, 1975, 197 p.

In discussing the historical background of the period, Surburg takes a chronological approach, beginning with the Persian rule, then moving through Alexander the Great and the Ptolemies to other rulers, and ending with the Jews under the Romans. In discussing the religious background of the period he delineates the various Jewish sects and the theological teachings of the time. In his final section, on the literature of the time, he covers the Septuagint, the Dead Sea Scrolls, Apocrypha and Pseudepigrapha, and Philo and Josephus.

B144. Toombs, Lawrence E. *The Threshold of Christianity; Between the Testaments*. Philadelphia: Westminster Press, 1960, 96 p.

Toombs discusses the literature of the intertestamental period in a thematic fashion, dealing with conceptions of the present age, the age to come, and life under the law. He also includes a section on the Dead Sea Scrolls. This very brief discussion is typical of many of the books in this series, the Westminster Guides to the Bible.

B145. Vermes, Geza. *Post Biblical Jewish Studies*. Leiden: E. J. Brill, 1975, 246 p.

Vermes has gathered twelve previously published papers appearing between 1960-1974, and has himself written a thirteenth specifically for this volume. The three major areas covered are: Qumran, Bible Exegesis, and Rabbinic History. Of special interest is his paper on ancient Judaism in the light of the Dead Sea Scrolls, and "Bible and Midrash: Early Old Testament Exegesis." In discussing the text of the Bible and the light which the Qumran Scrolls have thrown on the issue, Vermes writes: "The traditional biblical manuscripts established by early medieval scholars known as the Masoretes (guardians of tradition) display practically no worthwhile variant readings. Already before the discoveries at Qumran, it was conjectured that this uniformity was due not to an unwavering transmission from the start until the Middle Ages, but to a revision achieved by the rabbis of the first two centuries of the Christian era. Twenty-five years ago, this was probable hypothesis; today it is a near certainty"—p. 4.

B146. Whitelocke, Lester. *The Development of Jewish Religious Thought in the Inter-Testamental Period.* New York: Vantage Press, 1976, 143 p.

This small self-published volume covers Judaism in the Graeco-Roman period, and then reviews religious developments, the rise of the Pharisees, the influence of Apocalypticism on Pharisaic teaching, and the Pharisaic ideas of judgment, resurrection, and the world to come. An example of the way in which Whitelocke often does *not* examine his sources thoroughly enough can be seen in this quotation: "Even though the Pharisees have been labelled hypocrites in the New Testament, still they represented that element in the Jewish nation which was most zealous for the religion of the Torah, and they were thorough-going in the application of the principles of the Torah"—p. 65.

B147. Yadin, Yigael. *Bar-Kokhba: The Rediscovery of the Legendary Hero of the Second Jewish Revolt Against Rome.* New York: Random House, 1971, 271 p.

Yadin provides an account of an archaeological expedition to Israel to find hard information on the Jewish rebel, Bar-Kokhba. Yadin writes: "In the following pages I have striven, therefore, to let the reader share with the archaeologists, their thoughts, planning, frustrations and joys before, and during, the two short seasons of digging in the remote caves of the Judean Desert"—p. 13 of the Preface. What results is a fascinating illustrated diary of this adventure in excavation. On almost every page there are plates showing the artifacts discovered, with detailed printed explanations of what each means in the context of the known history of the time.

B148. Zeitlin, Solomon. *Solomon Zeitlin's Studies in the Early History of Judaism.* Vol. 1 of 4 v. New York: Ktav Publishing House, 1973-78.

Of special importance in volume one are the chapters: "The Temple and Worship: A Study of the Development of Judaism. A Chapter in the History of the Second Jewish Commonwealth," "The Judaean Calendar During the Second Commonwealth and the Scrolls," "The Political Synedrion and the Religious Sanhedrin," "Herod: A Malevolent Maniac," and "Hillel and the Hermeneutic Rules."

JEWISH LITERATURE

B149. Bowker, John. *The Targums and Rabbinic Literature: An Introduction to Jewish Interpretations of Scripture.* London: Cambridge University Press, 1969, 379 p.

After discussing pre-Rabbinic and non-Rabbinic literature as well as classical Rabbinic literature, Bowker spends much of his time translating Pseudo-Jonathan on selected chapters of Genesis. In the Preface he writes: "This book has two purposes. The first is to provide an introduction to the Aramaic Targums, which preserve some of the most basic and popular elements of Jewish biblical interpretation; the second is to show how the Targums form a part of Jewish exegesis in general, and thus the book is also intended to be a brief introduction to rabbinic literature"—p. ix. The Targums are Aramaic translations of Old Testament texts. "The Targum chosen for translation is one known as Pseudo-Jonathan (Ps.Jon.). It was chosen partly because it is the latest and most developed example of the 'Targum-tradition,' showing what that tradition became in its most extended form..."—p. xii.

B150. Buchler, Adolf. *Studies in Sin and Atonement in the Rabbinic Literature of the First Century.* New York: Ktav Publishing House, 1967 (c1928), 461 p.

Buchler's book is broken into a number of description chapter heads: "Obedience to the Torah, Its Source and Sanction," "The Service of God for the Love or the Fear of Him and the Right Attitude to Suffering," "The Defiling Force of Sin in the Bible," "The Defiling Force of Sin in Post-Biblical and the Rabbinic Literature," "Atonement of Sin by Sacrifice." Buchler's point of view is shown in the first sentences of his Introduction: "Sin and atonement occupy a central position in the system of every monotheistic religion, and may be presumed to have also formed an important part in the religious thought and experience of post-Biblical Jewry in Palestine. These two experiences of the individual soul in their various aspects and manifestations are reflected in the early Rabbinic literature, and should therefore hold a prominent place in every presentation of the religious life and the religion of the Jews in Palestine in the first century"—p. xiii. Although this book is somewhat dated, it still will help Christians become more aware of the importance of the concept of atonement in Judaism, both early and present-day.

B151. *Cambridge Commentaries on Writings of the Jewish and Christian World, 200 B.C. to A.D. 200.* New York: Cambridge University Press, 1985- , v.

The *Commentaries* promise to be an outstanding series for understanding each time and place covered. Volumes already published cover: *Jews in the Hellenistic World,* and *Sources Outside the Old Testament and the Qumran Community.* I have included the volume by Alfred Leaney (*The Jewish and Christian World, 200 B.C.-200 A.D.* [see B218]) separately in this bibliography.

B152. Charlesworth, James H. *The Old Testament Pseudepigrapha and the New Testament.* New York: Cambridge University Press, 1985, 213 p.

Charlesworth begins with a review of the modern study of pseudepigrapha and the challenges they present to the scholar. He also writes about the relation of pseudepigrapha to early Judaism and Christian origins, specifically their relationship to the New Testament, with special attention to the ideas of Messianism and Christology. He closes the book with accounts of seminars held on pseudepigrapha from 1976-1983. Charlesworth notes the criticisms of E. P. Sanders concerning those who compare early Judaism and early Christianity. He also points out that in studying the documents of early Judaism, we must read the complete texts themselves, and not some selection in an anthology. As with the books of the New Testament, we must consider the "historical matrix of the documents, the possible layers of tradition, and the alterations of traditions evident thanks to years of form critical analysis and redaction criticism"—p. 49.

B153. Charlesworth, James H. *The Pseudepigrapha and Modern Research, with a Supplement.* Chico, CA: Scholars Press, 1981, 329 p.

Charlesworth provides a brief discussion of each document of the Pseudepigrapha, including the Prayer of Joseph, and then records secondary sources (books and periodical articles) under each entry. In his discerning introduction he discusses the importance of Pseudepigrapha in relation to the Dead Sea Scrolls, Gnosticism, and the New Testament, stating that it "...is important to the Humanist,

Jew, and Christian. All three find these documents valuable because of their importance in the history of ideas since they advance significantly man's understanding of sin and the origin of evil, man's awareness of God's grandeur with the exaltation of Him progressively to more distant heavens, and man's belief in a resurrection with the subsequent speculation upon the place and qualities of paradise. The often bizarre, usually rich apocalyptic traditions upon which the Pseudepigrapha almost has a monopoly were determinative for the thoughts of Dante, Bunyan, and Milton"—p. 25.

B154. Collins, John J. *The Apocalyptic Imagination: An Introduction to the Jewish Matrix of Christianity.* New York: Crossroad, 1984, 280 p.

Collins first considers the genre of apocalyptic literature, and then examines such specific examples as the Enoch literature, the book of Daniel, some Qumran material, the Similitudes of Enoch, material written after the fall of Jerusalem in 70 C.E., and material from the Diaspora in the Roman period. "The importance of apocalypticism for Christian origins centers on the most basic of all Christian beliefs, the resurrection of Jesus from the dead. The resurrection was never viewed as an isolated miracle but rather as a revelatory event that provided a new perspective on life and history. The new perspective could be articulated in various ways and in time was found to be compatible with various theological and philosophical systems. In the earliest stages of Christianity, however, the context in which the understanding of the resurrection developed was distinctly apocalyptic"—p. 207.

B155. Corre, Alan, ed. *Understanding the Talmud.* New York: Ktav Publishing House, 1975, 468 p.

This anthology includes essays which provide a general understanding of the Mishnah and Talmud, as well as discussions of the world within the Talmud (such as the economic conditions of Judaea reflected in the Talmud), of the world outside the Talmud (including Graeco-Roman views of the Jews), of movements such as the Pharisees, of the law (including an essay on Rabbinic methods of interpretation), and of the religion of the Jews at the time of Jesus. The thirty-five articles provide an excellent background matrix for further examinations of the Talmud.

B156. Fischel, Henry A., ed. *Essays in Greco-Roman and Related Talmudic Literature.* New York: Ktav Publishing House, 1977, 600 p.

This multilingual anthology includes a number of English-language essays on such topics as Hillel and Shammai, Palestinian polemics against idolatry, Roman and Jewish law, Palestinian Judaism in the first century, the number of Greeks living in Palestine, and "Talmudic-Midrashic Affinities of Some Aesopic Fables." Also included is an annotated bibliography of monographs, articles, and chapters on Greco-Roman philosophical and rhetorical literature and Talmudic-Midrashic writings from 1850-1975. The articles cover most of the topics necessary for a basic understanding of the variety of approaches to the study of first-century Judaism.

B157. Fitzmyer, Joseph A., and Daniel J. Harrington, eds. *A Manual of Palestinian Aramaic Texts: Second Century B.C.-Second Century A.D.* Rome: Biblical Institute Press, 1978, 373 p.

Fitzmyer and Harrington include a diverse number of texts, among Biblical commentaries, intertestamental literature, letters, business documents, and contracts, all arranged in chronological order (insofar as it can be determined). "The kind of Aramaic that is found in these texts belongs to the period of Middle Aramaic, as this had been defined by J.A. Fitzmyer in *The Genesis Apocryphon of Qumran Cave 1: A Commentary...*"—p. xi. Matching Aramaic and English translations are given on facing pages.

B158. Ginzberg, Louis. *The Legends of the Jews.* Philadelphia: Jewish Publication Society of America, 1956 (c1909) , 7 v.

Coverage of these legends begins with Volume 1, "Bible Times and Characters from Creation to Jacob" and extends through Volume 6, "From Moses in the Wilderness to Egypt." Volume 7 provides an index to the entire set. Ginzberg has gathered "...from the original sources all Jewish legends, in so far as they refer to Biblical personages and events...."—Vol. 1, p. xi—including material from Talmudic-Midrashic literature from the second to the fourteenth century C.E., from the Targumim (4th-10th century C.E.), from Medieval Bible commentators and homilists, and from the

Kabbalah, which quotes various items of Midrashim now lost in their original forms.

B159. Goodblatt, David M. *Rabbinic Instruction in Sasanian Babylonia.* Leiden: E. J. Brill, 1975, 322 p.

Goldblatt examines the traditions of the Babylonian Amoraic schools and the views of modern scholars on this issue. In Part 2 he discusses the names of Rabbinic academic institutions in the Babylonian Talmud, believing that "rabbinic academic activity in Sasanian Babylonia was not dominated by large academies on the model of the Geonic yeshivot." Though there were some schools, most were "disciple circles." The author concludes: "In addition to relating details about the disciple circle system, the anecdotes cited above all illustrate the centrality of the individual master rather than the institution"—p. 270.

B160. Guttmann, Alexander. *Rabbinic Judaism in the Making: A Chapter in the History of the Halakhah from Ezra to Judah I.* Detroit: Wayne State University Press, 1970, 323 p.

Guttmann begins with a review of the Soferic period, examining Ezra and the Great Assembly. He then discusses the Pharisaic-early Tannaitic period and the Sanhedrin, Hillel and Shammai, the Pharisees, Sadducees, and Essenes, and Gamaliel I. The final section reviews the Tannaitic period and Johanan Ben Zakkai, Gamaliel II, and Judah I, among others. In explaining why Rabbinic Judaism survived, Guttmann writes, "Deep devotion to God and His law, while a *conditio sine qua non*, cannot be the only reason, since this was a quality of some other branches of Judaism as well. An analytical study of Judaism shows that rabbinism prevailed through the ages due to the clear vision and effective guidance of its leaders, the rabbis. These men possessed a deep understanding of the need for a warm and practical religious expression, genuinely Jewish, and at the same time harmonious with the spiritual and material life of the peoples surrounding them"—p. xii. Although Guttmann does review the lives of his subjects, he tends to focus more on their specific contributions to the interpretation of the Law.

B161. Halivni, David. *Midrash, Mishnah and Gemara: The Jewish Predilection for Justified Law.* Cambridge, MA: Harvard University Press, 1986, 176 p.

Halivni uses a chronological approach to approach his subject, as can be seen in his chapter titles: "The Biblical Period," "The Post-Biblical Period," "The Mishnaic Period," "The Amoraic Period," "The Stammaitic Period," "The Gemara as Successor of Midrash," and "The Legacy of the Stammaim." In his introduction the author discusses the redactional changes to the Talmud, which he says shows that some of the texts were originally transmitted haphazardly: "All this sounds strange and runs counter to the general belief that every statement of the sages was meticulously preserved—until one notices that the overwhelming majority of redactional changes occurred in the discursive passages of the Talmud, the ones that contain arguments and discussions, rather than in the apodictic passages, the ones that contain fixed law"—p. 2). The redactors of the Talmud, whom Halivni calls "...Stammaim, which is Aramaic for 'anonyms'..." were not just arrangers but were involved in the process of the creation of the Talmud—p. 3. The Midrashic form ties the law to Scripture and was intended to justify portions of the text. The redactors contributed to the process by re-examining the nature of Midrashic and Mishnaic forms. "The Stammaim captured the Jewish imagination, which was prepared all along to become captive to them by its natural reluctance to accept categorical law"—p. 92.

B162. Heinemann, Joseph, and Jakob J. Petuchowski, eds. *Literature of the Synagogue.* New York: Behrman House, 1975, 292 p.

The editors have collected the prayers, sermons, and poetry of the synagogue, giving the historical background to each piece, and showing how they have been used in synagogue services throughout the ages. Biblical material as well as the Mishnah and Talmud are included.

B163. Hoenig, Sidney B. *Solomon Zeitlin, Scholar Laureate: An Annotated Bibliography , 1915-1970, with Appreciations of His Writings.* New York: Bitzaron, 1971, 296 p.

The volume begins with "Recognitions" of the work of Zeitlin and then appreciations for Zeitlin's work written by nine different scholars. The annotated bibiliography which follows is arranged chronologically by year and then alphabetically by title. An index of subjects is also included. Dr. Zeitlin's work includes some of the most important materials yet written on the intertestamental period and the Second Jewish Commonwealth.

B164. Idelsohn, Abraham Z. *Jewish Liturgy and Its Development.* New York: Sacred Music Press, 1932, 404 p.

"This book attempts to give a comprehensive presentation of Jewish liturgy in all its phases. It describes the growth and the forms the liturgy assumed during the ages. Public services and private devotions, Synagogue and Home worship, are equally treated"—p. iii. A particularly relevant section focuses on worship during the Second Temple period. Idelsohn also describes the beginnings of the synagogue.

B165. Kadushin, Max. *The Rabbinic Mind.* 3rd ed. New York: Bloch Publishing Company, 1972, 414 p.

Kadushin conflates materials from the Rabbis and shows how they relate to certain modern conceptions such as the self, God, values, mysticism, and psychology of religion. His approach can be seen in this quotation from his preface to the second edition: "On the one hand the rabbinic mind is expressed in Halakah: law and juristic discussions and interpretations; and on the other it is expressed in Haggadah: nonjuristic interpretations and statements. Since both Halakah and Haggadah are aspects of the rabbinic mind there must be a large factor common to both, a factor that ought to be identified at the very beginning of our inquiry. It cannot possibly consist of statements, however inclusive, nor of the laws in Halakah and all the statements in Haggadah. What is common to both Halakah and Haggaadah are rabbinic concepts embodied in the particular laws and statements"—p. xi. Thus, Kadushin is dealing not just with the content of the law, but a demonstration of the processes by which the Rabbinic mind deliberated, as well as the transmission of social values through these texts.

B166. Koch, Klaus. *The Rediscovery of Apocalyptic: A Polemical Work on a Neglected Area of Biblical Studies and Its Damaging Effects on Theology and Philosophy.* Naperville, IL: A. R. Allenson, 1972, 157 p.

Chapter titles include: "The Gulf between Prophecy and Apocalyptic," "The Agonized Attempt to Save Jesus from Apocalyptic," "Systematic Theology turns to Eschatology,"

"Apocalyptic as a Disquieting Motif in Non-theological Thinking," and "Why Things Must Change: A Highly Subjective Epilogue." Koch believes that Biblical scholars who write about the apocalypse often fling down judgments which are based on outdated methods of research and "secondary literature of the era before the first World War..."—p. 123. Part of Koch's complaint is shown in this quotation: "The non-biblical material which is used is employed in a purely illustrative way; its exegetical application seems superficial and a matter of chance; the material is not fitted together with biblical statements into one overall context of life, since it is not understood as being the product of one and the same history"—p. 124. Koch also thinks there is a fear among the theologians that Jesus may be akin to apocalyptic, and belives we should look for the uniqueness of Jesus not in his preaching but in his ministry.

B167. Lipman, Eugene J., ed. *The Mishnah: Oral Teachings of Judaism*. New York: Schocken, 1974, 318 p.

"The purpose of this brief selection of Mishnaic material is to present to serious readers some interesting and relevant passages with a straightforward, traditional commentary. The hope is that it will illustrate the role of this classic in the evolution of Halakhah—Jewish law—and of Judaism in general."—Preface. Lipman arranges his material in the same order of the Mishnah itself. His general introduction to the book as well as his prefaces to each section are quite useful. This commentary helps illuminate what to many Christians are relatively unknown references.

B168. Marmorstein, Arthur. *The Old Rabbinic Doctrine of God.* London: Oxford University Press, 1927-1937, 2 v.

Volume 1 covers the names and attributes of God. These include: omnipresence, omniscience, omnipotence, eternity, truth, purity, and holiness, among others. Marmorstein gives each name in Hebrew, quotes a passage in Rabbinical writings where it occurs, and then offers commentary on the passage.

B169. Metzger, Bruce M. *An Introduction to the Apocrypha*. New York: Oxford University Press, 1957, 274 p.

After providing some background on each book of the Apocrypha, Metzger composes a summary of each book and shows how they may have been used throughout history. Metzger has chapters on the Apocrypha and the New Testament, a brief history of the use of the Apocrypha in the Christian church, and illustrations of how the Apocrypha has influenced literature, music, and art.

B170. Mielziner, Moses. *Introduction to the Talmud.* 4th ed. New York: Bloch Publishing Company, 1968, 415 p.

Essentially an unchanged reprint of the 1925 third edition, *Introduction to the Talmud* does include "a selected list of relevant literature printed after 1924." Mielziner begins with a historical and literary introduction which includes a listing of the Talmud and its component parts. He then presents information on the Mishnah and its expounders, a separate chapter on Gemara, and a discussion of commentaries on the Talmud. At length he then discusses the legal hermeneutics of the Talmud and the terminology and methodology of the Talmud. A final section includes an outline of Talmudical ethics. Mielziner gives his summary of the content of the Talmud in his first paragraph: "The Talmud is the work which embodies the mental labors of the ancient Jewish teachers during a period of about eight hundred years (from about 300 before, to 500 after, the Christian era) in expounding and developing the civil and religious law of the Bible. Besides, it contains the theosophical views, ethical maxims and exegetical remarks of those teachers; it is inter-woven with many valuable historical and ethnographical records and occasional references to the different branches of ancient knowledge and sciences."—p. 3.

B171. Moeller, Henry, ed. *The Legacy of Zion: Inter-Testamental Texts Related to the New Testament.* Grand Rapids, MI: Baker Book House, 1977, 212 p.

The documents are arranged under three headings: namely, "The Maccabean Freedom Struggle," "The Hasmonean Heyday," and "Judea Under Rome." Under each section there is a historical sketch with reprints of selected passages from the literature of the time. Moeller scatters commentary throughout the readings.

B172. Montefiore, Claude, and H. Loewe. *A Rabbinic Anthology.* Cleveland: World Publishing Company, 1960 (c1938).

Although anthologies of this type have fallen out of favor in recent years because the selections do not allow the reader to see or understand what was selected (and omitted) in its broader context, I have included it so the reader may become aware of this type of publication and become acquainted with the information in its introductions. The material is arranged under such broad subjects as: "The Nature and Character of God and His Relations with Man," "The Law," and "On Prayer." There are helpful tables at the back of the volume, including one listing the major Rabbis. The material is selected from the Talmud.

B173. Montefiore, Claude J. *Rabbinic Literature and Gospel Teachings*. New York: Ktav Publishing House, 1970, c 1930.

Eugene Mihaly points out in a prolegomenon to this new printing of Montefiore's work that much of what appears in this volume is really not new, but an expansion of several chapters of an earlier work entitled *Old Testament and After*. Montefiore wanted to show rabbinic parallels to the Gospels, and he covers both Matthew and Luke. In his Introduction, the author writes: "The present book is intended as a sort of supplement to my Commentary on the Synoptic Gospels, to which I am often obliged to refer (second editon, 1927). In that Commentary I gave very few parallels to the religious and ethical teaching in the Gospels which can be gathered from the Rabbinic literature. Here the omission, to some extent at any rate, is supplied. I limit myself entirely to the religious and ethical teaching of the Gospels and the Rabbis."—p. xxxv. "I have to admit that the 'parallels' are not allowed to speak for themselves, for I have added a certain amount of commentary."—p. xxxvi.

B174. Moore, George Foot. *Judaism in the First Centuries of the Christian Era: The Age of Tannaim*. Cambridge, MA: Harvard University Press, 1927-30, 3 v.

Moore's work has been recognized in recent years as a watershed work. Though a Protestant scholar, he gave a much more sympathetic, even informed, presentation of Judaism during the first centuries than had been done before. Rather than thinking of Judaism as dry legalism (these two words have often been joined together by non-Jewish scholars in the past), Moore saw a vital and dynamic religion. Volume 1 contains a historical introduction and a review of the sources used for the study. Moore then gives material under three headings: "Revealed Religion," "The Idea of God," and

"Man, Sin and Atonement." Volume 2 contains sections on "Observances," "Morals," "Piety," "The Hereafter," and the Indexes. Volume 3 contains a set of extensive notes for the first two volumes. Though one may question whether Judaism could be so neatly packaged together into the categories that Moore uses, his work is still fundamental to the study of this area.

B175. Nadich, Judah, ed. *Jewish Legends of the Second Commonwealth*. Philadelphia: Jewish Publication Society of America, 1983, 508 p.

"It is the aim of this book to set forth Jewish legends of the Second Commonwealth, that period in Jewish history between the return of the Jews from exile in Babylonia during the last third of the sixth century B.C.E. to the destruction of the Second Temple by the Romans in 70 C.E." "What we mean by legends is the equivalent of that classic body of Jewish lore known as Aggadah. In the rabbinic sense the word Aggadah is coupled with its opposite Halakhah ('law'); it is thus that part of the rabbinic literature, Talmud and Midrash, which is not Halakhah. Such Aggadah is the primary source of our material. It may include stories and anecdotes, fables and myths, sometimes told about biblical personalities, sometimes told independently."—p. xi. Nadich arranges the material chronologically beginning with the Persian period, followed by the Greek period, the Hasmonean period, a section on the Apocrypha, then the Second Temple period, the time of the Great Assembly and the Sanhedrin, the early sages, the first generation of the Tannaim, and finally the last years of the Second Commonwealth. Each section is followed by extensive notes, and a very helpful bibliography is also included.

B176. Neusner, Jacob. *Ancient Israel After Catastrophe: The Religious World View of the Mishnah*. Charlottesville: University Press of Virginia, 1983, 82 p.

In Part 1, "Reconstruction in an Age of Defeat," Neusner talks about why the Mishnah is important and the place of the Temple in the Mishnah. He further states that one would expect to find in the Mishnah only an interpretation of history, since it was written between two very important wars; instead, it talks about what is permanent and enduring, such as the conduct of civil society. Part 2 is entitled, "Stability in an Age of Disorder," and among other things discusses how the Mishnah made use of the five books of

Moses. The final section, "Sanctification in an Age of Pollution," discusses the Temple, the Mishnah's system of sanctification, and how this concept actually applied to everyday life.

B177. Neusner, Jacob. *Early Rabbinic Judaism: Historical Studies in Religion, Literature and Art*. Leiden: E. J. Brill, 1975, 226 p.

Part One (on religion) contains essays on a clarification of "Pharisaic-Rabbinic" Judaism and the meaning of Oral Torah. In the literature section, Neusner reviews the Rabbinic traditions about the Pharisees and the written tradition in Pharisaism before the year 70. The art section is commentary on Goodenough's Jewish Symbols. Neusner's examination of the formation of Rabbinic Judaism can shed light on the preceeding era as well, and when he examines the meaning of Oral Torah, he says that he prefers to look directly at the nature of Mishnah-Tosefta, rather than citing numerous rabbinic passages on the subject.

B178. Neusner, Jacob, ed. *The Formation of the Babylonian Talmud: Studies in the Achievements of Late Nineteenth and Twentieth Century Historical and Literary-Critical Research*. Leiden: E. J. Brill, 1970, 187 p.

Various scholars contribute chapters on the Babylonian Talmud. The first section focuses on the historians, while the second covers the literary critics. Part Three, "By Way of Comparison" consists of one chapter only, "Saul Lieberman on the Talmud of Caesarea and Louis Ginzberg on Mishnah Tamid," by Herman J. Blumberg. The final section focuses on the *sugya*, or what Neusner calls "the building block of the Babylonian Talmud"—p. xii. In the Foreword, Neusner writes: "These papers, originally prepared for my seminar in Talmudic studies at Brown University and then revised for publication, offer an account of the achievements of some of the more important late nineteenth and twentieth century historians and literary critics. We have concentrated on a single fundamental question, namely, how and when did the Babylonian Talmud take shape"—p. x.

B179. Neusner, Jacob. *Formative Judaism: Religious, Historical and Literary Studies*. Chico, CA: Scholars Press, 1982, 5+ v.

The first volume is arranged into parts dealing with religion, history, and literary study. "Religion" in this context includes such topics as a comparison of Zorastrianism and Judaism, while the "history" section covers subjects such as the quest for the historical Hillel, and the third part deals with topics such as the Mishnah as literature. The final section in the first volume discusses "Scripture, Mishnah, and the Birth of Judaism." Volume Two includes a study of the Messiah in the context of the Mishnah. Volumes Three through Five have their own individual subtitles, respectively: "Torah, Pharisees, and Rabbis," "Problems of Classification and Composition," and "Revisioning the Written Records of a Nascent Religion." In Volume Four, "classification" refers to such topics as whether the Mishnah is folklore, while the word "composition" incorporates such subjects as how the Babylonian Talmud was created. The application of historical critical methods to the classic texts of Judaism has provided fruitful work for Neusner and his students.

B180. Neusner, Jacob. *History of the Mishnaic Law of Purities*. Leiden: E. J. Brill, 1974-77, 22 v.

"The literary and historical study of Mishnah-Tosefta, the fundamental phase in the investigation of the growth of Talmudic and later rabbinic law and religion, furthermore, is simultaneously to be undertaken from two directions. From the first, we begin and work forward from the sayings attributed to the Tannaitic masters reviewed in historical sequence, beginning to end. From the second, we start with the end product and work backward from unnamed traditions in the Mishnah itself, with cognate sayings in Tosefta, the Tannaitic Midrashim, and the Palestinian and Babylonian Talmuds"—p. xii. Thus writes Neusner in the preface to Volume One of this set. This massive work of scholarship takes an historical and literary approach to various texts of the Mishanh dealing with purity. Each volume has its own very helpful introduction, and the text includes Neusner's discerning commentaries. Neusner not only discusses the meaning of each text, but shows how they relate to each other, and gives his opinion on the authors of the text, the original settings of each piece's composition, the meaning of the texts, and the intentions of the original editors.

B181. Neusner, Jacob. *Judaism and Scripture: The Evidence of Leviticus Rabbah*. Chicago: University of Chicago, 1986, 664 p.

For 120 pages, Neusner discusses the background of the composition of Leviticus Rabbah. Topics include: the logic of its composition, its plan (including an analysis of the building blocks of the text), and an outline of its contents. Neusner then gives the literary and political context of the composition. The commentary is followed by Neusner's own translation of the text, and then by the author's careful critical analysis.

B182. Neusner, Jacob. *Judaism: The Evidence of the Mishnah.* Chicago: University of Chicago Press, 1981, 420 p.

Neusner acknowledges in his introduction that there were many more ideas within Judaism in the first century C.E. than those represented within the Mishnah. He says it "is the first document to be redacted in something very like the character in which it now reaches us"—p. 2. Neusner begins by examining those paths not taken by Judaism, such as apocalyptic literature and Gnosticism. He then examines the divisions and tractates of the Mishnah, and the principal ideas in vogue before the Jewish wars, ideas which were later incorporated into the Mishnah. He also examines the Torah of Moses before focusing on the evidence provided by the Mishnah itself. In his conclusion he writes: "The characteristic mode of thought of the Mishnah is to try to sort things out, exploring the limits of conflict and the range of consensus. The one thing which the Mishnah's framers predictably want to know concerns what falls between two established categories or rules, the gray area of the law, the excluded middle among entities, whether persons, places or things"—p. 281. Four appendices cover such topics as "Scripture and Tradition in Judaism."

B183. Neusner, Jacob, ed. *The Modern Study of the Mishnah.* Leiden: E. J. Brill, 1973, 283 p.

A review of the major scholars who have worked on this classic text, *the Modern Study of the Mishnah* includes a beginning chapter on the achievements of Jacob N. Epstein, plus critical studies and reviews of the work of Zecharias Frankel and his colleagues, coverage of historians such as N. Krochmal and H. Graetz, and mention of such literary critics as David Weiss Halivni. The volume closes with a look at recent Israeli contributions to Mishnah scholarship, including the work of Abraham Goldberg. Neusner writes in the Foreword: "Traditional study of the Mishnah, as of other ancient holy books of rabbinic Judaism, pays close attention to the exegesis of individual words and sentences, to the interpretations of their meaning, and to the application of that meaning to legal problems." "A second form of study of the Mishnah is historical. Historical study stands outside the Mishnah and asks questions extrinsic to the individual sentences and to their meanings." "When, however, the answers to historical and literary questions are arrived at from other criteria in addition to the information supplied by the early students of the Mishnah on the basis of their theological presuppositions, and when that information is critically evaluated in the light of the motives behind it and the external evidence, then we have entered the modern era in the study of the ancient text"—p. xi-xii.

B184. Neusner, Jacob. *Torah: From Scroll to Symbol in Formative Judaism.* Philadelphia: Fortress Press, 1985, 208 p.

This volume forms Part Three of the Foundations of Judaism series, covering method, teleology, and doctrine. Chapter titles are: "The Mishnah and the Torah," "Abot: From the Torah to Torah," "Tosefta: Torah in the Mishnah's First Talmud," "The Talmud of the Land of Israel," "The Compilations of Scriptural Exegesis," and "The Talmud of Babylonia." Neusner writes: "...the inherited doctrine of the Torah as a canon of Scripture, attested in Israelite writings of diverse origin in the centuries from the fifth B.C.E. to the second C.E., underwent radical revision. The word Torah ceased to refer in particular to a scroll and its contents. The advent of the Mishnah, demanding entry into the canon, carried with it the need to reframe the meaning of the word Torah. Once the narrow, literary limits of the word had given way, 'Torah' came to encompass an entire way of life"—p. xiv.

B185. Neusner, Jacob, ed. *Understanding Rabbinic Judaism.* New York: Ktav Publishing House, 1974, 422 p.

This anthology begins with an exploration of the beginnings of Rabbinic Judaism and then examines Talmudic theology. As part of the former investigation, Rabbinic writings are examined along with the life of the synagogue. Rashi's work is discussed together with the impact of Maimonides, the latter in a section examining theology within Rabbinic Judaism. Other chapters focus on Jewish mysticism and Judaism on the "threshold" of modernity. Many of the men whose thoughts are examined are considered "medieval" scholars, but Neusner in his preface shows us their importance for our time: "Three of the masters before us, Elijah, the Gaon of Vilna, Moses Sofer, and Israel Salanter, lived at the threshold of modern times and in their setting they faced the same intellectual, social, and cultural issues confronting Western Jewry as well"—p. 2.

B186. Nickels, Peter. *Targum and New Testament: A Bibliography Together with a New Testament Index.* Rome: Pontifical Biblical Institute, 1967, 88 p.

The Targum is an Aramaic translation of what Christians now call the Old Testament. The criteria for inclusion in this work was the use of Targumic material in the treatment of a New Testament text. A brief list of books and articles which treat broad topics is provided first. The second section covers the books of the New Testament with passages noted within them, along with citations to books or articles which treat the passage.

B187. Nickelsburg, George W., and Michael E. Stone, eds. *Faith and Piety in Early Judaism: Texts and Documents.* Philadelphia: Fortress Press, 1983, 272 p.

The editors use this selection of documents to explore several themes on early Judaism. In the "Sects and Parties" section they focus on the Samaritans, Hasideans, Pharisees, Essenes, and Zealots. The "Temple and Cult" chapter includes passages from the Psalms, Apocryphal Psalms, Jeremiah, Testament of Levi, and others. The editors treat the broad topics of piety and deliverance, as well as agents of divine deliverance such as the Messiah. A final section examines the conception of Wisdom in Israel.

B188. Nickelsburg, George W. *Jewish Literature Between the Bible and the Mishnah.* Philadelphia: Fortress Press, 1981, 352 p.

The author sketches the historical background from which the various sacred works of Jewish literature derive, and then describes the "forms and directions" that the literature took and how to interpret them. For example, in Chapter 5, after discussing the settling of "Israel in Egypt," he covers The Sibylline Oracles, Book

3: Aristeas to Philocrates, 3 Maccabees, and other documents. Nickelsburg writes: "One important factor that holds together the largest part of this corpus of literature is its common setting in hard times: persecution; oppression; other kinds of disaster; the loneliness and pressures of a minoirity living up to its convictions in an alien environment"—p. 5. Extensive notes and a bibliography of other works on the literature are given at the end of each chapter.

B189. Patte, Daniel. *Early Jewish Hermeneutic in Palestine.* Missoula, MT: The Society of Biblical Literature, 1975, 344 p.

In Part One, "The Use of Scripture in Classical Judaism," Patte covers such subjects as the doctrine of scripture in classical Judaism, scripture and synagogue, and the use of scripture in the schools. In Part Two, "The Use of Scripture in Sectarian Judaism," he covers Apocalyptic texts and the use of scripture in the Qumran community. Patte says that classical Judaic scripture features the open and complete revelation of God, whereas in sectarian Judaism such revelation is not complete.

B190. Rost, Leonhard. *Judaism Outside the Hebrew Canon: Introduction to the Documents.* Nashville, TN: Abingdon Press, 1976, 205 p.

After some introductory comments on the Hebrew canon, the Greek canon and "Apocrypha," the "Pseudepigrapha," and a historical summary, Rost examines the individual books of the Apocrypha and Pseudipigrapha, discussing each text, placing it in context, and translating it. He then cites various commentaries and other secondary sources relating to each item. The Dead Sea Scrolls are covered in the section on Pseudepigrapha.

B191. Rowland, Christopher. *The Open Heaven: The Study of Apocalyptic in Judaism and Early Christianity.* New York: Crossroad, 1982, 562 p.

Rowland writes extensively about the nature of the apocalyptic in relation to the revelation of divine mysteries, eschatology, and the Apocalypse. He then talks about the content of the heavenly mysteries, including God, man, and the past and future. He looks at the origins of apocalyptic, the esoteric tradition in early Rabbinic Judaism, and apocalyptic in early Christianity. "There is now a widespread recognition, however, that apocalyptic (as we have used the word throughout this study) and eschatological beliefs had a significant, perhaps central, role to play in early Christian belief. Few would deny the importance of eschatological concepts for the proclamation of Jesus, though whether an imminent expectation formed a central platform of his and the Church's message is still a debated issue." "Whereas the evidence which we possess seems to support such an assessment of the contribution of apocalyptic to earliest Christianity, the same cannot be said unequivocally for all aspects of Jewish religion. No doubt apocalyptic did have its part to play within first century Judaism, but the question is whether it is at the heart of the Jewish religion or merely a fringe phenomenon"—p. 443.

B192. Rowley, Harold H. *The Relevance of Apocalyptic: A Study of Jewish and Christian Apocalypses from Daniel to the Revelation*. 3rd ed. New York: Association Press, 1964 (c1963), 240 p.

Rowley studies the rise of apocalyptic, examinging the literature of this genre during the last two centuries BC as well as those composed during the first century AD. His final chapter focuses on the enduring message of apocalyptic, which includes the ideas that history can be divided into certain periods, that God is in control of history, that there is to be a great and final act of history, and that the end of the world is to be preceded by suffering. "Let it be observed," Rowley writes, "that their faith in God was born of their experience of God. The unseen world was very real to them, and they could contemplate its glories as vividly as they could contemplate the sufferings of the seen world around them, because God was so real to them in their experience"—p. 179.

B193. Russell, David S. *Between the Testaments*. Revised edition. Philadelphia: Fortress Press, 1981 (c1965), 176 p.

In Part One, "The Cultural and Literary Background," Russell looks at the relation between Judaism and Hellenism before examining what he calls "Torah religion" as well as the canon and Apocryphal literature. In Part Two, "The Apocalyptists," he discusses the message of these writers, including their ideas of the Messiah, the Son of Man, and the resurrection. "For Judaism unlike Hellenism represented not so much a way of life as a national religous movement"—p. 14. In explaining how the interpretation of the Torah took on such significance, Russell continues: "The method which they used in their teaching was of the nature of a running commentary on the words of Scripture. The particular custom or practice or precept which they sought to elucidate was brought into relation with a text or passage of Scripture which was then expounded and an interpretation given. This method was known as the Midrash form (Hebrew darash, to interpret) and was a feature of the Sopherim's teaching"—p. 64.

B194. Russell, David S. *The Method and Message of Jewish Apocalyptic, 200 B.C.-A.D. 100.* Philadelphia: Westminster Press, 1964, 464 p.

After discussing the milieu of apocalyptic and the literature of apocalyptic, Russell examines the method of Jewish apocalyptic literature, including the decline of prophecy, the characteristics of apocalyptic writing, the apocalyptic consciousness, and inspiration. He then discusses the message of these documents under several broad categories, including human history and divine control, angels and demons, the Messianic kingdom, the Son of Man, and life after death. An extensive and still useful bibliography concludes the book.

B195. Schechter, Solomon. *Some Aspects of Rabbinic Theology.* New York: Macmillan Company, 1923 (c1909), 384 p.

Some of the aspects treated by Schechter include: God and the world, God and Israel, the kingdom of God (invisible), the kingdom of God (national), the joy of the Law, and forgiveness and reconciliation with God. Concerning the joy of the Law Schechter writes: "Law and commandments, or as the Rabbinic expression is, Torah and Mizwoth, have a harsh sound and are suggestive to the outsider of something external, forced upon men by authority from the outside, sinister and burdensome. The citations just given show that Israel did not consider them in this light. They were their very love and their very life"—p. 148. Further, "The institution of the Sabbath is one of those laws the strict observance of which was already the object of attack on the part of the compilers of the Synoptic Gospels. Nevertheless, the doctrine proclaimed in one of the Gospels that the Son of man is Lord of the Sabbath, was also current among the Rabbis. They too teach that the Sabbath is delivered into the hand of man (to break it when necessary) and not man into the power of the Sabbath"—p. 153.

B196. Schiftman, Lawrence H. *Who Was a Jew?: Rabbinic and Halakhic Perspectives on the Jewish-Christian Schism.* Hoboken, NJ: Ktav Publishing House, 1985, 131 p.

Schiftman discusses the Tannaitic definition of Jewishness, the Biblical imperative of becoming a Jew by birth, and then examines the question of conversion to Judaism, defines both apostates and heretics, and investigates Tannaitic Judaism and the early Christians as well as Jewish Christians in Tannaitic narrative. He closes with a look at the final break between the two faiths. "By the time of the Bar Kokhba war (132-35 C.E.), Gentile Christianity had most probably still not taken over the Jerusalem Church nor become the dominant element in the Palestinian Christian community. Accordingly, the tannaim would still have seen the early Christians as Jews"—p. 75. Schiftman says that because Bar Kokhba was seen as a Messianic figure, the Christians did not support or participate in the rebellion of the Jews against the Romans, and that this became a major factor in the final separation between Jews and Christians.

B197. Sloan, William W. *A Survey Between the Testaments.* Paterson, NJ: Littlefield, Adams, 1964, 231 p.

Sloan surveys the religious development of the intertestamental period (444 BC to the beginning of Christianity, as he defines it), as shown in the Dead Sea Scrolls, the Apocrypha, the Pseudepigrapha, and other writings of the period. He intertwines the historical and literary, discussing Apocalyptic literature, for example, in relation to the Maccabean revolt and the Hasmoneans. The book is designed as a text for a college course, with assignments and suggested readings appended to the end of each chapter.

B198. Smith, Morton. *Tannaitic Parallels to the Gospels.* Philadelphia: Society of Biblical Literature, 1951, 215 p.

In addition to providing verbal Tannaitic parallels, Smith covers parallels of idiom, meaning, literary form, and association, plus those with fixed differences and complete parallels. By Tanaitic literature, Smith means "...the Mishnah, Tosefta, Mekilta, Mekilta of Rabbi Simon, Sifra, Sifre on Numbers, Sifre Zutta, Sifre on

Deuteronomy, Midrash, Tannaim, and certain of the oldest prayers of the Jewish liturgy, especially the Eighteen Benedictions"—p. xi. He classifies the parallels according to their nature and begins each chapter with an effort to define the nature of the parallels discussed. He also tries "to emphasize the difference between the facts actually revealed by the texts, and the explanations of these facts current in the form of historical theories. However, the primary concern of this book is rather philological than philosophical, therefore, as directly concerned with fact, it could give only occasional and passing notice to theory"—p. xii. "Jesus=God. Here must first be mentioned the verbal parallels between the Gospels and the TL, for the Gospels frequently describe the relationship between Jesus and his disciples in words which might be the Greek translations of those used by TL to describe the relationship of all Israel (or of some Israelites) to God"—p. 153.

B199. Stewart, Roy A. *Rabbinic Theology: An Introductory Study.* Edinburgh: Oliver and Boyd, 161, 202 p.

After an introduction in which he discusses the beginnings of Rabbinic literature and the contents of the Talmud, Stewart moves thematically through the literature, covering such topics as the nature of God, the Messiah, angels and demons, creation, the origin of sin, atonement, and the Rabbinic estimate of man. Twelve subjects are covered in all, plus an apologia and epilogue. There is an appendix on "The Statutory Daily Prayers." Stewart reveals his own persuasion when he writes, "The present writer is an evangelical Christian, holding firmly to all the doctrines of the Apostles Creed. This has inevitably coloured his appraisal of Rabbinic religion, just as the books of Montefiore and others on Christian themes have been coloured by their Judaism"—p. 172. "Talmud and Midrash are perhaps as familiar to most modern Jews—and certainly to all modern Christians excepting only a handful of theological research students—as the lost books of Livy"—p. 174-175.

B200. Stone, Michael, ed. *Jewish Writings of the Second Temple Period: Apocrypha, Pseudepigrapha, Qumran Sectarian Writings, Philo, Josephus.* Philadelphia: Fortress Press, 1984, 656 p.

Each of the fourteen chapters of this work was written by a different scholar. The chapters are for the most part arranged by literary type.

Thus, the Wisdom literature is grouped together as are the Testaments. Chapter One gives an historical background with comments on the Hellenistic and Hasmonean period. A chapter on Jewish sources in Gnostic literature is included, as well as one on Psalms, hymns, and prayers. Writing in the introduction about the importance of this book's inclusion in the series, *Clompendia Rerum Iudaicarum ad Novum Testamentum*, and that this is a joint Jewish and Christian effort, editor Stone quotes from his work *Scriptures, Sects and Visions*: "The understanding and view that we have of Jewish history of the age of the Second Temple are conditioned by these two main factors—the presuppostion of historiography and the character of the sources..."—p. xvii. A very useful fifty-one-page bibliography completes this work.

B201. Strack, Hermann L. *Introduction to the Talmud and Midrash*. New York: Harper & Row, 1965 (c1936), 364 p.

In Part One, "Introduction to the Talmud," Strack provides a definition of terms and a sketch of the history of the Talmud. He outlines the contents of the sixty-three Tractates according to the order of Maimonides. He discusses both the Babylonian and Palestinian Talmuds and reviews some of the most important teachers among the Amoraim. In Part Two, "Introduction to the Midrashim," Strack reviews the Tannaitic Midrashim Mekiltha, Siphra and Siphre, the Homiletic Midrashim, and the oldest expositional Midrashim, among others. An interesting personal note appears at the front of the volume: "Although Professor Strack was active in the conversionary Institutum Judaicum, he was vigorous in his defense of Jews and Judaism against resurgent German anti-Semitism."

B202. Urbach, Efraim E. *The Sages: Their Concepts and Beliefs*. Jerusalem: Magnes Press, 1975, 2 v.

The entire second volume (over 400 pages) of this massive work is the set of footnotes for the first volume. Urbach covers the concepts and beliefs through a topical approach, including such items as the belief in one God, the Shekhina or presence of God in the World, the power of God, man, the commandments, and others. In a helpful first chapter on "The Study of the History of the Beliefs and Concepts of the Sages," he discusses the nature of the sources for his study and the methods of Jewish and Christian scholars, and comments on the work of G. F. Moore.

B203. Vermes, Geza. *Scripture and Tradition in Judaism: Haggadic Studies.* 2nd rev. ed. Leiden: E. J. Brill, 1973, 243 p.

This book follows the development of exegetical traditions by means of historical criticism. "It is my intention to show that such an historical approach is possible, to suggest how to apply it, and to illustrate its advantages for a better understanding of Jewish exegesis"—p. xi. Some of the themes treated by Vermes include: "Pharaoh—An Exegetical Tradition and Its Literary Analysis," "The Story of Balaam—The Scriptural origin of Haggadah," and "Redemption and Genesis xxii—The Binding of Isaac and the Sacrifice of Jesus." In his conclusion, Vermes notes: "In general, the period of great creative activity began in the fourth or third century BC and relaxed only towards the end of the second century AD. The first task was one of literary harmonization; harmony had first to be established within the Torah itself. Haggadah achieved this by combining and interweaving parallel accounts, eliminating discrepancies, and completing bare patches of the narrative. It carried the process still further. On the principle that the whole of Scripture is informed by the same Word of the same God, Torah, Prophets, and later even Hagiographa were considered and treated synoptically. The result was exegetical symbolism and a consequent doctrinal evolution and enrichment"—p. 228.

B204. Wicks, Henry J. *The Doctrine of God in the Jewish Apocryphal and Apocalyptic Literature.* New York: Ktav Publishing House, 1971 (c1915), 371 p.

Originally a doctoral thesis, *The Doctrine of God* is organized around three topics: the transcendence of God, the justice of God, and the grace of God. Under each section Wicks takes a chronological approach, covering the second century BC and the first century BC, and ending with the first century AD. In the section on the grace of God, Wicks shows his approach when he writes, "On the whole, it must be maintained that the conception of God implied in the notion of these writers as to what He requires from men is not a lofty one. It is often supposed that He tolerates feelings and actions in men which are unworthy, judged by a true ethical standard"—p. 346.

JOHN THE BAPTIST

B205. Kraeling, Carl H. *John the Baptist.* New York: Charles Scribner's Sons, 1951, 218 p.

Kraeling looks at the wilderness as the setting for John the Baptist, and then examines the proclamation and exhoration aspects of John's preaching. He writes about the rite of baptism practised by John, the relationship of John and Jesus, and the later history of the Baptist movement. This book focuses upon the great importance of John among the people of his time, and shows how Jesus contributed to the perpetuation of the Baptist's influence.

JOSEPHUS

B206. Farmer, William R. *Maccabees, Zealots, and Josephus: An Inquiry into Jewish Nationalism in the Greco-Roman Period.* New York: Columbia University Press, 1956, 239 p.

Farmer begins with an examination of the writings of Josephus, and then discusses the work of Emil Schurer and Joseph Klausner. In Part Two he examines Jewish nationalism in relation to the Torah and the Temple, the Maccabees, the Scrolls' presentation of the war of the Sons of Light against the Sons of Darkness, and Jewish nationalism and Jesus. He concludes that the Maccabees were the concious prototypes of later nationalists. "It follows, therefore, that the example and teaching of the Maccabees probably exerted a much greater influence on Jews during the New Testament period than is generally recognized"—p. 203.

B207. Feldman, Louis H. *Josephus and Modern Scholarship, 1937-1980.* New York: W. de Gruyter, 1984, 1055 p.

This massive one-volume work is arranged topically, including: bibliographies, the text of Josephus, Josephus's life, Josephus's sources, Josephus and archaeology, and Josephus's influence until the twentieth century. Books, journal articles, dissertations, and chapters from books in many languages are covered. After listing the resources in each subsection, Feldman gives summaries of each and analyses of selected items.

B208. Foakes-Jackson, Frederick J. *Josephus and the Jews: The Religon and History of the Jews as Explained by Flavius Josephus.* New York: R. R. Smith, Inc., 1930, 299 p.

Foakes-Jackson covers the life and religion of the Jewish-Roman historian, Flavius Josephus. Turning to the Josephus's works, he describes the Temple, the High Priesthood, the Law, and the hopes of Josephus. In a section discussing the independence of the Jews, Foakes-Jackson reviews the High Priests as warrior priests. He then covers what he calls the "Roman yoke." In a final section he delineates the events after the fall of Jerusalem, giving special attention to Josephus's *Antiquities*. The last section of the book deals with Josephus and the New Testament.

B209. Mason, Steve. *Flavius Josephus on the Pharisees: A Composition-Critical Study.* Leiden: E.J. Brill, 1991, 424 p.

After an introduction in which he reviews scholarly opinion on Josephus's interpretations of the Pharisees and gives an assessment of Josephus as an author, Mason reviews what Josephus says of the *Pharisees in the Jewish War, Antiquities,* and *Life.* He discusses the purpose of each of these three works, summarizing what Josephus says in the *Jewish War* and the *Antiquities* concerning the Pharisees in relation to Alexandra Salome, Herod's court, and the Jewish schools. When speaking of the *Life,* Mason looks at the Pharisaic allegiance of Josephus in modern scholarly opinion and Josephus's religious quest, as well as "Josephus, Simon, and the Delegation." Mason concludes that Josephus is responsible for all of the deliberate descriptions of the Pharisees which appear in his works, and that he consistently presents them as the dominant religious group among the Jews who had the support of the masses. "As the source critics well realized, Josephus displays a marked and consistent antipathy toward the Pharisees"—p. 373.

B210. Thackeray, Henry St. John. *Josephus the Man and the Historian.* New York: Ktav Publishing House, 1968 (c1967), 160 p. Originally published 1928.

George Foot Moore wrote the introduction to this volume. The result of a series of lectures by Thackeray, this volume covers the life of Josephus, his *War* and *Antiquities*, his use of Biblical texts, the affect of Hellenism on his work, and his comments on the "so-called testimonium Flavianum—the well known statement on the Founder of Christianity in the eighteenth book of the *Antiquities*...."—p. 125.

JUDAISM AND CHRISTIANITY

B211. Ayers, Robert H. *Judaism and Christianity: Origins, Developments and Recent Trends.* Lanham, MD: University Press of America, 1983, 466 p.

Though Ayers also covers the Reformation and Modern periods, in his introduction he writes about "The Study of Religion and the Judeo-Christian Tradition." In Part Two, he covers "The Biblical Period," including the New Testament and "The Emergence of Rabbinic Judaism." In this latter section, he reviews for the novice the various groups of the period, such as the Essenes, Sadducees, and Pharisees. He also defines important terms in the study of this period, and reviews some of the important themes in the Talmud.

B212. Baeck, Leo. *Judaism and Christianity.* Philadelphia: Jewish Publication Society of America, 1958, 292 p.

This group of essays, translated from the German, was selected by Baeck, and includes a biographical sketch of him by Walter Kaufmann. The five essays generally cover the subject of Judaism in conjunction with the origins of Christianity, and include writings on the Son of Man, the Gospels as documents in the history of the Jewish faith, and one section on what Baeck calls "romantic religion," by which he means a type of religion which includes Chrisitianity, where "tense feelings supply its content, and it seeks its goals in the now mythical, now mystical visions of the imagination"—p. 189-190. He emphasizes the varieties of the oral tradition which originally formed what became the Christian Gospels.

B213. Bonsirven, Joseph. *Palestinian Judaism in the Time of Jesus Christ.* New York: Holt, Rinehart and Winston, 1964, 271 p.

Bonsirven organizes his material around such topics as God, angels, the Torah, man and general ethics, religious life, Messianism, and others. This approach has been criticized by some, who think it brings too much order to what was a very fluid situation within Judaism at the time of Jesus. Putting together material from the Gospels along with apocryphal and rabbinic documents is problematic, unless attention is paid to the date and context of the material. Though Bonsirven acknowledges that we have few statements from the rabbis of the first century, he says they undoubtedly believed in the Messiah. He concludes: "...they shared one of the essential beliefs of the Jewish religion of their times, as it appears in official prayers, the Apocrypha, and as we can discover it even in the books of Philo and Josephus..."—p. 173.

B214. Callan, Terrance. *Forgetting the Root: The Emergence of Christianity From Judaism.* New York: Paulist Press, 1986, 131 p.

Callan covers a number of topics of specialized interest, including the Jewishness of Jesus, conservative Jewish Christianity, and liberal Jewish Christianity. In his "Conclusion" Callan writes: "We have seen that Christianity emerged from Judaism chiefly as a result of two things: first, the decision made by most of the church that Gentile Christians need not keep the Jewish law; and second, the adoption of this position by Gentile Christians, who understood it to mean that neither Jewish Christians nor Jews should keep the law. As we have noted, Jesus himself stood in some tension with the Judaism of his time, but perhaps no more so than some of the prophets. The belief that Jesus was the messiah, when it arose among some of the Jews, certainly set them apart from the rest of Israel which did not share this belief; but it is conceivable that the Christians might have remained a sect of Judaism if they had not admitted Gentiles to their company without requiring that they keep the law"—p. 106.

B215. Davies, William D. *The Gospel and the Land: Early Christian and Jewish Territorial Doctrine.* Berkeley: University of California Press, 1974, 521 p.

Davies first examines the concept of the land in the Hexateuch, the Prophets, and extra-Biblical sources in which he includes Apocrypha, Pseudepigrapha, the Qumran writings, and Rabbinic sources. In Part Two he discusses the concept of land in the New Testament and includes a section on Jesus and the land. Davies thinks a certain strand of the tradition views the land and the Temple in a negative light, such as Acts 7. "But, secondly, there are other strata in which the land, the Temple, and Jerusalem, in their physical acutality, are regarded positively; that is, in a certain way they retain a significance in Christianity"—p. 366. "The witness of the New Testament is, therefore, twofold: it transcends the land, Jerusalem, the Temple. Yes: but its History and Theology demand a concern with these realities also"—p. 367.

B216. Fiorenza, Elisabeth Schussler, ed. *Aspects of Religious Propaganda in Judaism and Early Christianity.* Notre Dame, Indiana: University of Notre Dame Press, 1976, 195 p.

Some of the items in this anthology include the introduction by Fiorenza, "Miracles, Mission, and Apologetics: An Introduction," in which she sets the one of the volume by examining the relation of miracles and magic in the Christian mission. She also writes: "The publication of this collection of essays hopefully will show that the history of the early Christian movement cannot be understood solely as a sectarian struggle. It has to be seen in the context of the Hellenistic and Jewish religious propaganda and its public dimensions"—p. 20. Other essays include: "Socioeconomic Reasons for the 'Divine Man' as a Propagandistic Pattern" by Dieter Georgi, and "Jesus and the Disciples as Miracle Workers in the Apocryphal New Testament" by Paul Achtemeier.

B217. Gerhardsson, Birger. *Memory and Manuscript: Oral Tradition and Written Transmission in Rabbinic Judaism and Early Christianity.* Uppsala: C. W. K. Gleerup, 1961, 379 p.

In Part 1, "Oral Tradition and Written Transmission in Rabbinic Judaism," Gerhardsson covers the transmission of the both the written and the oral Torah. In Part 2, "The Delivery of the Gospel Tradition in Early Christianity," he discusses the testimony of the post-apostolic Church, the witness of Luke, the evidence of Paul, and the origins and transmission of the gospel tradition. In his introduction, Gerhardsson also points out that he does define what he means by tradition in his work: "It is a remarkable fact that neither of the two pioneer works on the form-criticism of the gospel tradition makes any attempt to define the concept of tradition in early Christianity"—p. 13. The great detail of this work provides a good background for understanding the importance of Torah and the careful way in which it was passed on to the next generation.

B218. Leaney, Alfred R. *The Jewish and Christian World, 200 B.C.-200 A.D.* New York: Cambridge University Press, 1984, 259 p.

In Part One, Leaney describes the political situation, beginning with the Babylonian captivity and restoration and moving to the Roman empire, covering Judaea under Roman rule, and including Egypt as well. In Part Two, he takes a thematic approach to discuss the synagogue, the Law, Prophets, and Writings, then moves to the Septuagint, the Qumran writings, early Rabbinic Judaism, Christian writings. He closes by examining contemporary writers other than Jewish or Christian. In the Author's Foreword, he writes: "This book is intended as a student beginner's guide to the history of Judaism and Christianity in the period 200 BC to AD 200, and to the literature associated with both the Jews and Christians which fall outside the list of accepted books of the Old Testament, Apocrypha and the New Testament."

B219. Levison, Lahum. *The Jewish Background of Christianity: A Manual of the Political, Religious, Social and Literary Life of the Jews from 586 B.C. to A.D. 1.* Edinburgh: T. & T. Clark, 1932, 205 p.

Although his book was published in 1932, Levison in 1932 mentions the Apocrypha and Pseudepigrapha, and the Mishnah and the Talmuds. For the religious background he discusses pre-Exilic theism as well as the "dogmas" of post-Exilic Judaism, such as the nature of man, sin, Messianism, and demonology. He concludes with chapters on feasts and fasts such as the Passover, public and family life, including a section on women in Judaism, and a section on parties and personalities that influenced the period (*e.g.,* the Pharisees, Samaritans, Galileans, and Philo and Hillel). His concerns can be seen in the "Retrospect," when, in discussing the idea that Christianity took over from Judaism the idea of the universality of God, he writes, "So long as Christianity kept this principle to the fore as one of its doctrines it made true and enlightened followers; but when it transferred its allegiance to Rome and sought a vicar of God and a seat of authority it lost its power, and that power is still lacking in the greatest section of the Church"—p. 188-189. In writing on the Pharisees, he says, "A learned American theologian has asked us to discredit the gospel story about disagreement between Jesus and the Pharisees [*Jesus and the Pharisees*, by Donald W. Riddle]. This is because the scholar has studied Pharisaism in the library and cloister, rather than the Palestine of Jesus' day and today"—p. 156.

B220. Meeks, Wayne and Robert L. Wilken. *Jews and Christians in Antioch in the First Four Centuries of the Common Era.* Missoula: Scholars Press, 1978, 127 p.

The chapters in this book cover: "Jews and Christians in Antioch," "Archaeological Remarks," "Letters of Libanius Concerning the Jews," "Libanius' Oration on Systems of Patronage," and "John Chrysostom's Homilia Adverus Judaeos." The chief purpose of this book is "to provide resources for the study of early Christianity in its setting within the urban culture of the Roman Empire." "We have also tried to show that, for the understanding of early Christianity, it is necessary to study Judaism, not only as it existed in the so-called 'intertestamental period,' *i.e.*, as 'background' to Christianity, but as a vital social and religious force during the early centuries of the Common Era"—p. vii. This work brings together the disciplines of New Testament studies and early church history. In evaluating some of their sources, the authors note, "For the story of Christianity's beginnings in Antioch and consequently of the first interactions between Jews and Christians there, we have to depend upon the account in the book of Acts, together with the clues in a few verses of Galatians. If there is one thing that has been made clear by scholarship from F. C. Baur until the most recent 'redaction critics,' it is that historians have to read the Acts' account with a sharp eye open for its functions within the literary and theological plan of the whole two-volume work. When that is done, however, it becomes a very useful document for our purposes"—p. 13.

B221. Meyers, Eric M., and James F. Strange. *Archaeology, the Rabbis and Early Christianity.* Nashville: Abingdon Press, 1981, 208 p.

The authors argue that data from archaeological finds should be used in the reconstruction of early Judaism and Christianity (the usual approach only considers literary material). One example cited is the method used by certain Jewish groups to store water in religious buildings, and the function played by this water in religious ceremonies. Meyers and Strange cover the languages of Roman Palestine, Jewish burial practices, and early churches and early synagogues, and demonstrate how they propose to develop this combination of literary and archaeological material.

B222. Mussner, Franz. *Tractate on the Jews: The Significance of Judaism for Christian Faith.* Philadelphia: Fortress Press, 1984, 339 p.

Among the nine chapters of this book are sections describing the heritage of the faith of Israel, the "Jew" Jesus, and Paul and Israel. In the chapter on Jesus, Mussner begins with a survey of Jewish authors on Jesus, including Joseph Klausner, David Flusser, and Schalom Ben-Chorin. Mussner notes: "Is this 'law' of the Messiah Jesus of Matthew brought into opposition with the Torah of Israel? This appears not to be the case, even not in the 'antitheses' of the Sermon on the Mount..."—p. 116. He points out that the answer concerning the double commandment of love is given by Jesus in Mark and Matthew, but in Luke by a Jewish teacher of the Law; Mussner wonders whether there was already in existence at the time of Jesus a section of the Torah dealing with this topic. In the final paragraph of the chapter, he writes, "When we say that Jesus is 'Israel,' we do not make the claim in our mind that the Church likewise is Israel. The Church remains forever the 'wild shoot' grafted onto the noble olive tree of Israel..."—p. 134.

B223. Neusner, Jacob. *Judaism in the Beginning of Christianity.* Philadelphia: Fortress Press, 1984, 112 p.

Neusner begins with a study of the Jewish people in Israel at the time of Jesus, and presents what he calls three types of Judaism: sage, priest, and Messiah. His last chapters cover the Pharisees, and Hillel and Judaism after the destruction of the Temple. He also speaks of how Christians and Jews of the time both recognized a paradox of God: namely, that out of weakness God was bringing his victory.

B224. Neusner, Jacob. *Judaism in the Matrix of Christianity.* Philadelphia: Fortress Press, 1986, 160 p.

A large portion of this book is devoted to a discussion of how the material comprising the Palestinian and Babylonian Talmuds was gathered together in the fourth and fifth centuries C.E., and, later,

how the Mishnah was put together around 200 C.E. Since much of
the documents in the Mishnah were originally based on oral
tradition, scholars think that many of the items therein were
developed much earlier than 200 C.E. This helps us understand the
many components of first-century Judaism. Neusner shows how the
rabbis' answers in documents like the Mishnah were a response to
an ever-spreading Christianity. In writing about the challenge faced
by the rabbis, he notes: "The Christianization of the Roman Empire
presented the Jews with a challenge more severe than the destruction
of the Temple. The reason? Christianity claimed to be Judaism,
Christians to be Israel. More subtle and more insidious, the
challenge of Christianity addressed not the frontiers of the people
from without but the soul and heart of the people from within. The
shift in the condition of Israel marked by Christ's rise to political
power and the Torah's loss of a place in political institutions has
defined the context of Judaism from then to nearly the present
day"—p. 9.

**B225. Neusner, Jacob, William Scott Green, and Ernest
Fredrichs, eds.** *Judaisms and Their Messiahs at the Turn
of the Christian Era*. New York: Cambridge University
Press, 1987.

The various chapters of this book, each by a different author, deal
with subjects such as salvation, Messianism in the Maccabean
period, Qumran's view of the Messiah, Philo and the Messiah, and
the relation of the Gospel to the idea of the Messiah. Green begins
the volume with his "Introduction: Messiah in Judaism: Rethinking
the Question." One of his conclusions states: "We have seen that in
Jewish writings before or during the emergence of Christianity,
'messiah' appears neither as an evocative religious symbol nor as a
centralizing native cultural category. Rather, it is a term of disparity,
used in few texts and in diverse ways"—p. 6.

B226. Neusner, Jacob, ed. *The Social World of Formative
Christianity and Judaism*. Minneapolis: Augsburg/Fortress
Press, 1988.

This work includes essays by 20 different scholars, some of whom
use sociological methods to focus on societal aspects on New
Testament times. The first section of the book is entitled "Social
Studies: Ancient Israel, Christianity, and Judaism. Part Two is

"Literary Studies: Paul," and Part Three is "Literary Studies: Jesus and the Gospels." Among the essays are the following titles: "Sociohistorical Research and the Contextualization of Biblical Theology," by Michael LaFarge; "The Social Class of the Pharisees in Mark," by Anthony Saldarini; "Paul, God and Israel: Romans 9-11 in Recent Research," by Heikki Raisanen; and "Pharisees, Sinners and Jesus," by James D. G. Dunn. Since the book is a tribute to Howard Clark Kee, there is a bibliography of his work to Sept. 1, 1986.

B227. Nickelsburg, George W. *Resurrection, Immortality, and Eternal Life in Intertestamental Judaism.* Cambridge: Harvard University Press, 1972, 483 p.

A reworking of the author's dissertation, Nickelsburg's book uses the theme of religious persecution as the overall setting in which he discusses various intertestamental texts. For example, in Chapter 3, "Religious Persecution—The Story of the Persecution and Vindication of the Righteous," he discusses 2 Maccabees 7 and 4 Maccabees. In his conclusion, he writes: "The investigation has shown that in intertestamental Jewish theology the beliefs in resurrection, immortality, and eternal life are carried mainly within the framework of three forms"—p. 170. The three forms are: 1) the story of the righteous man and the Isaianic exaltation tradition; 2) the judgment scene; and 3) what Nickelsburg calls two-way theology, which "describes right and wrong modes of behavior and their respective rewards and punishments—here eternal life and eternal death" (p. 173).

B228. Pfeiffer, Robert H. *History of New Testament Times with an Introduction to the Apocrypha.* New York: Harper, 1949, 561 p.

Part One, "Judaism from 200 B.C. to A.D. 200," consists of two sections, one focusing on Palestinian Judaism, including the political, religious, and literary history of the time, and a second focusing on Hellenistic Judaism, including a section on Alexandrian-Jewish literature. In Part Two, "The Books of the Apocrypha," 1 Esdras, Tobit, Judith, and the Wisdom of Solomon, as well as 1 and 2 Maccabees, are covered along with five other books. In the section on Religious History, Pfeiffer comments: "The Pharisees were presumably the successors of the Hasidim, although we lack all information about their origin. Their name means 'separated,' but has been variously interpreted"—p. 54). "The Pharisees were progressive not only in their constant reinterpretation of the Law to adapt it to new conditions, but in all religious fields. They advocated the enlargement of the canon of Scriptures, adding the Prophets (200 B.C.) and the Writings (A.D. 90) to the Torah...."—p. 55. He also quotes from G. F. Moore, saying, "Certain members of the movement may well have deserved criticism in the Gospels and in the Talmud, but let us not forget that 'Judaism is the monument of the Pharisees'" (G. F. Moore, *Judaism*, II, 193)—p. 55.

B229. Purinton, Carl Everett. *Christianity and Its Judaic Heritage: An Introduction with Selected Sources.* New York: Ronald Press, 1961, 534 p.

Though this work covers Judaism from its beginnings to the Reformation era, it concentrates on the formative period, which Purinton identifies as the age of the Mishnah. After giving the religious, political, and social background of the particular time under discussion, Purinton then provides source material for the period. Thus, in the chapter on "The World of the Talmud," he gives the text of "The Sayings of the Fathers" (Pirke Aboth). In addition, there are chapters on Judaism under the Romans, on the life and teachings of Jesus, and on the beginnings of Christianity, with a separate chapter on the first three centuries A.D. In the sections on the life and teachings of Jesus, Purinton uses non-Christian literature such as the Psalms of Solomon 17:23-51, which discusses the "Son of David" Messiah. He also covers material about the Essenes.

B230. Rosenberg, Stuart E. *The Christian Problem: A Jewish View.* New York: Hippocrene Books, 1986, 241 p.

Part One covers "Christian Myths About Jews and Judaism," and includes essays on the ideas that Jesus was not a Christian, that the Jewish Messiah was not Jesus, that the Synagogue is neither Temple nor Church, that the Hebrew Bible is not the "Old Testament," and that the Church is not the new Israel. Part Two covers "Restoring Jews to the Mainstream of History," and includes a section on appreciating the Pharisees. Part Three is entitled, "The "New Jews" and Their Christian Neighbors: Continuing Problems in the Dialogue." The volume is dedicated to Rosenberg's grandfather, who died in the Holocaust. Rosenberg writes, "It cannot be forgotten that there were Christian martyrs who willingly endangered, or even sacrificed themselves, in the hope that they could save their Jewish neighbors. Jews have especially remembered. In Jerusalem at Yad Vashem—the national shrine memorializing the six million Jewish victims of the Holocaust—an honored place is reserved for those 'righteous Gentiles,' as the Jewish tradition refers to them, who served the cause of justice and mercy in their own godly ways"—p. 184.

B231. Sandmel, Samuel. *The First Christian Century in Judaism and Christianity: Certainties and Uncertainties.* New York: Oxford University Press, 1969, 241 p.

Originally a series of lectures, Sandmel's book includes: "The Significance of the First Century," "Palestinian Judaisms," "Hellenistic Judaism," and "Christianity." Even in 1969, Sandmel recognized the diversity within the Judaism of Palestine of the first century. Sandmel says we must distinguish between the history of Judea during the first century and the history of Judaism during this time. For the former we should use the writings of Josephus, but for the latter we must use the Rabbinic writings and other literature. "To Josephus, then, we can look primarily for events, but not for clear information on the doctrines, institutions, and underlying currents that fashioned Rabbinic Judaism"—p. 60. In the section on Christianity, Sandmel points to a central issue which is still much debated: "By all the testimony, the Pharisees and the Sadducees were quite aware of the difference between them, but they appear uniformly to have assumed that this difference existed within a Judaism common to them. When and how did the Christians' comparable awareness of difference within Judaism lead to their awareness of a difference from Judaism?"—p. 158-59.

B232. Sandmel, Samuel. *Judaism and Christian Beginnings.* New York: Oxford University Press, 1978, 510 p.

Sandmel divides this book into four parts, the first two of which have no overall title. Part III is called "Hellenistic Jewish Literature," and Part IV is "Early Christianity." In Part I Sandmel uses 94 pages to discuss sources, including what he calls the historical writings (I Maccabees and Josephus, for example), and what he refers to as religious writings, including the Apocrypha and Pseudepigraphical writings, plus various Dead Seas Scrolls and Rabbinic literature, such as the Talmud, Midrash, and Targum. Part

II includes a review of institutions such as the Temple and Sanhedrin, the Calendar, and various theological themes, such as the Divine and Messiah as well as studies of various sages. In the portion on Hellenistic Jewish literature, Sandmel includes the Septuagint and Philo among others. In the last section on "Early Christianity," he covers the Gospels, Jesus and Judaism, and closes with a section on Synagogue Judaism and Christianity.

B233. Sandmel, Samuel. *Two Living Traditions: Essays on Religion and the Bible.* Detroit: Wayne State University Press, 1972, 336 p.

This volume is made up of 25 articles which appeared previously. Among the most relevant for this bibliography are the following. "Judaism, Jesus, and Paul: Some Problems of Method in Scholarly Research," "'Son of Man' in Mark," "Modern and Ancient Problems in Communication: Rabbinic Judaism, Hellenistic Judaism, and Early Christianity," and "The Parting of the Ways." In the essay on the parting of the ways, Sandmel closes with these words: "There is a sense in which Christianity is the logical development from the premises of Paul, and rabbinic Judaism the logical development from a premise concerning the Law which is exactly the opposite of Paul. To zealous partisans of our day the separations of the past are not only complete, but also must be rigidly maintained. Yet perhaps the historian, whose perspective is that of the centuries, can be impelled to say, as I would myself say, that the threads were not all of them cut; rather, some threads have defied all the vicissitudes of history, and these hold the two communities to each other in our day, however tenuously"—p. 264.

B234. Streatfeild, Frank. *Preparing the Way: The Influence of Judaism of the Greek Period on the Earliest Developments of Christianity.* London: Macmillan and Co., 1918, 205 p.

Streatfeild discusses politics and propaganda, worship and education, including the synagogue, apocalyptic thought, and the imporance of language. Reflecting his time (1918), Streatfeild notes that the idea of whether the New Testament writers knew of the Jewish literature of the intertestamental period which had been excluded from the Jewish canon has been answered in another way, with the canon not being settled until after New Testament times. Streatfeild speaks of the "Jewish religion," when we now know that there were many competing ideas in Judaism during the time of Christ. Streatfeild's orientation, now certainly offensive to Jews, is shown by comments in his "Conclusions" section: "...the conclusion cannot be avoided that as the people of Israel were chosen of God to receive training as the nation from which Christianity should grow, so in this training and preparation not the least part is that included in the years which may roughly be called the Greek Period of History"—p. 128.

B235. Whittaker, Molly. *Jews and Christians: Graeco-Roman Views*. New York: Cambridge University Press, 1984, 304 p.

"The aim of this volume is to give access to sources which illustrate Graeco-Roman views of Judaism and Christianity from 200 BC to AD 200. Almost all the authors quoted are pagan, a word used here and throughout the book as a convenient term to cover any religion other than Judaism or Christianity, without implying any value-judgement"—p. viii. The three sections of the book covering Judaism include quotes from the original commentators, with clarifying remarks by Whittaker; the same format is followed in the section on Christianity. "The third section of this book, 'The Pagan Background,' is not a collection of sources but an attempt to sketch the cults and superstitions and general climate of thought. Passages have been chosen to illustrate the practices and beliefs which would influence men's reactions to such strange and alien cults as Judaism and Christianity"—p. ix. A chronological chart is also given to help put the classical authors in historical perspective.

THE LAW

B236. Banks, Robert. *Jesus and the Law in the Synoptic Tradition*. New York: Cambridge University Press, 1975, 310 p.

In Part One, Banks examines the view of the Law in the Old Testament and later Jewish literature in three areas: namely, the Law as achievement or purpose, the Law as rigid or flexible, and the Law as eternal or provisional. Part Two is entitled "Law in the Synoptic Tradition," in three subsections. The first covers what Banks calls incidental sayings and actions, such as attitudes toward customs and the Law. The second reviews debates and controversies, such as those regarding table-fellowship, Sabbath controversies, and the greatest commandment. Finally, Banks examines "extended teaching," such as the speeches against the Pharisees and the Sermon on the Mount.

B237. Falk, Zev W. *Introduction to Jewish Law of the Second Commonwealth.* Leiden: E. J. Brill, 1972-78, 2 v.

In Volume One, Falk studies the growth of Halakha, the sectarian Halakha (such as that of the Samaritans), what he calls "constitution" (institutions such as the Great Synagogue, the Temple, and local government), procedure (how the law was used in judgment), and evidence (as it was understood in this legal system). In Volume Two, the author organizes the law into areas such as crimes, torts, contracts, property, etc. He explains his purpose with these words: "This book is an attempt to describe Jewish Law in actual operation in the days of the Second Temple." "In this way I hope to prove 'the historical unity and uninterrupted development of Jewish Law' from the time when Scripture was determined until the Oral Law was edited in the Midrash and the Mishna."

THE MACCABEES

B238. Eisenman, Robert. *Maccabees, Zadokites, Christians, and Qumran.* Leiden: E. J. Brill, 1983, 110 p.

Eisenman covers such topics as Qumran research, the Zadokite Priesthood, the Maccabees as Zealots, and Zadokites and archaeological problems. In Chapter Nine, "Summing Up," he says that no member of the Maccabee family, not even Alexander Jannaeus, can be identified with the "wicked Priest" mentioned in the Qumran scrolls. Judas Maccabee is seen by Eisenman as the "prototype of the warrior priestly Messiah of the War Scroll"—p. 35. "What is new in 4 B.C. is the appearance of the 'Messianic' variation of the 'Zealot' movement"—p. 36. He places Jesus in the overall Messianic movement when he speaks of Jesus purifying the temple in good Maccabean style, after the example of Judas Maccabee, and he finds a Zadokite priesthood developed at Qumran, where the emphasis was not on a hereditary priesthood but on those who kept the Law. The lengthy footnotes provide much supplemental material.

THE MESSIAH

B239. Dahl, Nils A. *The Crucified Messiah and Other Essays.* Minneapolis: Augsburg Publishing House, 1974, 190 p.

Dahl's essays cover the Messiahship of Jesus in Paul, the problem of the historical Jesus, Bultmann's *Theology of the New Testament*, eschatology and history in the light of the Qumran texts, and "The Atonement—An Adequate Reward for the Akedah?" In his essay on the crucifixion, Dahl writes, "The contradiction between Jesus' non-messianic public appearances and his messiahship is to be explained neither from the nature of Jewish messianic ideas nor by the tension betwen historical facts and the conceptions of the evangelists. There is a third possiblility. Indeed many things can and must be explained by analysis of sources and traditions, and it is conceivable that Jesus appropriated certain ideas of Jewish messianism. The real explanation, however, is to be sought in the historical event itself; the inconsistency stems from Jesus' crucifixion as the Messiah despite the fact that he never made an express messianic claim"—p. 33-34.

B240. Klausner, Joseph. *The Messianic Idea in Israel: From Its Beginning to the Completion of the Mishnah.* New York: Macmillan, 1955, 543 p.

Klausner's book is divided into three sections: The Messianic Idea in the Period of the Prophets, The Messianic Idea in the Books of the Apocrypha and Pseudepigrapha, and The Messianic Idea in the Period of the Tannaim. In the Prophets Klausner finds a plan of the idea of sin, the need for punishment at the Day of the Lord, the repentance of the people, and then material and spiritual prosperity. For most of the prophets, there was never a human Messiah, only God himself to save mankind. Deutero-Isaiah and Daniel bring forth the new ideas of a spiritual, suffering Messiah, and a politically and materially successful Messiah. Klausner states that Jewish redemption can be considered without an individual Messiah: "Second, there is an irrational side even in the Jewish Messianic conception: where there is no mysticism at all there is no faith. Third, the Jewish Messiah is the redeemer of his people and the redeemer of mankind. But he does not redeem them by his blood; instead, he lends aid to their redemption by his great abilities and deeds"—p. 530.

B241. Levey, Samson H. *The Messiah: An Aramaic Interpretation—The Messianic Exegesis of the Targum.* Cincinnati: Hebrew Union College Press, 1974, 180 p.

The targums to the Pentateuch, Prophets, and Hagiographa are covered in the initial three sections. In the fourth chapter, "Conclusions," Levey writes that the offical Targumim are quite circumspect about adducing Messianic interpretations, and he speculates that the reason for this may be "...that the official Targumim stem from Maccabean times when hope for a restoration of the Davidic kingship would constitute treason to the Hasmonean dynasty"—p. 142. On the characteristics of the Messiah in the Targumim, he states: "The Messiah will be the symbol and/or the active agent of the deliverance of Israel. He will be of Davidic lineage, though he may have a non-Davidic predecessor, the Ephraimite Messiah, who will die in battle. Elijah will herald his coming and will serve as his High Priest"—p. 142-43.

B242. Neusner, Jacob. *Messiah in Context: Israel's History and Destiny in Formative Judaism.* Philadelphia: Fortress Press, 1984, 304 p.

This volume is part of a series, "The Foundations of Judaism." Neusner first examines the conception of the Messiah in the Mishnah and then in the Palestinian Talmud. Next, he examines the conception in the exegetical work of the Rabbis as they worked through the Bible. The last chapter concerns the conception of the Messiah in the Babylonian Talmud, and an appendix deals with the Messiah in works outside the Rabbis' canon, such as the synagogue liturgy.

B243. Scholem, Gershom G. *The Messianic Idea in Judaism, and Other Essays on Jewish Spirituality.* New York: Schocken, 1971, 376 p.

In addition to his essay, "Toward an Understanding of the Messianic Idea in Judaism," Scholem also discusses the idea of the Messianic idea in Kabbalism. Continuing his interest in mysticism, he looks at Martin Buber's interpretation of Hasidism. He also includes an essay on the history of the star of David as a symbol. In discussing the relation of Jewish mysticism and Messianism he writes: "About half the papers in this book are concerned with this relationship, which I consider of primary importance for the understanding of Jewish history in general and of Jewish mysticism in particular"—p. vii.

THE NEW TESTAMENT

B244. Bammel, Ernst, Charles K. Barrett and William D. Davies, eds. *Donum Gentilicium: New Testament Studies in Honor of David Daube.* Oxford: Clarendon Press, 1978, 342 p.

This collection of twenty essays (eight in English) includes work by some of the greatest scholars writing on the New Testament and early Judaism. The English-language essays include topics such as: "Jesus and the Pharisees," by B. Lindars and "On the Question of Fulfilling the Law in Paul and Rabbinic Judaism," by E. P. Sanders. Lindars sees common elements in Jesus's teaching and that of the Pharisees, but he wars against the assumption that formal criticism will close the gap between Jesus and the Pharisees. He examines Luke 16:1-8 and John 7:53-8:11, and argues that previous interpretations which try to place Jesus in a rabbinic mold are unsound.

B245. Barrett, Charles K., ed. *The New Testament Background: Selected Documents.* New York: Harper and Row, 1961 (c1956), 276 p.

Since it was published in 1956, this book does not give much space to the Dead Sea Scrolls, though it includes a few items in an appendix. It does encompass such items as the Roman writers (Tacitus, Suetonius), Papyri (*i.e.,* Oxyrhynchus papyri), and the Philosophers (Heraclitus, Zeno), as well as the usual authors (Josephus and Philo). Barrett gives a general introduction to each chapter, and then provides brief notes on each document, explaining how it is relevant as background for the study of the New Testament.

B246. Black, Matthew. *An Aramaic Approach to the Gospels and Acts.* 3rd ed. Oxford: Clarendon Press, 1967, 359 p.

Black reviews previous work on the Aramaic of the Gospels and Acts, and then looks at their syntax, grammer, and vocabulary. He then examines the Semitic poetry form in the Gospels, and presents some examples of mistranslation and misinterpretation of the Aramaic. Black writes: "A survey of the results of this study in this connexion yields one conclusion only which can be regarded as in any degree established, that an Aramaic sayings-source or tradition lies behind the Synoptic Gospels. Where any one Semitic or Aramaic construction could be observed recurring, its distribution showed that it tended to be found most frequently, and sometimes exclusively, in the words of Jesus"—p. 206).

B247. Cook, Michael. *Mark's Treatment of the Jewish Leaders.* Leiden: E. J. Brill, 1978, 104 p.

Cook discusses whether Mark was really familiar with the Jewish leadership in the light of his dependence on sources. The idea of the nature and number of sources used by Mark is also presented. The influence of the pre-Markan passion tradition on Mark is also examined, and the implications of this for the historian is presented. In his last chapter, Cook comments, "...even if the 'scribes' in the Passion narrative were only a construct, or civil servants, or Sadducees, we nevertheless believe that Mark viewed them as identical with the 'scribes' in the pre-Markan scribe collection. Had he realized that 'scribes' in this latter collection were synonymous with 'Pharisees,' he very likely would have perceived the 'scribes' in the Passion tradition also as Pharisaic; and he may then even have felt disposed to introduce the term 'Pharisees' into the Passion narrative proper"—p. 96-97.

B248. Cope, O, Lamar. *Matthew: A Scribe Trained for the Kingdom of Heaven.* Washington: Catholic Biblical Association of America, 1976, 142 p.

Cope looks at the use of Old Testament texts by Matthew, and studies the possibility of a controlled investigation of the Gospel writer, asking how the work of the final author/editors can be identified. He uses form criticism for his study as well, and applies redaction criticism to those areas where the gospel writer may have used an Old Testament passage to construct a Gospel story. In his concluding paragraph, he writes, "The author of Matthew was a Jewish-Christian so thoroughly familiar with the OT and with Jewish traditions of its interpretation that it was natural for him often to employ this knowledge as a key to the organization of his gospel. Where he had done this, he reveals to the reader certain of his characteristic ideas and beliefs. He also reveals his understanding of the relationship between the tradition about Jesus and the OT and the relationship of both to the problems of Christians for his own day. He probably thought of himself as 'a scribe trained for the kingdom of heaven'"—p. 130.

B249. Cullmann, Oscar. *The Christology of the New Testament.* Rev. ed. Philadelphia: Westminster Press, 1963 (c1959), 342 p.

Cullmann treats several themes in first-century Judaism in order to understand the Jesus of history: namely, the idea of the eschatological prophet in Judaism, the Ebed Yahweh in Judaism, the high priest as an ideal figure in Judaism, the Messiah in Judaism, the Kyrios or Lord in Judaism, the Logos or Word, and the Son of God in Judaism.

B250. Daube, David. *The New Testament and Rabbinic Judaism.* London: Athlone Press, 1956, 460 p.

Among items of special interest in this book is Daube's consideration of Messianic types, including Moses, Samuel, and Elijah. He also examines the questions of Sabbath observance, divorce, and baptism. In the last section he compares the views of the rabbis and the New Testament on such subjects as Rabbinic authority, laying on of hands, redemption, and violence to the Kingdom.

B251. Doeve, Jan W. *Jewish Hermeneutics in the Gospels and Acts.* Assen: Van Gorcum, 1954, 232 p.

Doeve examines how New Testament scholars use the knowledge of Jewish hermeneutics to study the New Testament. He then looks at the scriptural exegesis of the early Tannaites, and the Jewish interpretation of scripture and the New Testament. He also covers themes such as the Son of Man, the Messiah, and the Kingdom of God. Finally, he examines two midrashim relating to the resurrection of Christ as they are given in the Book of Acts. Doeve believes that the Jewish approach to exegesis of scripture is used within the New Testament itself. In terms of its helpfulness, he writes, "It would appear to us that, if one takes account of the Jewish way of working with Scripture when one is dealing with various exegetical and isagogical form-critical problems, one does indeed arrive at solutions for these problems one does not find by other means"—p. 207.

B252. Dungan, David L., and David Cartlidge, eds. *Sourcebook of Texts for the Comparative Study of the Gospels: Literature of the Hellenistic and Roman Period Illuminating the Milieu and Character of the Gospels.* Missoula, MT: Society of Biblical Literature, 1973, 378 p.

In the first part, Duncan and Cartlidge include "Selections from pagan, Jewish and Christian literature illustrating form-critical categories and typical aspects of this kind of popular religious biography"—p. v. These feature passages from Plutarch on the birth of Alexander the Great, the infancy story of Jesus from the Gospel of Thomas, the account of a Jewish boy who calms the Mediterranean from Berakhot 9, sayings of Pythagoras from Iamblichus, and many others. The second section contains "Whole writings for purposes of comparative compositional analysis, Gospels and biographies"—p. ix. These include the Coptic Gospel of Thomas, the Gospel of Philip, Philo of Alexandria's *About the Life of Moses* and others. A bibliography on mystery religions of the Greco-Roman world is also included. A brief introduction precedes each document.

B253. Fitzmyer, Joseph A. *Essays on the Semitic Background of the New Testament.* Missoula, MT: Society of Biblical Literature, 1974, 524 p.

Fitzmyer first examines the use of the Old Testament in the Qumran literature and the New Testament, and secondly the Semitic background of the Gospel passages, the Pauline passages, and the Epistle to the Hebrews. He then turns to early Christianity, including a section on Jewish Christianity in Acts in the light of the Dead Sea Scrolls. He writes, "In my opinion, the influence of Qumran literature on Acts is not as marked as it is in other New Testament writings (e.g., John, Paul, Matthew, Hebrews). The parallels that do exist, striking though they may be, are not numerous"—p. 302. "The thread that links together the vast majority of the essays is a connection between New Testament passages and the Dead Sea Scrolls or contemporary Aramaic studies"—p. xviii.

B254. Goppelt, Leonhard. *Jesus, Paul, and Judaism: An Introduction to New Testament Theology.* New York: Thomas Nelson, 1964, 192 p.

Goppelt first reviews Judaism at the time of Jesus, and then relates Jesus to the Judaism of this period by discussing the religious movements in Judaism, Jesus relationship to the Phariseees, Jesus' authority as an offence to Judaism, and the place of Israel in redemptive history according to Jesus. The Church broke from Judaism under the influence of Paul. Goppelt sees Christianity as a primarily Jewish sect, until it became its own religion around 62-64 C.E. Goppelt's last sentence states: "The relationship between Christianity and Judaism was the central problem of Christianity's theology and the church's existence in the first generation and for all time"—p. 192.

B255. Goulder, Michael D. *Midrash and Lection in Matthew.* London: SPCK, 1974, 528 p.

Goulder first looks at the midrashic method, and then at Matthew's poetry, imagery, use of scripture, and the non-Markan traditions in Matthew. In the second part he examines the book of Matthew under the theme of "The Matthaen Year," looking first at "Pentecost: The Unity of the Sermon" in Matthew 5-7, and continuing through the season of Tabernacles, Hanukkah, and Passover. He also shows us Luke's use of Mark and Matthew. In his conclusion, Goulder makes several comments of interest: "The more closely a passage corresponds to the liturgical structure of the Gospel and the Matthaean manner, in so far as they can be established, the more heavily does the burden of proof rest upon those who claim underlying non-Marcan traditions." "Matthew's being a sopher enabled him to excel all the other churches' attempts: he had the tradition of the elders at his finger-tips." "Matthew provided a liturgical work of art which will not be transcended, and he provided it by adapting Mark in a cataract of epigram, poetry, and parable which has been the dominant influence in forming the Church's image of Jesus. He was the Church's liturgist and the Church's poet, adapting Mark by midrash and through lection"—p. 474-75.

B256. Grant, Frederick C. *Ancient Judaism and the New Testament.* New York: Macmillan, 1959, 155 p.

Grant reviews how "modern" [in 1959] research leads to different conclusions concerning Judaism than the prejudiced approaches of the past. He discusses the results of such misinterpretations, and then discusses ancient Judaism proper, with a section on the synagogue, followed by chapters on the theology of ancient Judaism, the idea of messiah, and Jewish apocalyptic. In his section on the New Testament he speaks of Jesus the Galilean, the gospel of the kingdom of God, and the Church's heritage from Judaism. His conclusion discusses the need for a new liberalism. Grant calls for Jews and Christians to work together for world improvement. He thinks we must understand Christianity not as a separate religion, but as a culmination of Judaism.

B257. Harrington, Daniel J. *The New Testament: A Bibliography.* Wilmington, DE: Michael Glazier, 1985, 242 p.

The last section of the work contains a section on the world of the New Testament, which in turn has chapters on Jewish history, Second Temple Jewish writings, Rabbinic writings, and a number of other topics relevant for the topic of this bibliography.

B258. Hyatt, James P., ed. *The Bible in Modern Scholarship: Papers Read at the 100th Meeting of the Society of Biblical Literature, December 28-30, 1964.* Nashville: Abingdon Press, 1965, 400 p.

Of special interest is Chapter Seven, "The First Christian Century," where Hans Conzelmann discusses the period as Christian history and Martin Cohen discusses it as Jewish history. Among the topics Cohen covers are the rule of Rome, the leadership of the Pharisees, the cardinal doctrines of the Oral Torah, and the divisions and sects among the first-century Jews.

B259. Jonsson, Jakob. *Humour and Irony in the New Testament: Illuminated by Parallels in Talmud and Midrash.* Leiden: E. J. Brill, 1985 (c1965), 299 p.

After providing a background discussion on the subject of religious humor, Jonsson covers Greek and Roman humor, humor in the Old Testament, Talmud, and Midrash, humor in the Synoptic Gospels, and the humor of Jesus as both a public speaker and in his conversations. He shows us the humor inherent in the Gospel of

John, Acts and the writings of Paul. Jonsson thinks that many passages in the New Testament will be more easily and better understood if the underlying humor of some passages is taken into account by the reader.

B260. McKelvey, R. J. *The New Temple: The Church in the New Testament.* London: Oxford University Press, 1969, 238 p.

McKelvey looks at the use of the Temple in the Old Testament, the idea of a new Temple in Jewish literature, and the notion of a heavenly or a spiritual Temple in Jewish and Greek literature. He then examines Jesus and the Temple, and the idea of the new Temple in the writings of Paul and some other New Testament writings. McKelvey writes, "The essence of biblical and post-biblical thinking on the eschatological age is the conviction that God will graciously condescend to dwell in the midst of his people in a new and unparalleled way and never again leave them"—p. 179. "As a metaphor of the church, the conception of the temple is perhaps most significant for our understanding of the New Testament doctrine of the church because of its theocentric character"—p. 180.

B261. Przybylski, Benno. *Righteousness in Matthew and His World of Thought.* New York: Cambridge University Press, 1980, 184 p.

Przybylski first examines the problem of meaning and significance in the Matthaean concept of righteousness, and then he looks at the concept of righteousness as presented in the Dead Sea Scrolls and in Tannaitic literature. He concludes: "The Matthaean concept of righteousness, in contrast to the Pauline one, is not a primary Christian theological concept. The Matthaean concept of righteousness is essentially a Jewish concept, used in a provisional way to provide a point of contact between contemporary Jewish religious understanding and the teaching of Jesus as Matthew understood it"—p. 123. Interestingly, he also notes, "In order to differentiate between the teaching of Judaism and Jesus it was necessary to make a terminological distinction. The term righteousness was discarded in favor of the expression will of God which included not only the concept of the greater righteousness but also salvation by means of Jesus"—p. 122.

B262. Reicke, Bo. *The New Testament Era: The World of the Bible from 500 B.C. to A.D. 100.* Philadelphia: Fortress Press, 1968, 336 p.

The most relevant section of this work is Chapter Five, which covers Palestine at the time of Jesus, which Reicke extends from 4 B.C. to A.D. 66. He takes a geographical approach to organizing his material, first focusing on Galilee-Perea and then on Judea and Samaria. He draws on Biblical material, as well as texts from Josephus, and some material from the Mishnah. He makes a casual but undocumented statement on the origin of the synagogue: "This type of community center and place of worship was undoubtedly borrowed from the Diaspora, where the social and religious need for a common meeting place was especially great and the environment furnished certain models"—p. 119.

B263. Sandmel, Samuel. *A Jewish Understanding of the New Testament.* Augmented ed. New York: Ktav Publishing House, 1974 (c1956), 336 p.

Sandmel begins with a description of the New Testament, offering a look at its Jewish background. He moves on to Paul and his writings, then to the Synoptic Gospels and Jesus, and then the other New Testament writings, concluding with a look at the "genius" of New Testament faith. In the section on the Jewish background of the New Testament, he writes, "The Jewish Messiah was expected to accomplish specific aims. He would destroy the sovereignty of Rome; he would set up a legitimate Jewish kingdom, not of the hated Hasmonean or Herodian stock, but of the genuine Jewish royalty, the stock of King David; he would gather in the exiles from all over the Diaspora; his coming would usher in the judgment day, and there would ensue a resurrection of at least the righteous dead"—p. 29. In an epilogue, Sandmel writes, "For Jews, the New Testament is not and cannot be a literature sacred to us. But the sacred literatures of others can be enlightening and broadening to us, even giving fresh perspectives on our own belief, if we try to understand sympathetically the profound complexities and deep aspirations which human beings have been inspired to express, and how the lives of contemporaries are moved by those ideals and institutions which embody them"—p. 321.

B264. Sherwin-White, Adrian N. *Roman Society and Roman Law in the New Testament.* Oxford: Oxford University Press, 1963, 204 p.

Roman Society consists of eight lectures, of which the second focuses on the trial of Christ. The author shows how a knowledge of Roman law at the time can help understand the proceedings of this event, and provide useful background information for understanding the other happenings of the time. He writes, "...the evidence should be considered in the light of the Roman criminal procedure extra ordinem"—p. 24. On the accusation against Jesus, he says, "The charge is clearly indicated, not as a charge against a particular Roman law, but as a charge on which Pilate is asked to adjudicate"—p. 24. In writing about the historicity of the Gospels, Sherwin-White thinks that when a story enters the "realm of Rome," its historical accuracy is thereby confirmed. "That the degree of confirmation in Graeco-Roman terms is less for the Gospels than for Acts is due, as these lectures have tried to show, to the differences in their regional setting. As soon as Christ enters the Roman orbit at Jerusalem, the confirmation begins"—p. 188-89.

B265. Stambaugh, John E. *The New Testament in Its Social Environment.* Philadelphia: Westminster Press, 1986, 208 p.

A growing body of literature approaches Jesus and his time from a sociological viewpoint. Stambaugh's book shows some of the topics covered when the New Testament is approached in such a way. The organization of the Roman province of Palestine and Roman law are each examined, and then the economy of the time, along with social classes, demography, and languages. City life is examined with special attention to the physical environment, work, play, education, family, and clubs. A late section also covers "Christian Adaptation of Urban Social Forms." The questions the authors seek to answer are: "What were the societies like in which the early Christian movement took root, and what characteristics of those societies can help us to understand that movement's rise and spread?"—p. 10.

B266. *Studies on the Jewish Background of the New Testament.* Assen, Van Gorcum, 1969, 86 p.

A short anthology of pieces on the Jewish background of the New Testament, featuring essays by the likes of O. Michel, S. Safrai, R. le Deavt, and others.

THE OLD TESTAMENT

B267. Beckwith, Roger T. *The Old Testament Canon of the New Testament Church and Its Background in Early Judaism.* Grand Rapids, MI: Eerdmans, 1986, 528 p.

Beckwith first examines the witnesses to the canon, covering the Hebrew Old Testament, the Apocrypha, the Dead Sea Scrolls, and Philo, among others. He then sifts through the factual evidence, looking for support for the idea of an Old Testament canon in the New Testament Church. His other chapters focus on the order and number of the canonical O.T. books and their identity, as well as those that should excluded from the canon. In addition to providing a helpful exploration of the various ways in which the word "canon" was used in relation to the sacred books, Beckwith also explores five "fallacies" concerning the canon, such as the difference between what was accepted by the community, and what certain individuals had to say about it.

B268. Chilton, Bruce D. *A Galilean Rabbi and His Bible: Jesus' Own Interpretation of Isaiah.* London: SPCK, 1984, 216 p.

In Part One, Chilton discusses Jesus and Judaism as well as Targum research and early Judaism. Part Two is given over to a discussion of Jesus and the Targum to Isaiah, while Part Three covers Jesus' style of preaching as Scripture fulfilled. In a concluding section to Part Two, Chilton writes, "Although the substantive agreement is that the kingdom refers to God's personal and dynamic intervention on behalf of his people, the coherence between Jesus and the Targum is far from perfect: the Targum's theology of messianic vindication puts the kingdom in a more nationalistic perspective, while Jesus' attitude to those on the fringes of our outside Judaism was notoriously liberal"—p. 137. On the other hand, he also writes, "We have repeatedly cautioned that Jesus did not depend on the Targum as we know it, but he does seem to have been influenced and informed by traditions which the Targum preserves better than anything else"—p. 139.

B269. Malina, Bruce J. *The Palestinian Manna Tradition: The Manna Tradition in the Palestinian Targums and Its Relationship to the New Testament Writings*. Leiden: E. J. Brill, 1968, 112 p.

Malina's conclusions can be illustrated by the following quotation: "Thus what we have in Jn 6, 31*ff.* is a Christian midrash on the manna tradition, a meditation on this tradition in the light of Jesus, an explanation of the true meaning of this tradition in terms of Jesus, an updating of this tradition called forth by the fact that the Word became flesh"—p. 106. He also examines 1 Cor. 10,3 and Revelation 2,17 to see "whether the manna tradition as handed down through the PT can shed any light on them"—p. 94.

B270. Smith, William Robertson. *The Old Testament in the Jewish Church*. 2nd ed. New York: D. Appleton and Co., 1892, 458 p.

I have included this old work to show the nature of the scholarship related to our topic common in the late 1800s. The manner of argumentation, the sources used, and the conclusions reached, all have to be examined with great care because of the age of the book. The use of the word "church" in the title certainly speaks to the time of writing. Of the essays which make up this volume, Smith wrote in the preface to the First Edition, "The Twelve Lectures now laid before the public had their origin in a temporary victory of the opponents of progressive Biblical Science in Scotland, which has withdrawn me during the past winter from the ordinary work of my Chair in Aberdeen, and in the invitation of some six hundred prominent Free Churchmen in Edinburgh and Glasgow, who deemed it better that the Scottish public should have an opportunity of understanding the position of the newer Criticism than that they should condemn it unheard."—p. ix. Among the topics Smith covers are the scribes, the Septuagint, the history of the canon, the Psalter, and "Christian Interpretation and Jewish Tradition."

B271. Vaux, Roland de. *Ancient Israel: Its Life and Institutions*. New York: McGraw-Hill, 1961, 592 p.

Though somewhat dated and covering a period before the time central to this bibliography, Vaux's volume is important for understanding the views of this scholar on ancient Israel, because they are still are important as background information. The development of the religious calendar and the Sabbath for Israel are covered in this work, which emphasizes these aspects of the development of cultic worship forms within the ancient Near East. The author's approach can be seen in his discussion of the importance of prayer in Israel: "Praying means "speaking to God"; prayer, therefore, establishes a personal relationship between man and God, and it is the basic act of religion. The reason why we are treating it here among the secondary acts of worship is because our theme is the institutions of Israel, and prayer is relevant only in so far as it forms part of the exterior worship"—p. 457.

PALESTINE

B272. Abrahams, Israel. *Campaigns in Palestine from Alexander the Great.* Chicago: Argonaut, 1967, 55 p.

This volume consists of three lectures delivered by Abrahams before the British Academy in 1922. Among the battles discussed are those of the Maccabees, Alexander the Great, Antiochus VII Epiphanes, Napoleon, and Allenby. Abrahams' interest focuses in the Jewish fight for freedom. While he occasionally discusses military tactics, he spends much of his time examining the meaning of these battles for the subsequent history of the region.

B273. Albright, William F. *The Archaeology of Palestine.* Rev. ed. Gloucester, MA: Peter Smith, 1971 (c1960), 271 p.

Twelve chapters make up this volume, beginning with "Art of Excavating a Palestinian Mound." Three sections which have special importance for this bibliography. Chapter Seven, "Palestine in Graeco-Roman Times," covers this region from 332 BCE to the fourth century AD. Chapter Nine, "Daily Life in Ancient Palestine," discusses New Testament times in seven pages. Chapter Eleven, "The New Testament and Archaeology," examines early New Testament manuscripts, the lack of discovery of really early synagogues, and Jewish tombs. Finally, Albright demonstrates the way he reached his conclusions, based on the evidence available to him at the time in 1960.

B274. Albright, William F. *From Stone Age to Christianity.* 2nd ed. Baltimore: John Hopkins Press, 1967, 432 p.

Albright's emphasis is on archaeological discovery and interpretation of documents, but with a recognition of oral interpretation. The book includes sections on differing views of the philosophy of history, the evolution of material civilization in the Near East (with special attention to Egypt), ancient Israel through the time of Hellenism, and the religion of Jesus.

B275. Avi-Yonah, Michael, ed. *Encyclopedia of Archaeological Excavations in the Holy Land.* Englewood Cliffs, NJ: Prentice-Hall, 1975-78, 4 v.

This work covers work done on sites through the end of 1971. This translation of a book originally published in Hebrew works "toward a fuller understanding of recent discoveries by incorporating evaluations of the archaeological results and achievements and discussing the dilemmas and difficulties they pose"—p. 1 of the Introduction to the Hebrew edition. Most of the contributors are Israelis, but a few are European or American. "The encyclopedia is arranged in alphabetical order of the names of the excavated sites. An individual article is devoted to each site. In addition, there are composite articles, *e.g.*, Churches; Megaliths; Monasteries; Synagogues; as well as articles on specific areas, *e.g.*, Accho, Plain of; Jordan Valley. Chronologically the encyclopedia ranges from prehistoric times through the Crusader period. The geographic limits are the historic borders of the Holy Land on both sides of the Jordan, from the Ladder of Tyre and Dan in the north to the Gulf of Elath in the south"—p. 2 of the Introduction to the Hebrew edition. "Each entry is followed by a selected bibliography. Since visual material forms an integral part of archaeology, many illustrations and plans have been included (most of them prepared specially for this work) and in large part provided by the contributors themselves. These have been carefully selected to supplement and elucidate the written text"—p. 2 of the Introduction to the Hebrew edition.

B276. Avi-Yonah, Michael. *Gazetteer of Roman Palestine.* Jerusalem: Hebrew University of Jerusalem, 1976, 112 p.

The *Gazetteer* was originally based on bibliographic notes which Avi-Yonah prepared for the Hebrew original of his book, *The Historical Geography of Palestine*, which was published in 1949. The material has been updated through 1970. In the Preface three items are listed as goals for the Gazetteer: firstly, "an attempt, as far as possible, to reconstruct the original form of the name as it was pronounced in ancient times, mostly by giving a Hebrew form, or, in some cases, a Greek form to the name"; secondly, "The collection under one heading of names which appear in the sources in various forms but which—in the author's opinion—refer to the same place"; thirdly, "A proposed identification of each and every place mentioned in the *Gazetteer*"—p. 7. Over 900 places are listed here, arranged alphabetically by name. A list of ancient sources and their abbreviations precedes the main body of the work.

B277. Avi-Yonah, Michael. *The Holy Land: From the Persian to the Arab Conquests, 536 B.C. to A.D. 640: A Historical Geography.* Rev. ed. Grand Rapids: Baker Book House, 1977 (c1966), 249 p.

Part One of this work covers the historical events of the time, such as Judea under Persian rule, Ptolemaic rule, Palestine as part of the Seleucid Kingdom, and the kingdom of Herod and its internal organization and eventual division. In Part Two, "City Territories," the boundaries of each of the territorial units making up the Holy Land are analyzed in detail. Finally, in Part Three the development of the Roman road system is presented along with an economic geography and studies of population in terms of the various peoples living in the land at the time.

B278. De Lange, Nicholas. *Atlas of the Jewish World.* New York: Facts on File, 1984, 240 p.

Arranged topically, the first section on the historical background of the period contains essays on the Jews in the ancient world and on Christianity and the Jews. The maps are enhanced by drawings, such as one on the Second Temple. Printed in color, the book includes a number of helpful photographs.

B279. Finegan, Jack. *Archaeology of the New Testament: Vol. 1. The Life of Jesus and the Beginning of the early church; Vol. 2. The Mediterranean World of the Early Christian Apostles.* Princeton: Princeton University Press, 1969-81, 2 v.

Volume One of this set begins with information on the life of John the Baptist. In the section on Jesus, a geographical approach is taken, with information on Bethlehem, Nazareth, Samaria, Galilee,

Decapolis, Caesarea, Jericho, the Mount of Olives, Jerusalem, and Emmaus. Then Finegan looks at evidence from various tombs, catacombs, sarcophagi, ossuaries, and places where the mark of the cross was used. Black-and-white photos and line drawings supplement the text. Finegan identifies two sites which may have been the ancient Emmaus, examines the history of those places, and looks at literary evidence from Josephus and the ancient church historian, Sozomen.

B280. Freedman, David N., and Jonas C. Greenfield, eds. *New Directions in Biblical Archaeology*. Garden City, NY: Doubleday, 1969, 191 p.

A collection of essays by major archaeological and biblical scholars such as W. F. Albright, Frank Moore Cross, James Sanders, and David Noel Freedman, *New Directions* covers such topics as the impact of archaeology on Biblical research, "The Israelite Sanctuary at Arad," and several essays on the relevance of the Dead Sea Scrolls for Biblical research. In a piece on the Scrolls and the New Testament, Floyd Filson finds that one of the most neglected areas in examining the Scrolls is fact that the Qumran community intended their teachings to be secret—therefore, it seems unlikely that the Christians actually knew much about them. A bibliography of some of the more important writings on Qumran through 1969 is included.

B281. Goodenough, Erwin R. *Jewish Symbols in the Greco-Roman Period*. New York: Pantheon, 1953-68, 13 v.

Volumes 1-3 cover "The Archaeological Evidence from Palestine and the Diaspora, with v. 3 having 1,209 illustrations. Volume 4 covers "The Problem of Method; Symbols from Jewish Cult. Volumes 5-6 are entitled, "Fish, Bread, and Wine." The remaining titles are: volumes 7-8, "Pagan Symbols in Judaism," Volumes 9-11, "Symbolism in the Dura Synagogue" (v. 11 has 354 illustrations and 21 color plates). Volume 12 is "Summary and Conclusions," with essays which summarize all of the earlier volumes. Volume 13 contains "Indexes and Maps." An outstanding presentation of the archaeological evidence for the period.

B282. Goodman, Martin. *State and Society in Roman Galilee, A.D. 132-212*. Totowa, NJ: Rowman and Allanheld, 1983, 318 p.

In his introduction Goodman discusses his sources and methodology, and then turns to the geography of the region, including the topography of Galilee. He analyzes the society of the time, including the Jews and Gentiles inhabiting Galilee, and the trade and culture of the Galilean villages. His discussion of the government and law of the area includes an interesting review of rabbinic authority in Galilee during this time. A concluding section contains a presentation of the events of the second century. Extensive notes and a bibliography add to the usefulness of the volume.

B283. *Joint Expedition to Khirbet Shema, 1970-1972: Ancient Synagogue Excavations at Khirbet Shema, Upper Galilee, Israel, 1970-1972.* Durham, NC: Duke University Press, 1976, 297 p.

This is Volume 42 of "The Annual of the American Schools of Oriental Research." Topics include the historical setting of Khirbet Shema" in Upper Galilee, the archaeological geology of the area, the synagogue and its environs, the "Soundings in the Southeast Quadrant and Other Areas," the tombs, and reports on numismatics, ceramics, and other artifacts. On the dating of the synagogue, the book says, "The task of dating was simplified by positive identification of materials associated with the first building; they have been buried and thus isolated during the rebuilding after the earthquake of 306 CE..."—p. 33. A fascinating look at the synagogue itself and the way archeologists do their work.

B284. Jongeling, Bastiaan. *A Classified Bibliography of the Finds in the Desert of Judah, 1958-1969.* Leiden: E. J. Brill, 1971, 140 p.

Listing both books and articles in several languages, Jongeling organizes his material under headings such as: "Bibliographical Material," "Linguistic Studies," "Archaeology and History," "Qumran and the Old Testament," "Qumran and Judaism: The Calendar," "Qumran and the New Testament," and "Qumran and Christianity." Useful for surveying publications on the Dead Sea Scrolls during the time covered by the bibliography.

B285. Kraeling, Carl. *The Excavations at Dura Europos Conducted by Yale University and the French Academy of Inscriptions and Letters, Final Report, VIII, Pt. 1: The Synagogue.* New Haven: Yale University Press, 1956, 402 p.

The major topics covered are: "Buildings," "Decorations," "Furnishings and Interior Appointments, Inscriptions," and "Interpretation." "That the dwelling which eventually became the earlier building of the Synagogue was originally erected by Jewish inhabitants of Dura for their own use is possible, but not demonstrable. Its actual relation to the Jewish community becomes evident only when it was adapted to synagogue use as described above. Of the date of this adaptation, important as it is for present purposes, only two indications are available. The first is implied in the fact that the doorsill of the house and the floor of its entrance passageway were raised approximately to the height of that of House B; namely, 1.73 m. above the level of the interior courtyard, when the building was remodeled for religious use. This would probably put the remodeling into the period after A.D. 150"—p. 327. A group of marvelous plates add considerably to the value of the volume.

B286. Levine, Lee I. *Caesarea Under Roman Rule.* Leiden: E. J. Brill, 1975, 298 p.

Levine uses a chronological approach in his book, beginning with the founding of Caesarea, and then covering the first century, when the city was under Herod and Roman rule. In the second century Caesarea was a Roman colony. Levine covers the third and fourth centuries CE by focusing on the economic life of the community. He provides an excellent overview of the successive Jewish, Samaritan, and Christian towns, and closes with a chapter on the Byzantine rule of Caesarea.

B287. Lieberman, Saul. *Greek in Jewish Palestine.* 2nd ed. New York: Feldheim, 1965, 215 p.

Lieberman shows the relation between the Jewish and non-Jewish cultural spheres in Palestine. He examines Talmudic and Midrashic literature from the second through the fourth centuries CE. Topics include: the Greek of the Rabbis, the Greek of the synagugue, Gentiles and semi-proselytes, and Greek and Latin proverbs in

Rabbinic literature. In the light of the controversy about the level of Hellenistic influence in Palestine, it is interesting to note that Lieberman writes, "The previously discussed instances of the house of the patriarch and the house of the head of the academy in Caesarea prove that these were inherent factors favoring the spread of Greek culture among the Jewish masses"—p. 27. "Between these two opposite poles of native Palestinian scholars, on the one hand, who lived in Hellenized towns and were at home in Greek culture, and Babylonian immigrants, on the other hand, who were entirely ignorant of it, we have to place the average Rabbi who lived in the provincial towns and villages"—p. 27.

B288. Merrill, Selah. *Galilee in the Time of Christ*. Boston: Congregational Publishing Society, 1881, 159 p.

It is interesting to note the topics chosen by an author writing in 1881 on this subject. Merrill begins with a look at how the country was governed, and then examines the names "Galilee" and "Galilee of the Gentiles." A chapter on the extent of Galilee and the "number of inhabitants to a square mile" is also included. In the last sentence of the aforementioned chapter, Merrill writes, "Considering the fact that Galilee had a number of large cities, and that the whole province was dotted with important towns, its 2,000 square miles may have supported 3,000,000 inhabitants"—p. 21. As might be expected for this period, Merrill depends on Josephus for much of his information. One chapter reviews the religion, education, and morals of the Galileans, while another is interestingly entitled, "Nazareth, its Character and Probable Size; Origin of the Name; Not so Isolated as is Supposed."

PASSOVER

B289. Bokser, Baruch. *The Origins of the Seder*. Berkeley, CA: University of California Press, 1986 (c1984), 188 p.

Bokser begins by examining the character of relevant material in the Mishnah, and then focuses on extra-Temple practices as continuity or departure from pre-70 CE practices. He continues with a look at the pre-rabbinic description of the Passover Eve ritual and the centrality of the Passover sacrifice. He examines the meaning of the meal without the Passover sacrifice, and concludes with a chapter on the significance of the Passover rite and its place in early Rabbinic

Judaism. A Glossary and extensive bibliography make this volume even more useful. For Bokser, the emphasis on the Passover sacrifice was crucial. He focuses on Mishnah Pesahim 10, "which provided a rich and meaningful rite without the sacrifice, fulfilling the needs of Jews in the second century while maintaining a sense of community with the past"—p. 106.

PAUL THE APOSTLE

B290. Byrne, Brendan. *Sons of God—Seed of Abraham: A Study of the Idea of the Sonship of God of All Christians in Paul Against the Jewish Background.* Rome: Biblical Institute Press, 1979, 288 p.

In covering the Jewish background, Byrne investigates the idea of Sonship of God in the Old Testament in intertestamental literature, Rabbinic literature, and the Targums. He then turns to the idea of the Sonship of God in Romans and Galatians. Paul's view of Christ as the Son of God is also covered, and an Appendix contains an essay on "Paul and Palestinian Judaism," as well as an extensive (and quite useful) bibliography.

B291. Davies, William D. *Jewish and Pauline Studies.* Philadelphia: Fortress Press, 1984, 419 p.

The section on Judaica includes an essay on Law in first-century Judaism, and a reflection on the territorial dimension of Judaism, plus other materials. The chapter on Pauline studies incorporates essays on Paul and the Law, Paul and the people of Israel, some thoughts on Paul's Letter to the Galatians, and other pieces. A section on the New Testament includes an essay on Law in the New Testament.

B292. Davies, William D. *Paul and Rabbinic Judaism: Some Rabbinic Elements in Pauline Theology.* 4th ed. Philadelphia: Fortress Press, 1980 (c1965), 403 p.

After an introduction discussing Palestinian and Diaspora Judaism, Davies looks at the old and new Israel, the old and new man, the old and new obedience, and the old and new hope. In his introduction Davies talks about the development of scholarship on Paul and Judaism since the publication of Albert Schweitzer's *Paul and His Interpreters*. Davies writes, "What has happened since Schweitzer is that the simple picture of a normative Pharisaic Judaism standing over against apocalyptic and Hellenism has vanished. Its fast colours have become blurred and mixed. Judaism has emerged as more varied, changing, and complicated than Schweitzer could have appreciated. In particular, the Dead Sea Scrolls have triumphantly confirmed the suspicions of those who had already suspected Schweitzer's neat dichotomies"—p. xii. In his conclusion, Davies adds, "Both in his life and thought, therefore, Paul's close relation to Rabbinic Judaism has become clear, and we cannot too strongly insist again that for him the acceptance of the Gospel was not so much the rejection of the old Judaism and the discovery of a new religion wholly antithetical to it, as his polemics might sometimes pardonably lead us to assume, but the recognition of the advent of the true and final form of Judaism, in other words, the advent of the Messianic Age of Jewish expectation."

B293. Sanders, E. P. *Paul and Palestinian Judaism: A Comparison of Patterns of Religion.* Philadelphia: Fortress Press, 1977, 627 p.

Sanders bases his study of Palestinian Judaism on Tannaitic literature, the Dead Sea Scrolls, and the Apocrypha and pseudepigrapha. His section on Paul includes studies of Paul's soteriology and view of the Law. He concludes that "...Paul's pattern of religion cannot be described as 'covenantal nomism,' and therefore, Paul presents an essentially different type of religiousness from any found in Palestinian Jewish literature." Sanders further notes, concerning Paul's view of grace, that "...salvation is by grace but judgment is according to works; works are the condition of remaining 'in' but do not earn salvation"—p. 543.

B294. Sanders, E. P. *Paul, the Law, and the Jewish People.* Philadelphia: Fortress Press, 1983, 227 p.

Most (160 pages) of this book is given over to Part I, a consideration of Paul's view of the law. Part II deals with Paul's relation to the Jewish people. Sanders says Paul's view of the Law comes not from a general discussion, but from considering soteriology, Christology, and Christian behavior. Though he sees some consistency in Paul's view of the law, Sanders writes, " I have come to the conclusion that there is no single unity which adequately accounts for every statement about the law"—p. 147. Sanders argues with the idea that because the Jews rejected the word of Christ that they also rejected grace.

B295. Sandmel, Samuel. *The Genius of Paul.* Philadelphia: Fortress Press, 1979, 236 p.

Sandmel covers Paul as a man, as a Jew, as a convert, and as an apostle. He also reviews Paul's relation to the Acts of the Apostles and the other New Testament writings. In his last chapter, on the stature of Paul, Sandmel writes, "Respecting the development by which Jewish Christianity became a religion of salvation, it would be saying too much to attribute to Paul the full measure of the transformation"—p. 210. "Perhaps the most lasting contribution in the legacy of Paul is not his doctrine, but his example. He rebelled, not for the sake of mere rebellion, but, in his own wish, to be nearer to God." "A modern Jew can certainly not follow Paul. But he can try to assess him more justly than Paul assessed Judaism"—p. 220. Sandmel shows us just how similar Philo's and Paul's philosophy is. For example, "... Paul and Philo have many elements in common. Both of them view the Bible as a vehicle for individual salvation. Both are preoccupied with the question of how the individual can enable his mind (or soul; the words are interchangeable) to triumph over his body"—p. 53.

B296. Schoeps, Hans J. *Paul: The Theology of the Apostle in the Light of Jewish Religious History.* Philadelphia: Westminster Press, 1961, 303 p.

Among the topics discussed by Schoeps are Paul's views on eschatology, soteriology, the Law, saving history, and his views on Judaism. The volume begins with sections on the problems involved in Pauline research, and an examination of Paul's position in primitive Christianity. One approach to understanding Paul is given by Schoeps when he writes, "For Saul, throughout his life, scripture remained the supreme norm of all thought and action. Thus, even Paul the Christian adduces no argument to which he does not try to give a Biblical basis, and this applies also to the Messianic character and the soteriological role of Jesus. Even the abolition of the law must be proved from the law, and this is done by means of a principle of the rabbinic law of inheritance"—p. 38.

THE PHARISEES

B297. Abrahams, Israel. *Studies in Pharisaism and the Gospels.* First and Second Series. New York: Ktav Pub House, 1967 (c1917-22), 2 v.

Abrahams is careful not to assume that the writings of the Tannim always reflected the thought of Judaism at the time of Jesus. Nevertheless, he is able to use those writings, in addition to the Mishnah and Josephus, to add background for our understanding the New Testament. He shows how Jews would be able to understand Jesus' prophetic-apocalyptic visions, and Jesus' concern for the moral and ritual life of his day. Abrahams also covers such areas as John the Baptist, the cleansing of the Temple, fasting, the Lord's Prayer, and many other areas.

B298. Baeck, Leo. *The Pharisees and Other Essays.* New York, Schocken Books, 1947, 164 p.

The "other essays" include a piece on tradition in Judaism, another on the origin of Jewish mysticism, and four others relevant for this bibliography, including a look at "The Pharisees." Some fifty pages in length, the essay on the Pharisees was actually penned during the late 1930s, and examines the origin of the term "Pharisee," which meant "separated." Baeck uses Midrashim to arrive at an understanding of the term Pharisee, and finds that a very similar word was used to translate the word "holy." The development of the Pharisees is outlined in relation to study of the Torah and the development of prayer in the synagogue. A study of the conflict of the Temple and synagogue and the conflict of the Pharisees with the state is also included.

B299. Bokser, Ben Z. *Pharisaic Judaism in Transition: R. Eliezer the Great and Jewish Reconstruction After the War with Rome.* New York: Arno Press, 1973 (c1935), 174 p.

Bokser looks at social motivations in the teachings of Rabbi Eliezer ben Hyrcanus. Eliezer adhered to the Pharisaic tradition of his time, and resisted all innovation. He was conservative due in part to his status as a landowner and aristocrat. Bokser looks at some of the Rabbi's teachings, and the folk legends that were spun around him. He reconstructs the major phases of his career, and then investigates his theological, social, and legal doctrines. Bokser thinks that

Eliezer has much in common with the halakah of the Sadducees and the Shammaites, because of the social interests they had in common.

B300. Bowker, John. *Jesus and the Pharisees.* Cambridge, England: Cambridge University Press, 1973, 192 p.

After an initial section in which he discusses the problem of identifying the Pharisees, the emergence and development of the Hakamic movement, and Jesus and the "Pharisaioi," Bowker turns to translations of passages from Josephus, the Mishnah, Tosefta, the Babylonian and Palestinian Talmuds, the Dead Sea Scrolls and a few other documents of importance. He thinks passages in Mark show the transition from the Pharisaioi of Josephus to the perushim, whom Bowker thinks are more extreme in their observance of the Law than the Hakamim.

B301. Bronner, Leah. *Sects and Separatism During the Second Jewish Commonwealth.* New York: Bloch Publishing Co., 1967, 174 p.

The subtitle of this books gives its content: "A study of the origin of Religious Separatism with special reference to the rise, growth, and development of the various Sects, including the Dead Sea Community. The role these sects played in moulding Jewish life and thought is described and evaluated." Topics include the Nazirite, the Pietists, the early Hasidim, the Haburah, the Pharisees, and the Essenes.

B302. Davies, William D. *Introduction to Pharisaism.* Philadelphia: Fortress Press, 1967, 34 p.

Davies examines the derivation of the term Pharisee, and then looks at the sect's basic tenets, including Scripture and tradition, the resurrection, free will vs divine determination, and ethical teaching. He then examines the Pharisees' setting within Judaism and their significance, before closing with an epilogue on Pharisaism and Christianity. This is part of the Facet Books Biblical Series, and though short and now dated, offers a sound introductions to the topic.

B303. Finkel, Asher. *The Pharisees and the Teacher of Nazareth: A Study of Their Background, Their Halachic and*

Midrashic Teachings, Their Similarities and Differences. 2nd ed. Leiden: E. J. Brill, 1974, 195 p.

Finkel covers the Great Synagogue, the scribe, the collecting and preserving of holy scripture, and oral tradition. When considering the controversial halachic teachings of the Pharisees, he examines the laws of separation and purity, festivals such as the Day of Atonement, and the education of the members of the sect. He also examines the oral and written traditions of the Pharisees during the Hasmonaean and Herodian periods. Finally, he looks at the message of Jesus in the light of Pharisaic teachings, including a section on the Jewishness of Jesus. "Although the sources suggest that Jesus, who was raised in a Pharisaic and Essene atmosphere, could not escape the teachings and the mode of life of these masters, yet during the course of his ministry he did deviate from the path of his contemporaries"—p. 133. "Jesus intended that his call to ministry will be in the towns and villages among his own people. In said manner his call was not to be accomplished as a Pharisaic teacher among the strict observers of a code of separation and purity. His intended mission required close contact with the sick, the poor, the unclean and the untouchable"—p. 134.

B304. Finkelstein, Louis. *Pharisaism in the Making; Selected Essays.* New York: Ktav Publishing House, 1972, 459 p.

The essays making up this volume were written over a forty-year period, with some dating back to the 1930s. Even so, there is still enough important scholarship here to offer the student valuable insights even today. A look at some of the chapter titles offers evidence of Finkelstein's important contributions: "The Origin of the Synagogue," "The Oldest Midrash: Pre-Rabbinic Ideals and Teachings in the Passover Haggadah," "Pre-Maccabean Documents in the Passover Haggadah," "The Origin of the Pharisees," and "Some Examples of the Maccabean Halaka." Finlelstein knows that much of the material in the Talmud and synagogue liturgy derive from much earlier traditions, and therefore offer important resources for the topic of this volume. Though the work of Jacob Neusner has brought new approaches to this material, Finkelstein's writings are still of tremendous significance for this subject.

B305. Finkelstein, Louis. *The Pharisees: The Sociological Background of Their Faith.* 3rd ed. Philadelphia: Jewish Publication Society of America, 1962, 2 v.

Volume 1 has information on Palestine and its customs, the origin of the Pharisees, the social background of their legislation, and several of the Pharisees" beliefs, such as the resurrection, angels, and providence. Volume 2 covers areas which form the "sociological background" of the faith of the Pharisees, such as the "ideals of peace and human equality during the exile," social and political conflict under the Persian rule, the struggle against assimilation, and the relation of the Hellenists and the Pharisees. Concerning the origin of the Pharisees, Finkelstein shows the conditions of Palestinian society which lead to their formation. He depends on the Talmud and Josephus for most of his information.

B306. Herford, Robert T. *The Pharisees.* Boston: Beacon Press, 1962 (c1924), 248 p.

Writing in 1924, Herford acknowleges his debt to the theories of Leo Baeck. In the Foreword to 1962 edition of this book, Nahum Glatzer writes, "Robert Travers Herford (1860-1950) was motivated by a deep-seated sense of justice in his study of the religion of the Pharisees. He recognized that neither the early Christian references to the Pharisees, written in a spirit of polemics, nor the account of Flavius Josephus, written for Roman readers, provided the scholar with an objective view of the movement, and that the scholars who preceded him—Julius Wellhausen, Ferdinand Weber, Adolf V. Harnack, Emil Schurer, and others—overstressed the ritualistic and legal aspects of pharisaic religious thought, ignoring in the main its piety, loving concern, and humanness"—p. 1. After giving an historical account of the Pharisees, Herford deals with the relationship of the Pharisees to the synagogue, offers a summary of their teaching, and closes with the relation of Pharisaism to Apocryphal literature and the New Testament. In a concluding chapter, Herford writes, "Yet the view that Judaism was a preparation for Christianity is capable of another meaning beside the one which has been usually assigned to it. A meaning, moreover, which takes in both Christianity and the Judaism which has kept even pace with it, as being both parts in one great whole, each having there a necessary place, and neither being the rival of the other or implying the supersession of the other"—p. 228.

B307. Neusner, Jacob. *The Rabbinic Traditions About the Pharisees Before 70.* Leiden: E. J. Brill, 1971, 3 v.

In volume 1, "The Masters," Neusner reviews the rabbinical traditions about the Pharisees by looking at several major figures, including Simeon the Just. He then examines each of these major figures for their relevance. Neusner analyzes Pharisaic-rabbinc traditions from "formal, redactional, synoptic or comparative, and literary-critical perspectives...."—p. 1. Volume 2, "The Houses," consists of two parts; namely, "Tannaitic Midrashim" and "Mishnah-Tosefta and some Beraitot." Neusner poses two questions. "First, what was the substance of the law attributed to the Houses?" "The second question is this, What words are essential to the pericope, and what are glosses, interpolations, developments, or supplements? What are the mnemonic patterns?"—p. 5. In volume 3, "Conclusions," Neusner examines the literary and historical traits of the tradition as a whole. He also compares the "types and forms of rabbinic traditions about the Pharisees with those of other groups in ancient Judaism"—p. 1. He then deals with the "substantive problems in the history of rabbinic traditions about the Pharisees."

B308. Riddle, Donald W. *Jesus and the Pharisees.* Chicago: University of Chicago, 1928, 193 p.

Riddle writes in his preface, "It is hoped that the following study may be useful in three fields: First, it supplements the existing literature on the Pharisees, in which Christian sources are slightly utilized, by placing beside the thoroughly adequate studies based upon the Jewish sources the data of the Christian traditions. Second, the development of the social-historical method needs several monographs upon certain subjects. This is one such, which, with others, may serve as undergirding for a distinctly new study of early Christianity and the life of Jesus. Finally, an important, though incidental, purpose, is its contribution to the correction of an injustice"—p. vii. Riddle's approach is to take the traditions on this subject, such as those in the earliest and latest Gospels, and analyze them with an eye to what the evangelist's interests may have been. He also looks at the tradition in the Pauline communities and in the Roman milieu, and the development of tradtion in Antioch. In his last section on "Jesus, the Pharisees, and the Tradition," he summarizes how the traditions about the Pharisees developed within the Christian community, concluding, "it requires but a canvass of the sources to perceive that the portrait of the Pharisees in the Gospels is inconsistent, incomplete, and incorrect"—p. 169. He thinks we must look at sources more friendly to the Pharisees to reach a balanced view of their role, and cites the value of work from Herford, Montefiore, Abrahams, and Moore.

B309. Rivkin, Ellis. *A Hidden Revolution: The Pharisees Search for the Kingdom Within.* Nashville: Abington Press, 1978, 336 p.

The revolution to which Rivkin refers is that performed by the Pharisees upon Judaism. He acknowledges the influence of Solomon Zeitlin on his work, and in the preface writes, "I had already sensed that the Pharisees had carried through one of the most stunning revolutions in the history of humankind—a revolution they never acknowledged and of which they left no record other than their transmutation of Judaism"—p. 15. Rivkin first looks at the sources for his study; namely, Josephus, the New Testament, and the Tannaitic literature. He then does a historical reconstruction of the origin of the Pharisees, and describes their revolution in chapters such as "On the Cathedra of Moses" and "God So Loved the Individual...." Commenting on some of his differences with Zeitlin, he writes, "...I could not go along with Zeitlin's early dating of Pharisaic origins or with his unwillingness to call a revolution a revolution. I also was becoming aware that, though Zeitlin intuitively applied a method capable of solving the fundamental problems of definition and origins, he had never made this method explicit. As a consequence, he himself failed to follow his premises through to their logical conclusions. It thus occured to me I might some day try my hand at developing an explicit methodology that would yield both an objective definition of the Pharisees and a compelling hypothesis of their origins as a revolutionary class."—p. 17-18.

B310. Simon, Marcel. *Jewish Sects at the Time of Jesus.* Philadelphia: Fortress Press, 1986, 192 p.

Simon begins with a definition of Jewish sects and their characteristics. He then discusses the Sadducees, Pharisees, Zealots, Essenes, and what he calls the other Palestinian sects (such as Galileans, Baptist groups, Hellenists, and others). He then looks at Alexandrian Judaism, and the relation of the Jewish sects to Christianity. He cautions about comparisons when he writes, "We should not lose sight of the fact that certain traits identical or analogous in both the primitive church and at Qumran belonged also to what could be called the common Judaism of the epoch"—p. 79.

THE SAMARITANS

B311. Coggins, R. J. *Samaritans and Jews: The Origins of Samaritanism Reconsidered.* Oxford: Blackwell, 1975, 170 p.

The evidence Coggins studies includes the Old Testament, later Jewish literature, including the Apocrypha, Pseudepigrapha, and Josephus, the evidence of archaeology, and Samaritan traditions. Coggins is heavily dependent on secondary sources. In his chapter on conclusions, he cites N. H. Snaith's hypothesis, "...the 'schism,' as having taken place between the time of Ezra and that of Alexander the Great"—p. 162. This idea opposes the notion that the schism can be traced to the eighth century BCE. The use of the word "schism" is problematic, because the breakup of the Samaritans and Jews is seen by Coggins as a very gradual process. As he states, "Here again, there is a danger that standards imported from the study of the history of the Christian church might be misleadingly applied to Judaism"—p. 164. "It is not easy to make the transference from this position to one in which a wide variety of belief and practice within certain rather loosely defined norms was entirely acceptable"—p. 164.

B312. Lowy, Simon. *The Principles of Samaritan Bible Exegesis.* Leiden: E. J. Brill, 1977, 544 p.

In this work, Lowy reviews previous research on the subject, and looks at the authentic Samaritans and their origins. He then examines the theories underlying Samaritan exegesis, such as the authority of the Torah and its true version, the Samaritan Midrash, and the issue of tradition versus Scripture, as well as their hermeneutics, such as their use of a literal approach versus allegory. He also reviews syntactical problems, etymological and lexical interpretations, and hermeneutical rules. Lowy points out the stubborn independence of the Samaritan traditions, although some innovations did creep into their way of interpreting Scripture. He notes, "If we steadily bear in mind the fact that religious leaders were regarded rather as the exegetes of existing traditions than as legislators, we realize that their freedom of manoeuvre was in fact very limited. This point is particularly weighty in reference to the Samaritans, for their whole mentality was aligned to the convicition of being guided by the Divine Legislator and His sole messenger. Any major innovation in hermeneutical legislation would thus amount in their view to sacrilege. Unlike the Rabbis, who attributed Sinaitic authority to an 'ORAL LAW' which allowed constant developments, the Samaritans maintained their tradition in a static condition"—p. 504-05.

B313. MacDonald, John. *The Theology of the Samaritans.* London: SCM Press, 1964, 480 p.

After a 58-page introduction, MacDonald arranges his material topically with sections covering: God and the world, Moses, lord of the world, the life of man in the world, eschatology, the world to come, and Samaritanism assessed. In this final section, he writes of three periods in the development of the Samaritan religion: first, the Golden age of literature and religion, which was "the age of the Targum, of Amram Darah the formulator of the doctrine of God, of Markah the great thinker and exegete"; second, the Silver Age, which "saw the incoming of the Eastern Samaritan christological tradition; third, the period of decline, "...begun about the late sixteenth or early seventeenth century. It was the time when Islamic beliefs found their way into liturgical and exegetical works"—p. 447.

B314. Mayer, Leo A., ed. by Donald Broadribb. *Bibliography of the Samaritans.* Leiden: E. J. Brill, 1964, 49 p.

After Mayer's death, Broadribb completed his bibliography, so that it now contains 646 entries arranged alphabetically by author. Items from several languages are included, some of them published in the 1800s, with the latest entries dating from 1963. Books and periodical articles are included. The volume is especially good for its retrospective material on the Samaritans.

B315. Montgomery, James Alan. *The Samaritan, the Earliest Jewish Sect: Their History, Theology, and Literature.* Philadelphia: John C. Winston Co., 1907, 358 p.

Montgomery discusses the land of Samaria and the city of Shechem, the modern Samaritans, and the Samaritans under the Hellenic and

Roman empires, along with other topics. There are two large sections on the theology of the Samaritans and the language and literature of the Samaritans. The discussion of their theology includes their belief in God, angels, and Creation. Also reviewed are their concepts of Moses, the Law, eschatology, and the importance of Mount Gerizim.

B316. Purvis, James D. *The Samaritan Pentateuch and the Origin of the Samaritan Sect.* Cambridge, MA: Harvard University Press, 1968, 147 p.

Purvis looks at the Samaritan script, and at the orthography and textual tradition of the Samaritan Pentateuch. He then reviews theories of the pre-Exilic or post-Exilic origins of the Samaritan sect. Purvis states his conclusions on the Samaritan Pentateuch and their origins with these thoughts, "Whereas previous generations had considered it to have been promulgated by the Samaritans at the time of the construction of their sanctuary on Mt. Gerizim, it is now evident that the work was produced in the late Hasmonean period. This observation enables the historian to determine when the rupture in relations between Jerusalem and Shechem was made complete and the time when Samaritanism emerged as a Jewish sect. It now appears that previous estimates of the origin of the Samaritan sect placed the time of this decisive breach too early. The complete and irreparable break in relations between the Samaritans and the Jews occurred neither in the Persian nor the Greek periods. It occurred in the Hasmonaean period as the result of the destruction of Shechem and the ravaging of Gerizim by John Hyrcanus"—p. 117-18.

THE SERMON ON THE MOUNT

B317. Betz, Hanz D. *Essays on the Sermon on the Mount.* Philadelphia: Fortress Press, 1985, 170 p.

The topics covered include: the literary genre and function of the Sermon on the Mount, the hermeneutical principles of the Sermon, the cosmogony and ethics of the Sermon, and "A Jewish-Christian Cultic Didache in Matt. 6:1-18: Reflections and Questions on the Problem of the Historical Jesus." Betz says in the Preface that though the Sermon on the Mount seems simple and straightforward, "In reality, the Sermon on the Mount is the New Testament text most remote from modern men and women"—p. ix. He also says it is necessary to apply "...philology, form and redaction criticism, literary criticism, history of religions, and New Testament theology..." to understand the text—p. ix. He also offers the hypothesis that "...the Sermon on the Mount was a pre-Matthean source composed by a redactor. This source presents us with an early form—deriving from Jewish Christianity—of the Christian faith as a whole which had direct links to the teaching of the historical Jesus and thus constituted an alternative to Gentile Christianity as known above all from the letters of Paul and the Gospels as well as later writings in the New Testament"—p. x.

B318. Davies, William D. *The Setting of the Sermon on the Mount.* Atlanta: Scholars Press, 1989 (c1964), 546 p.

A reprint of one of the most thorough studies of this subject. After a general introduction, Davies covers the setting in Matthew by studying the Pentateuchal motifs, the idea of a new Exodus and a New Moses, and how the Mosaic categories are transcended. He then examines Jewish Messianic expectation, and looks at the Old Testament, Apocrypha, Pseudipigrapha, Dead Sea Scrolls, and the Rabbinic writings. When he returns to what he calls "Contemporary Judaism," he discusses Gnosticism, the Qumran community, and the events at Jamnia. His study of the setting in the early church covers Paul's work on this tradition, and the sources behind Matthew called "Q" and "M." When he writes about the ministry of Jesus, he notes the ways in which Jesus' words were transmitted, the ideas of Jesus as teacher, eschatological preacher, and rabbi, as well as the demands of Jesus in their setting. Some of his conclusions are: 1. The Sermon on the Mount (SM) in the Gospel tradition "preserves only the whisper of the voice of Jesus."—p. 436. 2. Jesus sayings and the "law of Christ" and his commandments "...played a more significant part in the New Testament as a whole than is often recognized."—p. 437. 3. "Thus it is that our effort to set the SM historically in its place finally sets us in our place. And the place in which it sets us is the Last Judgement, before the infinite succour and the infinite demand of Christ."—p. 440.

B319. Friedlander, Gerald. *The Jewish Sources of the Sermon on the Mount.* New York: Ktav, 1969, 301 p.

Written in 1911, Friedlander's book a major contribution to comparative theology. He takes the Sermon on the Mount as the essential summary of the teachings of Jesus, and seeks to compare it to the Judaism of the time. He looks at Jewish sources for the Beatitudes, the "unfair treatment of the Pharisees," and has a chapter on "Falsifying the Torah to Praise the Gospel." He also examines the concept of the Fatherhood of God in Christianity and in Judaism at the time of Jesus and the Old Testament as a source for the Lord's Prayer. He further argues for the Jewish origin of the Golden Rule.

THE SYNAGOGUE

B320. Gutmann, Joseph, ed. *The Synagogue: Studies in Origins, Archaeology and Architecture*. New York: Ktav Publishing House, 1975, 359 p.

This anthology has chapters by such prominent scholars as Louis Finkelstein, Solomon Zeitlin, Martin Hengel, and Michael Avi-Yonah. One section covers the origins of the synagogue, with the last chapter being a review of the current (1975) state of research on the subject. The second section on archaeology covers art in the synagogue, then-recent excavations at Capernaum, and the idea of "the seat of Moses." The final section on architecture has chapters comparing synagogue and Protestant church architecture, and covering German and Egyptian synagogues.

B321. Kohler, Kaufmann. *The Origins of the Synagogue and the Church*. New York: Arno Press, 1973 (c1929), 297 p.

A brief biographical essay by the editor, H. G. Enelow, begins this book. Kohler discusses the Hasidim and their place in the history of the synagogue, as well as the prayers, liturgy, Scripture reading, and holidays which were a part of the life of the synagogue; and talks about the Pharisees and their ideas. In part 2, on the origins of the Church, he discusses the conditions of Jewry before the rise of Christianity, John the Baptist, the beginnings of the Church, the Essenes and Sadducees, and their relation to the Church and the Gnostic sects. He writes, "It was by no means either the life of Jesus or his teachings, however unique in grandeur of soul the one or in loftiness of spirit the other, that created the Christian Church, but rather his followers' visions of his resurrection, which gave unity and stability to their belief in him"—p. 232.

B322. Mann, Jacob. *The Bible as Read and Preached in the Old Synagogue: A Study in the Cycles of the Readings from*

Torah and Prophets, As Well As from Psalms, and in the Structure of the Midrashic Homilies. Cincinnati: Hebrew Union College, 1940-66, 2 v.

The subtitle says it all: a scholarly study of the portions of Biblical material read on certain Sabbaths, and of the homilies which went along with the Scriptural readings in the old synagogue.

THE TRIAL OF JESUS

B323. Bammel, Ernst, ed. *The Trial of Jesus: Cambridge Studies in Honor of C.F.D. Moule.* Naperville, IL: A. R. Allenson, 1970, 177 p.

This anthology includes chapters on "The Israel-Idea in the Passion Narratives," "The Problem of the Historicity of the Sanhedrin Trial," "The Charge of Blasphemy at Jesus' Trial Before the Sanhedrin," and "The Trial of Jesus in Jewish Tradition." The authors' footnotes are extensive and provide a basis for further study, and the fourteen essays cover a wide diversity of topics, including most of the primary points of controversy concerning the presentation of Jesus's trial in the New Testament.

B324. Catchpole, David R. *The Trial of Jesus: A Study in the Gospels and Jewish Historiography from 1770 to the Present Day.* Leiden: E. J. Brill, 1971, 324 p.

Catchpole begins by examining the influence of Talmudic material and other Rabbinic sources on such Jewish scholars as Joseph Klausner. He then turns to the question of the charge against Jesus in the Sanhedrin, and the problem of the Sanhedrin hearing in Luke. He closes with a look at the legal setting of the trial of Jesus. Catchpole discusses the issues raised by a Jewish approach to the trial of Jesus: "First, the debate about illegalities should be regarded as at a dead end, and at most able to make only a minor contribution....Secondly, the Passion narratives raise in a particularly clear way the phenomenon of the gospel material....Thirdly, the relationship between Jesus' career and his downfall continually requires re-examination....Fourthly and lastly, the old dominance of the traditions of Mark and Matthew can no longer, after the work of Winter as well as of non-Jewish writers, persist"—p. 268-71.

B325. Cohn, Haim. *The Trial and Death of Jesus*. New York: Harper & Row, 1971, 419 p.

Cohn discusses those involved in Jesus's execution, including the Romans, the Jewish chief priests, elders, scribes, and council. He then examines the arrest, the trial, the scourging, and the crucifixion. The acts of Pilate are also reviewed. Cohn was appointed a Justice on the Supreme Court of Israel in 1960, and he takes the point of view of a lawyer as he examines the sources for this event. Cohn shows that "...the trial before the Roman governor was conducted under Roman law and according to Roman procedures..."—p. 331. He writes that the forefathers of the Jews did not take part in the trial and the crucifixion of Jesus, and indeed tried to save him—p. 331.

B326. Juel, Donald. *Messiah and Temple: The Trial of Jesus in the Gospel of Mark*. Missoula, MT: Society of Biblical Literature, 1977, 223 p.

Juel begins by examining such topics as the legality of Jesus's trial and the mocking of Jesus as a prophet, and then looks at the decisive charge against him. He further discusses the concepts of the Son of God, Messiah, Son of Man, the charge of blasphemy, the charge of destroying the Temple, as well as the idea of the community as Temple at Qumran. He also examines Targumic and Rabbinic traditions concerning the Messiah and the Temple in the last days. Juel believes that Jesus's trial must be approached on a literary level and seen within the context of Mark's entire story. The trial is the place Mark chooses to introduce the themes necessary to understand Jesus's death.

B327. Mantel, Hugo. *Studies in the History of the Sanhedrin*. Cambridge: Harvard University Press, 1961, 374 p.

Mantel covers: "The Title Nasi in Jewish Tradition," "The Sanhedrin in Rabbinic and Greek Sources," "The Titles AB Bet Din, Hakam, and Mufla," "The Removals of the Sanhedrin from Jabneh to Usha," "The Offices of the Nasi," and "Jesus, Paul, and the Sanhedrin." In this final chapter, he writes, "According to the Gospels the trial of Jesus took place before the Sanhedrin with the high priest presiding; yet according to rabbinic tradition the presiding officer of the Sanhedrin was a Pharisaic scholar, not the high priest. In our first chapter we pointed out that there is no reason to doubt the trustworthiness of this tradition, while in the second we found that the Synedrion of the Gospels is not identical with the Sanhedrin in the Hall of Gazit. The one was a political, the other a religious body. So there is no contradiction between the rabbinic sources and the New Testament concerning the court before which Jesus was tried. The difficulty lies rather in the Gospel accounts of the circumstances of Jesus' trial, especially the day on which it occurred, on the one hand, and the nature of the charges brought against him on the other"—p. 254.

B328. Winter, Paul. *On the Trial of Jesus.* 2nd ed. New York: Walter de Gruyter, 1974, 225 p.

For this Second Edition, T.A. Burkill has taken supplementary notes written by the late Paul Winter, and placed them at the appropriate places in the text. Winter covers Jewish-Roman relations at the time, looks at the office of High Priest and the importance of the Sanhedrin, and examines the part of Pilate, the penalty of crucifixion, Jewish death penalties, and the inscription on the cross. The focus of Winter's approach to this subject is to identify the various levels of tradition which he calls primary tradition, secondary tradition, and editorial accretion. Explaining his approach, he says, "...we conducted an analysis of individual items in the Passion Narratives of the canonical Gospels in a sustained attempt to identify apologetic motives introduced by the particular evangelists into the traditional material at their disposal"—p. 190. In the chapter on crucifixion as a penalty, Winter says, "Crucifixion was not a punitive measure that can be shown actually to have been used by Jews during or after the lifetime of Jesus"—p. 96.

THE ZEALOTS

B329. Brandon, Samuel G. F. *Jesus and the Zealots: A Study of the Political Factor in Primitive Christianity.* New York: Charles Scribner's Sons, 1967, 412 p.

This work presents the factors surrounding the Roman execution of Jesus, the origin and ideals of the Zealots, the causes for Israel's unrest in relation to Rome, how the Zealot ideal affected Jewish Christians, how the Gospel of Mark's issues related to this topic, the concept of the pacific Christ, and a last chapter on Jesus and the Zealots. Brandon builds his argument on the idea that Jesus was put to death because of a charge of sedition. He attributes Mark's presentation of Jewish involvement in the death of Jesus to the fact that the Christians in Rome were in a very precarious position in 71 CE.

B330. Yadin, Yigael. *Masada: Herod's Fortress and the Zealots' Last Stand*. New York: Random House, 1966, 272 p.

As in his book on the Bar-Kokhba expedition, Yadin uses the format of plates showing the findings of the dig and the area under investigation to illustrate his text. He discusses how the dig was accomplished, what was found, and its significance. Chapters include information on how archaeologists work, the casement wall, the scrolls, the remains of the last defenders, and "the dramatic end."

C.

PERIODICAL AND SERIAL ARTICLES

THE DEAD SEA SCROLLS

C1.   **Amusin, Joseph D.** "The Reflection of Historical Events of the First Century B.C. in Qumran Commentaries (4Q 161; 4Q 169; 4Q 166)." *Hebrew Union College Annual* 48 (1977): 123-152.

Amusin presents various scholarly views, including his own, about the historical events are being referred to, both in coded language and in the Qumran Commentaries on Nahum and Isaiah. He favors the idea that the event mentioned in the Isaiah Commentary is the battle between Alexander Janneus and Ptolemy Lathyrus involving the coastal town of Acco-Ptolemaïs. In the Naham Commentary, Almusin believes he finds reference to the people's revolt under Alexander Janneus and under his widow, Alexandra Salomë.

C2.   **Baumgarten, Joseph M.** "The Pharisaic-Sadducean Controversies About Purity and the Qumran Texts." *Journal of Jewish Studies* 31 (Autumn, 1980): 157-170.

Beginning with the ritual of purification involving ashes from the red heifer as given in Numbers 19, Baumgarten examines the Sadducee, Pharisee, and Essene views on purity. In relation to the red heifer ceremony, the Sadducees required the priest to be immersed and to wait until sundown to perform the ritual, while the Pharisees had no such waiting period. 11 Q Temple from the Dead Sea Scrolls shows that the Essenes were often in agreement with the Sadducees, according to Baumgarten, and the Tebul Yom was considered unclean until sundown.

C3.   **Beckwith, Roger T.** "The Pre-History and Relationships of the Pharisees, Sadducees and Essenes: A Tentative

Reconstruction." *Revue de Qumran* 11 (October, 1982): 3-46.

Beckwith begins with the Qumran text of 1 Enoch in an attempt to reassess the prehistory—*i.e.*, before 175 BCE—of the Pharisees, Sadducees, and Essenes. He finds reason to question the idea that the Sadducees and Essenes were more conservative than the Pharisees, and he notes the tendencies that led to the development of these three groups as far back as the third century BCE. He believes that the Sadducean denial of angels and an afterlife was a reaction to Greek philosophy. In the final section, he traces the development of those responsible for teaching the law, from priest to Levite to scribe.

C4. **Brownlee, William H.** "The Wicked Priest, the Man of Lies, and the Righteous Teacher: The Problem of Identity." *Jewish Quarterly Review* 73 (July, 1982): 1-37.

Brownlee shows the difficulty of identifying the Wicked Priest with just one historical figure, and he argues for three persons: John Hyrcanus and his two sons. He uses various Qumran texts to show how the events of their lives are reflected in the texts, and he discusses various other interpretations and their weaknesses. The Habakkuk Commentary is a central document for Brownlee. He also shows how the Wicked Priest or Man of Lies was at first in favor with the Qumran community, but later was viewed as an apostate. He goes into great detail when reconstructing the history of the lives of King Hyrcanus and his sons.

C5. **Charlesworth, James H**. "The Origin and Subsequent History of the Authors of the Dead Sea Scrolls, Four Transitional Phases Among the Qumran Essenes." *Revue de Qumran* 10 (May, 1980): 213-233.

Charlesworth believes the Scrolls derive from the Qumran community of the Essenes, which existed from the middle of the second century BCE to 68 CE. The four phases described by him are: (1) Settlement at Qumran probably just before 135 BCE; (2) The buildings at Qumran acquire their definitive form and the community expands; (3) From 30 BCE to a few years into the first century CE the Essenes leave the community, perhaps as a result of a fire; (4) 64 C.E. to 68 CE., when Qumran is destroyed by military action. Evidence from Masada shows Essianism was still "flickering" in 74 CE, Charlesworth believes.

C6. **Davies, Philip R**. "Eschatology at Qumran." *Journal of Biblical Literature* 104 (March, 1985): 39-55.

Davies finds evidence of doctrinal reformulation and evolution in the eschatological beliefs at Qumran, and he thinks some of the Scrolls are non-Qumran Essene material. He traces the idea of dualism in the Scrolls as evidence of the distinctive Qumran developments among the Essenes.

C7. **Davies, Philip R**. "The Ideology of the Temple in the Damascus Document." *Journal of Jewish Studies* 33 (Spring-Autumn, 1982): 287-301.

Davies states that the Damacus Document has a qualified, even critical attitude towards the Jerusalem temple, and that there has been no general agreement among scholars to explain this. Davies examines the Document more closely and the scholarly opinion concerning it, and concludes that the community did participate in the Temple cult, but with a very scrupulous attitude. He also thinks that the Temple was not really an independent issue, but was connected to Qumran thinking on the law and the calendar.

C8. **Driver, Godfrey**. "Mythology of Qumran." *Jewish Quarterly Review* 61 (April, 1971): 241-281.

The first myth that Driver attacks is W. F. Albright's conception of the documents found at Masada. Driver presents what was and was not found there, and on that basis challenges some of Albright's assumptions. He then presents an outline of the history of the time for those who have trouble grasping it. He challenges the writing of Edmund Wilson on the Dead Sea Scrolls by pointing out that Wilson cannot read Hebrew and has only the sketchiest knowledge of the Scrolls. Driver continues with a list of words from the Scrolls which he thinks have been misunderstood. He finishes with a lengthy argument against some of the conclusions of Dr. Hoenig concerning the Essenes, especially their view of whether the Temple worship practices could be reformed.

C9. **Fitzmyer, Joseph A**. "The Contribution of Qumran Aramaic to the Study of the New Testament." *New Testament Studies* 20 (July, 1974): 382-407.

Three topics are covered in this article: "...(I) lexical matters that supply a first century Palestinian background to certain New Testament problems; (II) Jewish Palestinian practices or beliefs that emerge in these texts; and (III) literary parallels that have become known through them"—p. 385. Among the items Fitzmyer studies are: the absolute use of the word "Lord" as a title for God in the Qumran targum of Job, and the implications it has for the use of "kurios" for Jesus in the New Testament; the use of the term "Son of God" in the Pseudo-Danielic text from Qumran Cave IV; his belief that no matter how the term "Son of God" is interpreted, it will have to be considered in its apocalyptic setting; and some Aramaic parallels to the infancy story in Luke which appear in the Genesis Apocryphon. "Another instance of a Qumran tenet that has emerged from an Aramaic text confirms the notion of Melchizedek as a heavenly being. This seems to be the view presented in IIQ Melchizedek, a Hebrew text..."—p. 399. Fitzmyer closes his article with a list of the parallels, and a bibliography of periodical articles that have been written about them.

C10. **Golb, Norman**. "The Dead Sea Scrolls." *American Scholar* 58 (Spring, 1989): 177-207.

Golb disagrees with the scholarly consensus that the Dead Sea Scrolls were composed at Qumran. He points out what he considers several weaknesses with such a theory. The Qumran site where the Essenes were to have lived was destroyed in a military battle, and yet the Essenes were supposed to be peace-loving and weaponless. There is no general endorsement of celibacy in the manuscripts, and yet the Essenes were supposed to have been celibate. The supposed scriptorium where the manuscripts were to have been copied had no fragments of manuscripts when it was excavated. The Qumran settlement was supposed to have been the center of Essene activity, and yet there were no legal deeds, letters, or other similar documents found at the site. The treasures mentioned in the Cooper Scroll also seem out of character with a community that did not believe in the value of material possessions. Gold then argues that the Scrolls were written in Jerusalem, and when fighting with the Romans broke out were taken to the Qumran site.

C11. **Hoenig, Sidney**. "Garnet's Salvation and Atonement in the Qumran Scrolls." *Jewish Quarterly Review* 70 (October, 1979): 121-122.

In this book review of Paul Garnet's *Salvation and Atonement in the Qumran Scrolls*, Hoenig indicates that Garnet follows the theory of stages advanced by J. Starkey. He divides the Scroll Hymns into Founder, Leader, and Member Hymns, and looks at their idea of atonement and salvation. Garnet thinks the background for Jesus's understanding of these issues is not sectarian Judaism, but Rabbinic and Hellenistic Judaism. Hoenig points out that the notion of atonement by death is an apocalyptic concept found in II and IV Maccabees, which was later introduced into rabbinic Judaism.

C12. **Laurin, Robert B**. "The Problem of the Two Messiahs in the Qumran Scrolls." *Revue de Qumran* 4 (January, 1963): 39-52.

The Damascus Document had raised questions when it spoke of a Messiah of Aaron and Israel. The use of the plural for anointed ones or Messiahs in IQS IX, 9-11 and at other places in the Qumran Scrolls has raised even more questions. Laurin sets out to show that "a 'two Messiah' view is in opposition to the meaning of the term 'Messiah,' both in Jewish literature outside of Qumran and in the Scrolls themselves"—p. 40. Laurin concludes that the use of the plural is either a scribal error or a "general designation for the eschatological priest and king"—p. 51. "So the theory of two Messiahs in the Qumran Scrolls is really built on a tenuous interpretation of one text: Rule of the Community IX, 11(35). The overwhelming evidence elsewhere—the history of the development of the word, its use in Jewish literature, and other Scrolls—indicates that the messianic hope of the Scrolls was for a Davidic Messiah and a high priestly companion"—p. 52.

C13. **Marcus, Ralph**. "Qumran Scrolls and Early Judaism." *Biblical Research* 1 (1956): 9-47.

Though writing in 1956, at a time when Marcus acknowledges it had only been six years since "...the appearance of the first of the Qumran scrolls to be printed in complete form..." (p. 9), the author discusses five areas which have an impact upon the study of the Scrolls and early Judaism. These are: "1. linguistic problems; 2.

literary affinities; 3. the historical background; 4. the Jewish religious background; 5. Gnostic elements in the Qumran Scrolls"— p. 9. In the section on the religious background, he covers the Pharisees, the Essenes and Jewish Gnostics. He calls attention to the need to consult Talmudic literature when trying to understand the Damascus Covenant and the Manual of Discipline, because of their Halakic passages.

Marcus draws the interesting conclusion, even for 1956, that the Qumran community was a group of gnosticizing Pharisees. "If, then, we assume that in their observances and institutions the Qumran covenanters were predominantly Pharisaic and at the most only 'heterodox' Pharisees in some regards, and if at the same time we recognize that they inclined, far more than Pharisaic authorities of the Tannaite period, toward apocalypticism, cosmic-ethical dualism and determinism, we are, I think, inexorably led to the conclusion that they were gnosticizing Pharisees"—p. 28.

He summarizes his conclusions with the following words: "But even in the present state of knowledge I venture to present these conclusions as inherently probable: 1. Jewish Gnosticism antedates the Christian era; 2. the Damascus and Qumran covenanters were Essenes; 3. the Essenes were gnosticizing Pharisees; 4. Essene Gnosticism (and perhaps other forms of Jewish Gnosticism) significantly influenced both Christian Gnosticism and certain forms of pagan Gnosticism, particularly Mandaeism"—p. 40.

C14. Murphy-O'Connor, Jerome. "Judah the Essene and the Teacher of Righteousness." *Revue de Qumran* 10 (December, 1981): 579-585.

Jean Carmignac had come to the conviction that the Teacher of Righteousness of the Qumran Scrolls should be identified with Judah the Essene. The major premise in the argument had been what Josephus says about Judah the Essene in War, I, 78-80. Murphy-O'Connor reviews this argument and disagrees, in part because Carmignac's conclusion "...is obtained by a process of exclusion"— p. 580. After examining Carmignac's conclusions and showing their weakness, he writes, "The evidence of Josephus proves only that Essenes could frequent the Temple in 103 B.C. It does not prove what sort of Essenes they were. It proves Carmignac's conclusion only within the framework of assumptions whose truth he does not demonstrate and which, in my opinion, cannot be demonstrated. Finally, the evidence of Josephus does not refute the hypothesis that

Jonathan was the Wicked Priest because it is compatible with that hypothesis"—p. 585.

C15. **Neusner, Jacob**. "Qumran and Jerusalem: Two Jewish Roads to Utopias." *Journal of Bible and Religion* 27 (October, 1959): 284-290.

"The central issue of the Jewish Commonwealth was how to transform biblical precept into daily practice"—p. 284. Neusner says Qumran represented revolutionary a Utopianism which sought to build a new society on the ruins of the old by destroying the old in order to create anew. Other Jewish Utopian programs represented social Utopianism which sought to restore society to an ancient ideal. The Qumran community withdrew from wicked society to build their own holy society behind the walls of the desert and with their own discipline. The Pharisees sought to build holy communities in the villages of Israel and in Jerusalem. Neusner reviews the elements which made up each approach, and compares and contrasts them.

C16. **Nickelsburg, George W.** "The Epistle of Enoch and the Qumran Literature." *Journal of Jewish Studies* 33 (Spring-Autumn, 1982): 333-348.

Nickelsburg attempts to "...plot some possible relationships between a writing of unknown provenance found at Qumran, and some of the Qumran Essene literature. The writing is the Epistle of Enoch (I Enoch 92-105)"—p. 333. He discusses the author of this Epistle, his group and the religious conflict with the Jews and the author's purpose in writing (*Ibid.*). He then draws some comparisons with other Essene Scrolls, and suggests some ideas about why the Epistle was included in the Qumran library. He concludes with a section on the question of provenance, in which he offers some reasons why he thinks there is a historical connection "...between the author of this text and the authors of the relevant Qumran writings."—p. 347.

C17. **O'Dell, Jerry.** "The Religious Background of the Psalms of Solomon (Re-evaluated in the Light of the Qumran Texts)." *Revue de Qumran* 5 (May, 1961): 241-257.

O'Dell examines the arguments in support of the idea that the Psalms of Solomon had been written by the Pharisees. These arguments included the ideas that the authors saw the downfall of the Hasmoneans as the righteous punishment of God, that piety is in direct relation to obedience to the law, that although God ordains everything, man has freedom of will. O'Dell then shows that these beliefs were shared by several groups within Judaism at the time, including what he calls a third group which had a strong eschatological emphasis, among them the Essenes, Zealots, John the Baptist, and the early Christians. He documents this from the Qumran Scrolls, and says that though we cannot prove conclusively who the authors were, "It is much more likely that the milieu out of which these psalms originated was that of the Chasidim." He writes, "By Chasidim I do not mean a closed, narrow party, but rather a general trend of pious, eschatological Jews whose piousness was one of the individual nature rather than something imposed upon them by the group"—p. 257.

C18.   Smith, Morton. "The Dead Sea Sect in Relation to Ancient Judaism." *New Testament Studies* 7 (July, 1961): 347-360.

Smith acknowledges the vast difference of opinion on the Scrolls in 1961, and the fact that much of the material had not yet been published. He views the Qumran sect as a religious rather than a philosophical group. Smith then takes some time to review Old Testament material, especially the reforms of Nehemiah and their effects on later Jewish sects, and looks at how the Qumran material then published relates to these reforms. "The essential contribution, therefore, of the fuller picture of Jewish sectarianism which we have been given by the Qumran finds, is to increase our estimate of the importance of that side of ancient Judaism which conceived of it as the religion of the Law, and to do this by demonstrating the legal origin and nature even of the Jewish sects"—p. 360.

C19.   Vermes, Geza. "The Essenes and History." *Journal of Jewish Studies* 32 (Spring, 1981): 18-31.

Vermes begins with two points; namely, the importance of the discovery of the Qumran Scrolls for the understanding of the textual evolution of the Hebrew Scriptures, and the light the Scrolls throw on the community of the Essenes. Vermes assumes an identity or close relationship "...between the Qumran sect and the Jewish ascetics described by Philo, Josephus and Pliny the Elder"—p. 20. He explains his reasons for believing that Qumran was a location for a group of Essenes, and then gives a history of the Essenes. He examines some scholarly opinions about this community, and shows why he disagrees with several of them. He closes with a look at the Essene and Jewish historiography.

C20. Vermes, Geza. "The Impact of the Dead Sea Scrolls on Jewish Studies During the Last Twenty Five Years." *Journal of Jewish Studies* 26 (Spring-Autumn, 1975): 1-14.

Vermes outlines the problems with the study of Jewish history at the end of the nineteenth century. He then looks at the initial impact of the discovery of the Scrolls, and some of the early opinions of the scholars on the study of Judaism. He relates some of the intrigue necessary in gaining access to the Scrolls in the early days after their discovery. A review of various subjects on which the Scroll research has had an impact includes: transmission of the text of the Bible, Apocrypha and Pseudepigrapha, Palestinian Jewish history and culture, and haggadah and religious thought. In this last section he mentions the idea that pesher or interpretation of the fulfillment of prophecy has a very important place in Qumran. Furthermore, "The close links between the Dead Sea Scrolls pesher and the use of the Hebrew Bible in the New Testament have been noticed since the early days of Qumran research"—p. 11.

C21. Vermes, Geza. "The Impact of the Dead Sea Scrolls on the Study of the New Testament." *Journal of Jewish Studies* 27 (Autumn, 1976): 107-116.

Vermes thinks the Scrolls are not Judaeo-Christian documents. The areas of comparison Vermes considers are: eschatological expectation, the claims concerning who is the true Israel, the attitude toward the Bible in both Qumran writings and the New Testament, and the significance of the Jerusalem Temple. The Essenes considered their withdrawl as temporary until the replacement of the wicked priesthood. The Christians, on the other hand, thought of their withdrawal from the Temple as permanent. His main conclusion is, "...if the Qumran Scrolls are invaluable in shedding new light on early Christianity, rabbinic literature, skillfully handled, is still the richest source for interpretation of the original Gospel message, and the most precious aid to the quest for the historical Jesus"—p. 116.

C22. **Vermes, Geza.** "Pre-Mishnaic Jewish Worship and the Phylacteries from the Dead Sea." *Vetus Testamentum* 9 (January, 1959): 65-73.

Fragments of several phylacteries found in Qumran caves I and IV are important in part because their content differs from the phylactery of Murabba'at and the tefillah as described in rabbinic literature. Vermes focuses on the choice of texts used in these various phylacteries, and then lists five principal facts which emerge from his study. The first is, "The phylactery from Murabba'at proves that the Mishnaic reform was already in practice at the time of the Bar Kokhba rising (AD 132-135)"—p. 71.

C23. **Zeitlin, Solomon.** "The Essenes and Messianic Expectations: A Historical Study of the Sects and Ideas During the Second Jewish Commonwealth." *Jewish Quarterly Review* 45 (October, 1954): 83-119.

Zeitlin uses Josephus for a primary source for his information, and begins with an explanation of the Pharisees and Sadducees. He then uses sources such as Josephus, Philo, and the Apocrapha to examine the Essenes. After relating their history, Zeitlin turns to the organization of the Essenes, and discusses some of their beliefs, including their Messianic expectations. Of the Essenes he writes, "They cherished belief in immortality of the soul, and reward and punishment. They accepted the Pentateuch and perhaps the prophets, but rejected belief in a Messiah"—p. 114.

EARLY CHRISTIANITY

C24. **Torrance, Thomas F.** "Origins of Baptism." *Scottish Journal of Theology* 11 (June, 1958): 158-171.

Torrance acknowledges the complexity of his topic: the New Testament takes its background for granted. "Perhaps one of the most difficult things for us to do today, after a century of exhaustive Old Testament investigation, is to get ourselves into the position from which the New Testament writers regarded and interpreted and handled the Old Testament"—p. 158. He begins with a look at the sixteenth chapter of Ezekiel as background for understanding proselyte Baptism. It is Jewish proselyte Baptism which Torrance thinks provides the background for Christian Baptism. "...I do not mean at all that we are to see in proselyte baptism itself the source of the Christian rite, but that proselyte baptism helps us to see a line of interpretation embedded in the Jewish tradition, which throws considerable light upon what the New Testament writers took for granted in regard to the origins of the Christian rite"—p. 160-61). He then examines the three elements involved in Jewish proselyte baptism: namely, circumcision, the sprinkling of sin-offering water on the third and seventh days after circumcision, and ablution.

C25. Young, Frances M. "Temple Cult and Law in Early Christianity: A Study in the Relationship Between Jews and Christians in the Early Centuries." *New Testament Studies* 19 (April, 1973): 325-338.

Young reviews Hellenistic and Jewish arguments against sacrifice as the background of Christian arguments on the subject. He also shows a "spiritual" understanding of the Sabboth, Covenant, and Temple among early Christians. Having reviewed Jewish persecution of Christians, he says the main focus of Jewish hostility was not the Messianic claim of Christianity, but Jesus' message and that of early Christians to Jews of the need for repentance. He finds the background of the early Christian message in the prophets, and says Jesus saw morality as more important than the Law or the Temple cult.

GNOSTICISM

C26. Marcus, Ralph. "Judaism and Gnosticism." *Judaism* 4 (Autumn) 1955): 360-364.

"Gnosticism is a predominantly pessimistic kind of mystical nostalgia. It has no 'origin' in the sense in which Early Judaism or Christianity or Neo-Platonism has a recognizable origin, but, like mysticism in general, Gnosticism is older than any historical religion or religious philosophy. It appears that Gnosticism assumed a more or less concrete form as early as the Hellenistic period, after it had taken over important mythical elements from Zarorastrianism, Judaism, Platonism, Stoicism and other forms of thought"—p. 360. Marcus describes the content of the central myth of Gnosticism, and examines contrasts between Gnosticism and Platonism, and Zoroastrianism and Judaism. For example, whereas Gnosticism sees the world as having an incurable evil, the others recognize the battle between good and evil, but think of the world as essentially good, having been created by a good God. Marcus then looks at the Qumran Book of Discipline, and finds there a possible source for a type of Gnosticizing Judaism. Toward the end of his article he makes two especially interesting statements: "That Paul strongly Gnosticized early Palestinian Christianity seems to me beyond doubt." "Fortunately, Judaism and Greek philosophy unconsciously collaborated in the writings of Philo and his Christian successors to save later Christianity from complete Gnosticizing..."—p. 364.

C27.   Wilson, R. McL. "Jewish Gnosis and Gnostic Origins: A Survey." *Hebrew Union College Annual* 45 (1974): 177-189.

Wilson begins by reviewing the theories of various scholars on the origins of Gnosticism. The conflict between Bultmann and Alan Richardson on the possible influence of Gnosticism on Christianity is explored. Wilson then shows how the term has been used overbroadly, and asks for more specificity: "The only Gnosticism we know is that of the second century and later—at least so far as documents are concerned"—p. 180. Wilson wants the terms Gnosis and Gnosticism used in strictly defined contexts. After reviewing the theories of some scholars who wish to trace the origin of Gnosticism to Judaism, Wilson writes that we should recognize "...the transmutation which has taken place, and refrain from reading it back into the original contexts from which the motifs were derived"—p. 183. However, he recognizes that Judaism was one of the areas where new thoughts were being developed, and that some of these notions eventually led to Gnosticism. Next, Wilson reviews the areas of exploration for this topic, including the writings of Philo, the Qumran documents, the Jewish apocalyptic, and the Wisdom tradition. While he thinks Gnosticism must be reserved to second-century sects, the wider realm of Gnosis was at work in Platonism, Stoicism, Greek philosophy, and various aspects of Judaism.

THE HERODS

C28.   Braund, D. "Four Notes on the Herods." *Class Quarterly* n.s. 33:1 (1983): 239-242.

Braund deals with four items involving the history of the House of Herod, including some uncertainty deriving from accounts in

Josephus: 1. Josephus states that Herod sent 500 bodyguards to serve the Roman Emperor Augustus, yet they took part in the Gallus Expedition before assuming their new assignment. 2. Herod sent his sons to Rome to stay at the house of a certain Pollio; Braund says this need not have been a prominent Roman figure, since we know that this was also a popular Jewish name. 3. Two accounts have Gaius exiling Herod Antipas to Lugdunum or to Spain. Which is right? Braund presents a case for considering Lyons as the location. 4. The link of L. Iulius Agrippa to the Herods is dubious, and thus the theory of J. and J. Ch. Balty, who stated that the inscription on a statue-base from Apamea points to a connection, and that L. Iulius Agrippa was related to Herod Agrippa I or II of Judaea, is questionable.

C29. Bruce, Frederick F. "Herod Antipas, Tetrarch of Galilee and Peraea." *Annual of Leeds University Oriental Society* 5 (1963-65): 6-23.

Bruce begins his account with King Herod the Great, and talks about his several wives and the sons which are born from them, including Antipas. He reviews the latter's rise to power, his relations with John the Baptist, with Jesus, and with the Roman authorities. He compares the accounts in Mark and Luke concerning Antipas, and looks at the identity of the girl who danced for Antipas and cost John the Baptist his head. Finally, he reviews Herod Antipas' relations with Pilate, and summarizes the events that led to the exile of Antipas to Lyons in Gaul.

C30. Edwards, Ormond. "Herodian Chronology." *Palestine Exploration Quarterly* 114 (January-June, 1982): 29-42.

Edwards thinks Josephus' account in Jewish Wars was wrong concerning the calendars of the Herodian period. "He dated all the Herods' reigns from the spring new year, whereas the earlier Herods (excluding Agrippa II) dated their coins from the autumn civil new year's day preceding accession. The error only comes to light when the data in Josephus is compared with the coin dates"—p. 41. Edwards notes that Josephus corrected some of the information in his *Antiquities,* and Edwards thinks this was because he had new information about the lunar eclipse prior to Herod's death, and also that Josephus was free from the supervision of Herod Agrippa II when he wrote the *Antiquities.*

C31. **Ladouceur, D. J.** "Death of Herod the Great." *Classical Philology* 76 (January, 1981): 25-34.

Ladouceur says that whereas the death of a famous good man was described in standard way, the same is true of the death of a godless man. His death is described as the result of divine retribution, and the degree of loathsomeness recorded in contemporaneous accounts matched the degree of wickedness. Ladouceur lists and comments upon a number of examples, and then questions the presentation of Josephus concerning the death of Herod the Great. He then examines Josephus' account in detail, and shows how he often borrowed the style of classical authors. Josephus views Herod's disease as associated with God's judgment, and thus any attempt to take the symptoms as a literal description is highly questionable.

THE HIGH PRIESTS

C32. **Sievers, Joseph.** "The High Priesthood of Simon Maccabeus: An Analysis of 1 Macc 14:25-49." *Society of Biblical Literature Seminar Papers* no. 20 (1981): 309-318.

Sievers examines how and why the Hasmoneans obtained the high priesthood. He shows that 1 Maccabees has little to say about Jonathan becoming High Priest, and says this was probably because it met with great resistance. He then turns attention to Simon as High Priest. While there is more documentation related to Simon than any other Hasmonean, the material often seems repetitive and disorganized. Sievers thinks this shows the "...successive stages of Simon's accession to high priesthood..."—p. 315. It took two years before the Jerusalem aristocracy very hesitantly approved of Simon's position. With the state of present knowledge, Sievers thinks it best not to assign a role in these developments to the Pharisees and Sadducees.

C33. **Smallwood, E. Mary.** "High Priests and Politics in Roman Palestine." *Journal of Theological Studies* 13 (April, 1962): 14-34.

Smallwood writes, "The purpose of this paper is to consider the secular and political activities and achievements of those High Priests of the Roman period about whom Josephus gives more information than the bare fact of their appointment, and to study the development of their attitude towards Rome during the years leading up to the war"—p. 16. She accomplishes this purpose by discussing scholarly theories about the political impact of various High Priests on both the Roman and Jewish communities. She also criticises some information presented by Josephus, and closes with a list of the High Priests, the dates of their appointments, and where this information can be found in the writings of Josephus.

INTERTESTAMENTAL LITERATURE

C34. Collins, John J. "The Intertestamental Literature." *Listening: Journal of Religion and Culture* 19 (Winter, 1984): 41-52.

Collins defines intertestamental literature as a Christian designation for a corpus of Jewish literature written between 250 BCE and 132 CE. He spends a large portion of the article discussing apocalyptic literature, and then, in turn, the Dead Sea Scrolls, literature of the Diaspora, Greek Torah, and Common Ethic (meaning Hellenistic Jewish literature which lays emphasis on ethics, rather than circumcision or the dietary laws). Collins concludes with a brief summary of how this literature influenced Christianity more than Judaism.

C35. Doran, Robert. "Parties and Politics in Pre-Hasmonean Jerusalem: A Closer Look at 2 Maccabees 3:11." *Society of Biblical Literature Seminar Papers* no. 21 (1982): 107-111.

The mention of Hyrcanus, son of Tobias, in 2 Macc 3:11 has given rise to much speculation about the political parties in Jerusalem at the time. The accepted idea has been that this Hyrcanus is the same one mentioned by Josephus in his *Antiquities* 12.186-222. It is also thought that Onias III reversed the opinion of his father, who had expelled Hyrcanus from Jerusalem. Pro-Ptolemaic and pro-Seleucid parties in Jerusalem are posited on the basis of this speculation. Doran thinks this is wrong, because the context in 2 Maccabees doesn't favor support of the Ptolemaic party by Hyrcanus. Since Hyrcanus was such a popular name at the time, we cannot be sure that the one mentioned in Josephus is the same one noted in 2 Maccabees. Doran concludes, "There seems to be no basis for the posited pro-Ptolemaic and pro-Seleucid parties in Jerusalem—2 Macc 3:11 offers no support for it, and Hyrcanus as head of a pro-Ptolemaic faction seems unlikely." "For Jerusalem at this time, we now have the Oniads, the Tobiads, and those of the tribe of Balgea, Simon and Menelaus (2 Macc 3:4; 4:23). Rather than appealing to pro-Ptolemaic or pro-Seleucid parties, one should, I think, be content to see at play the ambitions of the rich families of a small town"—p. 111.

C36. **Fujita, Shozo.** "Metaphor of Plant in Jewish Literature of the Intertestamental Period." *Journal for the Study of Judaism in the Persian, Hellenistic and Roman Period* 7 (June, 1976): 30-45.

Fujita begins by pointing out that in Jewish literature of the intertestamental period the people of God are spoken of as His plants. He then moves to examine the messianic and eschatological implications of other metaphorical uses of the image of the plant. He examines the Psalms of Solomon, and says the plants there are the righteous Jews, and that they are opposed to those who in their view have incorrectly taken over the offerings in the Temple. Speaking of the authorship of the Psalms of Solomon, he says, "It appears likely that the book was written by a Jew, perhaps a left-wing Pharisee close to the Essenes, who was opposed to the priests and the officials in Jerusalem, *i.e.* the Sadducees"—p. 32. He then examines the metaphorical idea of the plant of righteousness in First Enoch and in the Book of Jubilees, where Abraham is connected to the plant of righteousness. After a lengthy analysis of how this metaphor is used, Fujita moves to the Thanksgiving Hymn 8 of Qumran, and looks at the image of the trees and water. The water which nourishes the trees from the fountain of mystery is the cosmic mystery of God. Interestingly, he concludes that "Geographically, Qumran exactly fits the description of the dry land which Ezekiel prophesied would be turned into a fertile land. It seems, therefore, understandable why the sect chose nowhere else but Qumran for the site on which to establish its community"—p. 43.

C37. **Lacocque, André.** "The Vision of the Eagle in 4 Esdras: A Rereading of Daniel 7 in the First Century C.E." *Society of Biblical Literature Seminar Papers* no. 20 (1981): 237-258.

Lacocque discusses ideas of the end time and how they relate to the vision of the eagle in 4 Esdras. He begins by looking at literary genre, and how the allegorical identification of parts of the eagle have parallels in Daniel 7. He also examines the role of the Messiah in eschatological events, and then turns to consider the fifth vision in 4 Esdras, which he says "...represents a Pharisaism open to Apocalyptic, and remarkably close to a mentality illustrated by Paulinism in the New Testament"—p. 237. He closes with suggestions for re-reading the apocalypse in the light of the dependence of the vision of the Eagle upon Daniel.

C38. Nickelsburg, George W. "1 and 2 Maccabees: Same Story, Different Meaning." *Concordia Theological Monthly* 42 (September, 1971): 515-526.

"The author sketches briefly the history of Israel two centuries before Christ and reviews various viewpoints about and interpretations of that history which are recorded in the books of First and Second Maccabees"—p. 515. Although 1 Maccabees maintains the idea that Israel was delivered by the Hasmonean family, 2 Maccabees seems to ignore the Hasmoneans. Nickelsburg thinks 2 Maccabees may have come from the Hasidim, who were opponents of the Hasmoneans.

C39. Page, Sydney H. "The Suffering Servant Between the Testaments." *New Testament Studies* 31 (October, 1985): 481-497.

Page examines five groups of literature to see if the allusions to and quotations from Isaiah could lead to the idea that there was a pre-Christian understanding that the Messiah and the servant, especially the suffering servant, were one and the same. The five groups are: 1. the Aprocryphal and Pseudepigraphal literature; 2. the Qumran texts; 3. various versions of the Old Testament; 4. the New Testament; and 5. Rabbinic literature. He concludes as follows. "It is clear from the survey presented that some of the claims that have been made concerning the existence of a messianic suffering servant figure in the pre-Christian period have been exaggerated." "If claims concerning a messianic suffering servant have been overstated, it is equally true that the denial of the possibility of such a conception having been entertained before the time of Christ is unwarranted"—p. 492-93.

C40. Russell, David S. "Intertestamental Period." *Baptist Quarterly* (London) 22 (October, 1967): 215-224. Bibliography.

"The purpose of this article is to trace in broad outline some of the developments which have taken place over the past ten or fifteen years or so in the intertestamental field and to indicate some of the more important books written during this time which have a bearing on this study"—p. 215. In this bibliographical essay, Russell describes recent (as of 1967) finds of papyri and other archaeological evidence, as well as the Qumran scrolls; and lists what he sees as some of the more important and useful books on the subject. He also summarizes the conclusions of the scholars on some of the topics important to the period, such as the relation of the Scrolls to the New Testament. "The chief value of the Scrolls for a study of the intertestamental period, however, is to be found in the contribution they make to our understanding of that complex Judaism which flourished at the beginning of the Christian era"—p. 219-20. He concludes his essay with material on the Zealots and on the Apocrypha.

C41. **Scott, J. Julius.** "On the Value of Intertestamental Jewish Literature for New Testament Theology." *Journal of the Evangelical Theological Society* 23 (December, 1980): 315-323.

Scott begins by describing his perspective as that of an evangelical Christian. In speaking of the diversity within Biblical theology, he quotes the *Westminster Shorter Catecism*, writing, "...I believe there is also a unified, divinely inspired, authoritative revelation of 'what man is to believe concerning God, and what duty God requires of man'"—p. 316. In the Jewish literature of the Second Commonwealth, Scott includes "...the LXX, apocrypha, the so-called pseudepigrapha, QL, inscriptions, official and private documents, the writings of Philo and Josephus, and parts of the rabbinic literature as well as the NT itself"—p. 317. He describes the various forms the literature takes and the distinctions of Hellenistic literature. Though he knows many critical questions remain unanswered, he thinks the literature can still be used by NT theologians, because they are "...windows through which we may catch glimpses of various aspects of that bygone world and culture...."—p. 318. He surveys the development of the use of such literature, and talks of the ways that it may illumine certain NT texts and help us understand the diversity of first-century Judaism. He concludes with a look at the eschatological views and methods of interpretation of sacred texts within the literature of the intertestamental period.

C42. **Suter, David W.** "The Measure of Redemption: The Similitudes of Enoch, Nonviolence and National Integrity." *Society of Biblical Literature Seminar Papers* no. 22 (1983): 167-176.

Suter thinks the most important question in relation to the Similtudes is the context "...in which this search for redemption takes place"—p. 168. Though most of 1 Enoch is concerned with angelic and demonic realms, the Similtudes deal with a polemic against the kings of the earth. Suter thinks this work was written before the fall of the Temple, and is of Jewish origin; part of its concern is nonviolent resistance to Rome. He rejects the idea that this work might have come from the Essenes, and finds the most likely authors to be the lower ranks of the priests. Interestingly, Suter compares the Similitudes with the Ghost Dance Religion of the American Plains Indians, because he thinks both are a type of millennarian movement which try to deal with the incursion of a foreign culture.

JERUSALEM

C43. **Fennelly, James M.** "The Jerusalem Community and Kashrut Shatness." *Society of Biblical Literature Seminar Papers* no. 22 (1983): 272-288.

Fennelly uses an economic approach to understand some of the events in early Christianity. He analyzes the use of temples by Rome and the exception made for the Temple in Jerusalem. He also looks at the problems with the economic system confronted by Christians. "In the hellenistic world, and during the subsequent Roman period, city temples and international cult centers performed complex socio-economic functions within the community." "The hellenistic temple pattern was disrupted by the arrival of the Romans who transformed the essential social consensus by means of strict central control"—p. 273. "The Jerusalem temple and market complex was granted permission to dominate several aspects of Roman-Parthian trade and political cooperation"—p. 274. "Jews sold and bought temple quality goods to and from their co-religionists, who were the dealers and suppliers of the Synagogue-agora"—p. 277. "Originally designed to provide support services for the practice of Jewish ceremonial law (first in Jerusalem and then in the diaspora), during the early Empire the synagogue developed into a vertical cartel"—p. 280. Writing about the problems Christians faced, he says, "The High Priest had the authority to expel them from the synagogue in so far as they had invested wealth in the Temple-synagogue economic structure"—p. 286. Mentioning Saul's persecution of the Christians, he writes, "Thus, if he found followers of the 'Way' within the Temple-synagogue system, Saul could lead them under ban (as performers of an unclean or forbidden act) to Jerusalem. Judged unclean (Christian, uncircumcised Jew, or proselyte), one would be separated from his synagogue and forbidden to participate in its activities. Cash resources and assets would be frozen"—p. 287.

C44. Fuks, Gideon. "Again on the Episode of the Gilded Roman Shields at Jerusalem." *Harvard Theological Review* 75 (October, 1982): 503-507.

In examining the issue of the guilded shields which Philo says were erected in Herod's palace in the holy city, Fuks says that he agrees with the conclusions of Michael Grant. He quotes the appropriate passages in Philo about the incident, as well as Josephus' account of a similar but different occurrence. Then he examines the conclusions of several scholars, and comments on what he sees as their weaknesses. At the end of the article, he writes, "In sum: it seems more probable than any other explanation that the orthodox and religiously sensitive inhabitants of Jerusalem were enraged by the unprecedented engraving of the name of an alien diety (divus Augustus) within the precincts of their Holy City"—p. 507.

C45. Maier, Paul L. "Episode of the Golden Roman Shields at Jerusalem." *Harvard Theological Review* 62 (January, 1969): 109-121.

Josephus describes a number of important events in the life of Pilate, but there is one event, designated the "golden shields affair," which is only described by Philo in his Embassy to Gaius. Pilate had placed some golden shields in Herod's palace, and they were dedicated to Tiberius. This infuriated the Jews. Eventually, the shields were removed under orders from Rome and were transferred to Caesarea. Maier discusses whether this event, described by Philo, is the same event as an episode involving Roman standards described by Josephus. He concludes that although there are some similarities, two different events are being described. Though the shields did not have an image painted on them, there were words of dedication inscribed. Philo says Pilate did this to annoy the Jews, but Maier says, "In view of Pilate's previous record in Judea and the new circumstances in Rome, he now had every reason not to want to 'annoy the multitude'"—p. 115. "The cause for Jewish ire at Pilate's imageless shields is an enigma. The theological protest which was so understandable in the case of numinous iconic standards dangling in the holy city of Jerusalem seems to have no justification whatever in this instance"—p. 116. "Where, then, was the offense? Possibly it lay merely in the inscribed name of the emperor, Tibrius Caesar, and the Empire he represented—not so much because of the man or the Empire, but because the shields hung in the sacred capital itself"—p. 117. Maier thinks that though Pilate certainly was ruthless, he may have been treated unfairly in Philo's account: "Quite naturally, the Jewish philosopher despised foreign administration of Judea, and in the citation above he seems to be unloading his holy ire at the loss of Judean independence on the man who represented Rome in Palestine..."—p. 120.

C46.   Mazar, Benjamin. "Herodian Jerusalem in the Light of the Excavations South and South-West of the Temple Mount." *Israel Exploration Journal* 28:4 (1978): 230-237.

The focus of this article is "...the area adjacent to the Temple Enclosure concerning the Herodian period, from the beginnings of Herod's huge construction project until the destruction of Jerusalem by the Roman legions in A.D. 70. Herod's building activities brought about a decisive change in the topography of this area, in which the Temple Enclosure was doubled in area, adjacent valleys were filled in, the entire platform was enclosed and porticoes were built all around the Temple..."—p. 230. Mazar describes what has become known as "Robinson's Arch" in this way: "During the excavations, it became clearly evident that his arch, together with a row of arches stretching to the south at regular intervals, each successively lower, formed a monumental stairway which led from the paved street up to the portal of the Royal Stoa. This discovery well suits the overall plan of the area, and conforms with Josephus, who mentions four gates in the Western Wall, from the southernmost of which descended many steps to the Tyropoeon Valley (*Ant.*, XV, 410)"—p. 232. Mazar says of the streets and surrounding area of "Robinson's Arch," "Indeed, the descriptions in

Josephus and in the Mishnah concerning this very area are in close accord with the archaeological findings, as revealed in our excavations"—p. 237.

C47.   Rahmani, L. Y. "Ancient Jerusalem's Funery Customs and Tombs." *Biblical Archaeologist* 44 (Spring, 1981): 171-177; 44 (Fall, 1981): 229-235; 45 (Winter, 1981): 43-53; 45 (Spring, 1982): 109-119.

Rahmani describes Early to Middle Canaanite tombs which may have represented reburials of nomads in a central family tomb. Middle and Late Canaanite tombs continued this concept of the ancestral tomb, which was supplied with clothing, weapons and food for use in the nether world. These concepts continued in Jewish tombs between the early monarchy and the destruction of the First Temple, with the deceased resting on benches hewn at right angles into the burial chamber. The practice continued till the end of the Hasmonean dynasty, reflecting upper and middle class customs. The burial chamber, however, was changed so that loculi were hewn into the rock at right angles to the walls. With the end of this period, new ideas about resurrection appeared, "emphasizing the separate deposition of bones bare of the decomposed flesh"—p. 118, part 4. The dead were to be recreated out of their entire skeleton. "This ossilegium took place about 12 months after burial, thus extending the work of the mourning of that period"—*Ibid*. "This set of ideas developed in the framework of the theological concepts of Jerusalem's Pharisaic middle-class circles, gaining eventually wide-spread acceptance"—*Ibid*. "After the mid 3rd century A.D., changing economic, political and demographic conditions, as well as martyriology and dispersion, made impossible any insistence on the preservation of the whole skeleton or of any remains at all, as prerequisite to resurrection. As a result, the custom of reburying bones in ossuaries disappeared"—*Ibid*.

C48.   Sperber, Daniel. "Social Legislation in Jerusalem During the Latter Part of the Second Temple Period." *Journal for the Study of Judaism in the Persian, Hellenistic and Roman Period* 6 (June, 1975): 86-95.

Sperber describes his study as "...a preliminary attempt to see the development of certain halachic legislation during the latter period of the Second Temple (*i.e.* c. 50 B.C.E. to 70 C.E.) in a socio-economic historical context. Here we have limited ourselves to only one or two examples, but these are, we believe, representative of a whole developmental trend"—p. 86. He first quotes a passage from Mishnah Pesahim 4.6 and the Tosefta, showing that the Sages allowed only three classes of craftsmen to work till midday on Passover eve. Sperber argues that the two passages of opposing views are "...grounded in two historically different periods, and reflect each their own conditions"—p. 88. He argues that as more of the poor took part in pilgrimage to Jerusalem, the restrictions were altered. He analyzes the passages further, and offers a socio-economic rational for the differences between the two passages.

C49. Vanderkam, James C. "2 Maccabees 6, 7a and a Calendrical Change in Jerusalem." *Journal for the Study of Judaism in the Persian, Hellenistic and Roman Period* 12 (July, 1981): 52-74.

Vanderkam begins with a look at the dispute over the religious calendar, which eventually led the members of the Qumran community to reject the Jerusalem Temple. "Because calendrical law came from God himself it was not a trifling matter; rather, punctilious obedience was absolutely essential"—p. 54. Vanderkam examines 1 Enoch 72-78 and Jubilees, which teach a 364-day calendar, and then adds the evidence of Daniel 7 and the Maccabees passage mentioned in the title, noting its relevance for understanding calendrical change. "There is, I think, adequate reason for postulating that a 364-day calendar regulated the cult of the second temple in its early centuries. It is known, moreover, that at the time of Jubilees (the generation after the beginning of the Maccabean uprising) calendrical debate had arisen between advocates of this calendar and those of a lunar system"—p. 68. Vanderkam thinks a non-orthodox calendar was used in the Temple beginning in 167, but this is too early as a date for the establishment of the Qumran community. "Hence I will conclude with a historical sketch of the developments which, I think, the evidence suggests took place within the priestly community after 167 and which eventually produced the Essene schism"—p. 69. After further discussion, Vanderkam concludes, "Armed with all this authority, Jonathan the high priest may simply have decreed an end to priestly calendrical discussion by opting for use of the Seleucid lunisolar arrangement in cultic matters and brooking no opposition. This stance, which fit conveniently into his pro-Seleucid policy at the time, and his displacement of the acting Zadokite high priest who supported the old calendar were, I think, the immediate occasion for the Essene schism. In this way the calendrical change of 167 that can be deduced especially from 2 Macc. 6,7a and 1 Macc. 1,59 eventually became a major factor in the exodus to Qumran"—p. 74.

JESUS

C50.   **Barnett, Paul W.** "The Jewish Sign Prophets—AD 40-70: Their Intentions and Origin." *New Testament Studies* 27 (October, 1981): 679-697.

Having explored the historical-political background of the time during which "sign prophets" arose, Barnett discusses his conviction that the sign prophets believed "...if only a 'sign' of the Exodus-Conquest could be performed, then the wheels of God would be set in motion for a re-run of His Great Saving Act"—p. 688. Barnett believes Jesus was the cause of the rise of the sign prophets, because no one before Jesus had all four elements of the sign prophet: namely, he was a prophet, had an Exodus-Conquest sign (the loaves to feed the 5,000), worked in a significant locale (the wilderness), and was followed by a crowd.

C51.   **Brandon, S. G. F.** "Recent Study of the Sources for the Life of Jesus." *Modern Churchman* n.s. 2 (March, 1959): 160-169.

Brandon begins with an acknowledgment that at the time of his writing no "Life" of Jesus had been written since the end of the Second World War. He thinks there are theological reasons for this. He shows how Form Criticism has focused on the literary tradition behind the Gospels. On the other hand, the idea that Christianity is a historical religion had led New Testament scholars to investigate the historical facts of the time of Jesus, and this in turn to the recognition that the Gospels are interpretations of his life, that it was not possible to get behind those interpretations. Thus, historical interest gave way to an interest in the Christ of the primitive Christian faith. The discovery of the Dead Sea Scrolls and the speculation that the Qumran community had been destroyed by the Romans has resulted to a greater interest in Jesus' political situation. Brandon then goes into an extensive examination of the Zealots, and how some of Jesus' actions and teaching can be seen as support for them. He points out that the Romans condemned Jesus to death as a revolutionary. He closes by writing, "And so I would end by saying that, although the 'quest for the historical Jesus' has declined in recent years with the majority of New Testament scholars, a re-assessment of the political factor in Primitive Chrisitianity, particularly as it concerns Jesus, is becoming more urgent, and it is likely to be productive of some useful conclusions from the historical point of view"—p. 169.

C52.   Charlesworth, James. "Jewish Prayers in the Time of Jesus." *Princeton Seminary Bulletin: Supplementary Issue* no. 2 (1992): 36-55.

After making some general comments about how Jewish prayers at the time of Jesus could unite persons with God, Charlesworth tells about six aspects of Jewish prayer that he will cover in the rest of his article. "The first three of these clarify the great need for God expressed in Jewish prayers: a dependence on God, an urgency for forgiveness, and finally a desire to converse with God and to know that he is present to hear and respond. Next we shall explore three dimensions of Jewish prayer: it was public and collective, it solidified Israel as a people who prayed, and it was cosmic, both clarifying and uniting times and seasons"—p. 40.

C53.   Culbertson, Philip. "The Pharisaic Jesus and His Parables." *Christian Century* 102 (January 23, 1985): 74-77.

Culbertson believes Jesus stood within the Pharisaic movement, and he interprets the parables of the prodigal son, the wise and foolish virgins, and the wicked tenants in the vineyard from this perspective. He believes that Jesus puts Israel at the center of God's action, and concludes, "the Christian tradition's anti-Jewish motif perpetuates violence against the choices God made in the Incarnation"—p. 77.

C54.   de Jonge, M. "The Use of the Word 'Anointed' in the Time of Jesus." *Novum Testamentum* 8 (April-October, 1966): 132-148.

De Jonge examines various meanings for the term "anointed" or "Messiah" by first reviewing Psalms 17 and 18 of the Psalms of Solomon. He also sifts through the various Qumran documents, and finds both earthly and spiritual aspects of the ideal descendant of King David. There are also aspects which go beyond this ideal figure. I Enoch is also reviewed. De Jonge concludes that the term 'annointed' is used in very few instances, and is not an essential term for a future redeemer. He also thinks it is not the person, as such, who is important, but rather his calling by God and his function.

C55. Derrett, J. Duncan. "Workers in the Vineyard: A Parable of Jesus." *Journal of Jewish Studies* 25 (February, 1974): 64-91.

Derrett says the vineyard parable of Matthew 20:1-16 is a Midrashic exegesis of several Old Testament texts, including Genesis 15:1, Deuteronomy 24:14-15, and Proverbs 24:1,19, as well as others. If the parable was originally a sermon, Derrett favors Jeremiah 31:31-32 as the background text. He writes, "...we know that we are hearing a parable describing the 'behavior' of God, a commercial parable, and thus fun." He uses economic principles to help interpret this story, and associates the parable with earlier writing that states that faithful adherents of an Biblical covenant will eventually receive their reward, even those who kept themselves ready for employment and were called at the last hour.

C56. Flusser, David. "Jesus and the World of Judaism." *Judaism* 35 (Summer, 1986): 361-364. Review essay.

In this review of Geza Vermes' *Jesus and the World of Judaism,* Flusser indicates Vermes' book is "a valuable contribution to a better understanding both of the Jewishness of Jesus and of the Jewish world in the period of the Second Temple"—p. 361. Vermes discusses the Dead Sea Scrolls and the Essenes, and seeks to understand the essentials of Jesus' piety in contrast to the spiritual thrust of the religion of which Jesus is the object—p. 362. Flusser also adds some of his own thoughts about the issues raised by Vermes.

C57. Geller, Markham J. "Jesus' Theugic Powers: Parallels in the Talmud and Incantation Bowls." *Journal of Jewish Studies* 28 (Autumn, 1977): 141-155.

Geller shows the similarities between the exorcisms of Jesus in the New Testament and the magical traditions of the Talmud and Aramaic incantation bowls. Beginning with Luke 4:34-36, Geller points to what he calls a direct parallel in the exorcism performed by R. Simon ben Yohai, the disciple of R. Akiba who flourished in the second century CE. He points out that both engaged the demon in dialogue, and Jesus command him to get out, while R. Simon's command is to go out. Geller then looks at a number of other New Testament passages, and draws out the comparisons with Talmudic and incantation items. Geller then writes, "In these cases of Jesus' healing which we have cited, the demons which attack human victims, the language of the exorcism, and Jesus' dialogues with demons, can all be identified in the magical literature of the period"—p. 145. Further, "The Gospels relate that Jesus taught magic to his disciples, 'giving them power and authority over all demons, and to heal diseases' (Lk. 9:1), indicating that Jesus' power was a theurgic art that could be transmitted to students"—p. 146. Geller then writes about the difficulties of making the same kind of comparisons with Babylonian magic bowls. Finally, he states: "It is, however, the Jesus exorcisms which are common to all three sources, since each describes incantations invoking Jesus' name, which demonstrates that exorcisms of the N.T., Talmud, and magic bowls form a single genre of magical literature"—p. 155.

C58. Kistemaker, Simon J. "Lord's Prayer in the First Century." *Journal of the Evangelical Theological Society* 21 (December, 1978): 323-328.

Kistemaker says that the apostles first taught the Lord's Prayer in the Jewish synagogues, and placed it in the "framework of the rich liturgical tradition of the Jews..."—p. 323. He thinks Luke's version of the Prayer was for Hellenists, while Matthew's was intended for a Jewish audience; and he gives close examination to the various phrases common to each Gospel. He then reviews the Biblical setting of the Prayer, and uses Jewish sources such as the Babylonian Talmud to review Jewish liturgy. He closes with a look at the use of the Prayer in the early church, by using the Didache and other sources to draw parallels.

C59. Mateos, Juan. "The Message of Jesus." *Sojourners* 6 (July, 1977): 8-16.

Mateos reviews the political history of the time of Jesus, and describes the religious groupings of the Jews. He thinks the contrast between Jesus and his fellow Jews was that they accepted the system, monarch, temple, and priesthood as permanent institutions—but he did not accept any of them. He then describes the attitude of groups such as the Pharisees and Zealots toward the idea of the kingdom of God. He thinks the message of Jesus is centered in the idea of the reign of God in a historical setting, which Jesus had come to set in motion, the final setting being the complete triumph of God. He then goes on to describe Jesus' idea of discipleship, which meant resisting the world of evil even though it might mean death. Mateos concludes by writing about Jesus' denuciation of the authorities and what this means for the modern church. Christians must reject the idea of "getting and having" as the basis of happiness, Mateos believes.

C60. Meyer, Ben F. "Jesus and the Remnant of Israel." *Journal of Biblical Literature* 84 (June, 1965): 123-130.

The question of whether Jesus consciously decided to gather a remnant of Israel as a nucleus of a new People of God has often been debated. Meyer reviews the scholars who had argued for this idea, as well as Bultmann, who had denied that this was ever Jesus' intention. After examining the evidence used by both sides of the argument, Meyer concludes that if a new examination of the evidence makes it clear that "...'the remnant of Israel' represents one of the ways—and a basic one—in which Jesus did in fact conceive his salvific mission..." then we will have found one element "...of a more satisfactory resolution of the surface antinomy of eschatology and church..."—p. 130.

C61. Raisanen, Heikki. "Jesus and the Food Laws: Reflections on Mark 7:15." *Journal for the Study of the New Testament* 16 (October, 1982): 79-100.

Raisanen considers whether Mark 7:15 is the authentic word of Jesus, as he examines various scholarly views that question whether these words were actually spoken by Jesus. He reviews issues such as the original context of each saying, and the idea that one of the charges against Jesus was that he set aside the Jewish purity laws. Raisanen concludes that based on later Christian developments, we should maintain our skepticism about this being an authentic saying of Jesus.

C62. Rosenberg, Stuart E. "The Christian Problem." *Midstream* 32 (November, 1986): 23-25.

"...in making him Christ, Christians had virtually rejected Jesus as a Jew." "If Jesus were somehow to arise, walk this earth, and wish to commune with 'his father in heaven,' where might he choose to pray?" "As the disciples of Jesus on earth—the man, the teacher, and the Jewish herald of their salvation—they must somehow acknowledge and appreciate his own Jewish ways. Yet they are to be found in their churches, which they call his, while he, as even their own sacred texts attest, never left his synagogue"—p. 23. If Christians had founded a religion unrelated to Judaism, Rosenberg states, there would be no "Christian problem," because Christians would not be as uneasy in the presence of the survival of Judaism. "And that Jews should have been as critical of Jesus as of all of their would-be messiahs—both before and after him—still remains unacceptable, or at best, inexplicable, to many Christians"—p. 23. Rosenberg argues that it is the Christians who rejected Judaism more than any rejection on the part of Jews.

C63.   Sanders, James A. "Torah and Christ." *Interpretation* 29 (October, 1975): 372-390.

For Sanders, Torah consists of two parts; muthos—gospel—story— haggadah; and ethos—laws—ethics—halachah. He thinks the split between the Pharisees or later Rabbinic Judaism and Christianity can be explained by their choice of a certain part of Torah. Sanders writes, "Rabbinic Judaism, following the emphasis of Pharisaism, stressed the ethos or halachah aspect of Torah, while Christianity emphasized the muthos or haggadah aspect"—p. 373-74. He argues that Paul understood Torah as primarily story, not laws, and that he viewed Christ as the last Torah story which demonstrated God's righteousness and salvation. He draws his article to a close by writing, "There is nothing wrong in continuing to hope, as Paul did, that Jews acknowledge the work of God in Christ so long as we do not go on then to insist that they 'become Christian'"—p. 389.

C64.   Stroumsa, Gedaliahu G. "Form(s) of God: Some Notes on Metatron and Christ." *Harvard Theological Review* 76 (July, 1983): 269-288.

The purpose of this article is to call attention to some early Christian and Gnostic texts that bear upon Jewish conceptions of the Divine Body or of the Hypostasis, or both, and might shed new light on the origin and evolution of those conceptions. Some of the documents examined by Stroumsa include the Greek Magical Papyri, certain writings of Philo, Justin Martyr's *Dialogue with Trypho*, Origen's *Homilies on Genesis*, Basil the Great's *Homilies on the Origin of Man*, Poimandres, several Nag Hammadi texts, a document from late Jewish antiquity, Shi'ur Qomah, and several Gnostic texts, including the Gospel of Philip. He closes with an examination of the possible etymology of the name metatron: "To the most serious challenge each posed to Jewish monotheistic theology, the Shi'ur Qomah preferred the dangers of crude anthropomorphism, those same dangers which paradoxically enough, the earliest doctrine of the hypostatic form of God had tried to overcome. Rabbinic macrocosmic conceptions of God, indeed, testify to the same dialectic confrontation of problems raised by the biblical text as do some of the earliest strata of christology and of Gnostic dualism"— p. 288.

C65.   Vermes, Geza. "The Present State of the 'Son of Man' Debate." *Journal of Jewish Studies* 29 (Autumn, 1978): 123-134.

Writing about the Greek phrase "The Son of Man," Vermes says, "The expression occurring in the Gospels, *ho huios tou anthropou*, is not a genuine Greek idiom." "It is in fact generally, though not universally, thought that the Semitic model from which the Greek derives is Aramaic. Hebrew is in disfavour because, with one possible exception, it never uses the definite article with ben adam"—p. 123. Vermes then reviews the research he has done on extant Aramaic texts where the words "son of man" were used. Next, he answers the various criticisms that have been made about his theory in terms of the meaning of the phrase in Aramaic. Vermes thinks this is an indirect way of referring to the self. The favorable response of the literary critics to Vermes' theory is covered next. Along the way the author notes developments in the debate over the phrase. For example, he writes, "I always remember with emotion and pleasure that admirable octogenarian, C. H. Dodd, who did not hesitate in 1970 to re-adjust a life-time of exegesis so that it accorded with freshly assimilated information concerning the Aramaic usage of the 'son of man'"—p. 133.

C66.   Yoder, John H. "Jesus and Power." *Ecumenical Review* 25 (October, 1973): 447-454.

Yoder begins with a discussion of various then-recent church documents concerning social justice, which point to research about Jesus' Zealot sympathies as justification for violent revolution. He then talks about the World Council of Churches focusing on Jesus and Power. He discusses Jesus' approach among conflicting attitudes to power by showing the different options Jesus could have chosen in his ministry. Yoder looks at Jesus and our desire for power and says, "We may learn from Jesus, it is argued, that we should take the side of the oppressed: but how to do so we must learn from our contemporaries"—p. 451. He concludes by examining Jesus and our power language as he explores the importance of terms for ethics and social change.

C67. **Zeitlin, Solomon.** "The Title Rabbi in the Gospels Is Anachronistic." *Jewish Quarterly Review* 59 (October, 1968): 159-160.

"...one fact remains that during the Second Commonwealth the term Rabbi was not used. The sages were quoted by their names without the prefix of Rabbi..."—p. 158. Zeitlin examines various rabbinic writings to prove his point, including quotations from Tosefta.

JEWISH HISTORY

C68. **Ackroyd, Peter.** "Archaeology, Politics, and Religion: The Persian period." *Iliff Review* 39 (Spring, 1982): 5-24.

As he surveys the scholarship on the Persian period in Palestine, Ackroyd emphasizes two points: first, the importance of the influence of Jews living outside Palestine on Palestinian affairs; and second, the importance of political control by Persia. He also investigates the political organization of Judah, relations between Samaria and Judah, and aspects of the Jews' religious situation. He concludes with a brief survey of the Davidic theme as treated in the later books of the Jewish Bible.

C69. **Aune, David.** "Orthodoxy in First Century Judaism? A Response to N. J. McEleney." *Journal for the Study of Judaism in the Persian, Hellenistic and Roman Period* 7 (June, 1976): 1-10.

Aune argues against the view that there was a Jewish orthodoxy in the first century which was replaced by two other orthodoxies:

187

namely, Pharisaic Judaism and Christianity. He argues that orthopraxy (right practice) was the central concern of first-century Judaism, not orthodoxy (right belief). Concerning first-century Jewish ideas of God, Israel, and Torah, Aune writes: "...it was the intentional-behavioral explications of those topics upon which Jewish religious life and thought centered"—p. 7.

C70. **Bokser, Baruch M.** "Recent Developments in the Study of Judaism, 70-200 C.E." *The Second Century: A Journal of Early Christian Studies* 3 (Spring, 1983): 1-68.

In this bibliographic essay, Bokser focuses on the changes from pre-70 CE to post 70 CE Judaism. He begins by reviewing material on the archaeology of the period, moves to review non-Jewish sources, and then returns to Jewish material on the Mishnah and Targum. He ends by pointing out issues of importance for future research, and comments on scholarly disagreements in each area he has covered.

C71. **Derfler, Steven.** "The Roman Fortress at Tel Michal and Jewish Piracy Based in Jaffa." *American Journal of Archaeology* 88 (April, 1984): 242.

This brief (¼-page) book review highlights the idea that this Roman fortress appears to be unique along the coast in the 1st century CE. It served as a watch station and lighthouse, and helps understand Josephus' reports about the Jewish fleet operating out of Jaffa.

C72. **Everett, Robert A.** "Dealing Honestly with Judaism and Jewish History: James Parkes as a Model for the Christian Community. *Journal of Ecumenical Studies* 23 (Winter, 1986): 37-57.

In order to correct what Everett says is a distorted view of Judaism in the New Testament, he recommends and reviews some of the writings of the Anglican scholar, James Williams Parkes (1896-1981), whom he says remains one of the best non-Jewish experts on Judaism, and whom he recommends as a model for Christians. Parkes' interpretation of early Judaism is examined, and its significance for Christianity is highlighted. Everett concentrates on Parkes' view of Ezra as the one who laid the foundations which led to the synagogue, and thus prepared the way for the change from the religion of Israel to Judaism.

C73. Grabbe, Lester L. "Orthodoxy in First Century Judaism? What are the Issues?" *Journal for the Study of Judaism in the Persian, Hellenistic and Roman Period* 8 (October, 1977): 149-153.

Examining issues concerning orthodoxy in first-century Judaism, which were not covered in earlier articles by Neil McEleney and David Aune, Grabbe examines the question of who is a Jew. Concerning whether Pharisaic/rabbinic Judaism was normative in the first century CE, he reviews the varieties within Judaism, and examines the amha'ares, scribes, Sadducees, and Essenes. The Temple worship in Jerusalem may have been the only basis of orthodoxy, but there are shortcomings with this view also.

C74. Hachlili, Rachel, and Ann Killebrew. "Jewish Funerary Customs During the Second Temple Period in Light of the Excavations at the Jericho Necropolis." *Palestine Exploration Quarterly* 115 (July-December, 1983): 109-139.

"The excavations at the Nericho necropolis have revealed that two completely different burial customs, one chronologically following the other, were practiced by Jews of the Second Temple period. The earlier custom (first century B.C.) was primary individual burials in wooden coffins..."—p. 128. "The second type of burial found in the Jericho cemetery, chronologically following the coffin burials, is conscious secondary burial of the bones either placed in individual ossuaries (Type 2a) or communal in nature (Type 2b)"—p. 129. "The rapid changes as well as the varied pagan influences evident in the burial customs of the Second Temple period are outstanding as burial practices are usually the most conservative customs in society"—p. 129.

C75. Horsley, Richard A. "'Like One of the Prophets of Old': Two Types of Popular Prophets at the Time of Jesus." *Catholic Biblical Quarterly* 47 (July, 1985): 435-463.

Horsley thinks the theological approach to the study of prophecy during the time of Jesus has led to too great an emphasis on the expectation of an eschatological prophet. He believes that it is time for a sociological and anthropological approach to the subject. He writes, "A sociological analysis of available materials will then indicate that there were two basic types of prophets contemporary with Jesus, the one being an oracular type of prophet basically similar to the classical oracular prophets in Jewish biblical traditions and the other type being patterned after the great liberators of early Israel. Our analysis will also indicate that both of these types of popular prophets stemmed basically from the peasantry and had little to do with the literate-scholarly groups, the Pharisees and the Essenes"—p. 436-37. He examines the evidence for the idea that there was an expectation of the appearance of an eschatological prophet during the time of Jesus, and thinks that the evidence is minimal and can be interpreted in other ways. He spends the rest of the article examining two movements which he says did exist. The first group was in the tradition of the "classical biblical oracular prophets" (p. 450), and the second had leaders who had so many followers that they could be said to have each founded a movement. Horsley thinks that scholarship must also make a more careful analysis of these prophets against the background of the Israelite-Jewish prophetic traditions, and analyze their social location against the background of their historical situation—p. 446.

C76. **Horsley, Richard A.** "Sicarii: Ancient Jewish 'Terrorists.'" *Journal of Religion* 59 (October, 1979): 435-458.

Horsley uses recent studies of modern anti-colonial movements to show that the Sicarii as presented in Josephus are best understood as Jewish "terrorists." While ordinary bandits were usually rurally based, Horsley finds that the Sicarri were primarily urban in origin, and engaged in assassinations. Thus, they should be understood in modern terms as "terrorist" groups, and not as criminals or individuals engaged in guerrilla warfare. Horsley examines the selective, symbolic assassinations, the general assassinations, and the kidnappings of the Sicarii, and then looks at their role in the Jewish revolt and the overall effects of their terrorist activities. He thinks that Josephus presents a clear and careful picture of this group in distinction from other groups at the time.

C77. **Kolenkow, Anitra.** "Genre Testament and Forecasts of the Future in the Hellenistic Jewish Milieu." *Journal for the Study of Judaism in the Persian, Hellenistic and Roman Period* 6 (June, 1975): 57-71.

"The last words of a man given just before he dies (sometimes called blessing, revelation, or testament) become an important genre in the Judaism of the Hellenistic era. The genre serves particularly as a vehicle for literature forecasting the future, written in the name of a patriarch. In this literature, the patriarch receives visions or knowledge of heaven and these make his forecasts of history and descriptions of heaven and judgment strong evidence in the argument for remaining among or joining the righteous"—p. 57. Kolenkow examines this kind of statement in the Old Testament, focusing on the Assumption of Moses, I Enoch 91-94, and the Testament of Levi, among others. He finds that whereas in the Old Testament the patriarchs give forecasts of the history of the Jewish people, later works influenced by Hellenism add stories of visions or trips to heaven. The Jews may have been trying to show to the world outside that they too had oracles. "...Hellenistic-Jewish testaments of patriarchs which forecast history (from their time to the end time with emphasis on the good future of the righteous) may have served apologetic purposes in the Hellenistic world"—p. 71.

C78. Ladouceur, D. J. "Masada: A Consideration of the Literary Evidence." *Greek, Roman and Byzantine Studies* 21 (Autumn, 1980): 245-260.

The only literary evidence for the events of Masada is the account of Josephus in *Bellum Judaicum*. Ladouceur asks why Josephus covered this event, since he seems to have had little use generally for the Sicarii. Yigael Yadin thought Jodephus was "genuinely overwhelmed by the heroism of the people...," although Trude Weiss-Rosmarin thinks the whole thing is a fiction to cover up the murder of all those at Masada by the Roman soldiers. Ladouceur mounts a case for considering that the historian's account was intended to bolster his own case for not committing suicide when Josephus and his men had been cornered by the Romans. The context of the times and the ongoing tensions with Rome during the period when Josephus composed his history is also an important factor to consider, Ladouceur asserts. He closes his article by examining the views of military suicide in various documents of the time.

C79. Landman, Leo. "Some Aspects of Traditions Received from Moses at Sinai." *Jewish Quarterly Review* 67 (October 1976-January 1977): 111-128.

Landman examines a category of Jewish law referred to as Halakhah le-Mosheh mi-Sinai (HLMM)—the laws handed down to Moses at Sinai"—p. 111-12. Landman thinks the Sages applied this label to customs whose origins could not be determined, and to a second category where the authority for them was under dispute. This created such a conflict that the extent of the power and authority of the Sages was questioned, Landman asserts. He then examines relevant passages in the Mishnah and Talmud to support his views. This entire approach is in contention with a more conservative approach among those Rabbis who sought to derive laws through hermeneutics applied to Biblical passages, as Hillel, for example, had done.

C80.   Levine, Lee I. "Jewish-Greek Conflict in First Century Caesarea." *Journal of Jewish Studies* 25 (Winter, 1974): 381-397.

Levine says the conflict between the Jews and the Greeks over control of Caesarea resulted because the Jews claimed the city was legally theirs, since it was founded by a Jewish king; the Greeks claimed ownership based upon the display of various Greek statues and temples erected by King Herod throughout the city. "The implications of the Caesarean conflict were far reaching owing not only to the fact that the city was a provincial capital and centre of Roman activity in the area, but also because powerful and influential Jewish and Greek communities were concentrated therein"—p. 381. Levine examines discrepancies in the accounts of Josephus, and then notes how unusual it was for the Jews to claim a city and opt for conflict over peace and compromise. The result of this wave of Jewish religious-nationalist sentiment was the eventual war with Rome, according to Josephus.

C81.   Loftus, Francis. "Anti-Roman Revolts of the Jews and the Galileans." *Jewish Quarterly Review* 68 (October, 1977): 78-98.

Loftus studies the references to the rebelliousness of the Galileans as presented in Josephus, and offers a suggestion as to why they were so difficult. The "traditions" which existed as part of the Galilean background is also explored, and he notes that most of the Galilean leaders came from one family. He shows that the extensive history of the various revolts by the Galileans was based upon their support of the Hasmonaeans, and this support is the key in Loftus' mind to understanding the ultimate rebellion of the Galileans against Rome.

C82. **Loftus, Francis.** "The Martyrdom of the Galilean Troglodytes: A Suggested Traditionsgeschichte." *Jewish Quarterly Review* 66 (April, 1976): 212-223.

During the war between Kings Herod and Antigonus (40-37 BCE), the Galileans supported Antigonus. Loftus relates an event described in Josephus of an old man who killed his wife and seven sons after they suggested going over to the enemy. Loftus thinks this tale derives from a folk tradition stemming from Jer. 15:9. In II and IV Maccabees and in the Assumption of Moses, there are accounts of the martyrdom of seven brothers, and Loftus thinks these are all based on the same tradition—and are therefore not historical. Loftus believes Josephus drew his account from this same source.

C83. **McEleney, Neil J.** "Orthododoxy in Judaism of the First Christian Century." *Journal for the Study of Judaism in the Persian, Hellenistic and Roman Period* 4 (July, 1973): 19-42.

McEleney believes there was a pre-Christian Jewish orthodoxy of belief the first century, and that the three beliefs which constituted it were 1) belief in the God of Israel, 2) belief in the people of Israel as the chosen people, and 3) belief in the law of Moses. McEleney's position is in contrast to those scholars who think that Judaism was about "right practice" and not "right belief." McEleney surveys the conflicts of belief between different groups within Judaism, including the Samaritans, Pharisees, and Sadducees. He shows who was excluded from these groups and on what grounds. The way in which a convert to Judaism was required to alter his life is also covered.

C84. **McEleney, Neil J.** "Orthodoxy in Judaism of the First Christian Century: Replies to D. E. Aune and L. L. Grabbe." *Journal for the Study of Judaism in the Persian, Hellenistic and Roman Period* 9 (June, 1978): 83-88.

In an earlier article, McEleney had argued for a Jewish orthodoxy in the first century, and David Aune and Lester Grabbe had written articles contesting such a viewpoint. (All three essays are covered in this bibliography.) McEleney now responds to those criticisms. He says that Aune "twists me into divorcing belief from action and then opting for belief as though action were unimportant"—p. 84. But McEleney asserts that he did not do this. He then goes on to show how other scholars, Louis Jacobs and Jacob Lauterbach, wrote articles which in effect supported his contention. He then says that while Aune obviously disagrees with him, he has not refuted what McEleney said. In response to Grabbe's question as to whether someone who denied the God of Israel would be unorthodox or un-Jewish, McEleney says that that person would be both. Lastly, McEleney states that he wrote that the Pharisees' ideas became the norm for subsequent Judaism, and that during the first century they were simply numbered among the orthodox Jews.

C85. Mantel, Hugo. "The Dichotomy of Judaism During the Second Temple." *Hebrew Union College Annual* 44 (1973): 55-87.

Mantel reviews seveal scholarly theories of the origins of the Pharisees and Sadducees. His own intention in the article is to "...show that the controversy between the Sadducees and the Pharisees was nothing but a continuation of the one between the Zadokite high priests and the Sons of the Golah, both strongly coherent groups, in the first part of the Persian era; and that, moreover, the nucleus of the dispute may have already been there during the period of the First Temple"—p. 57. Mantel then turns to the figure of Ezra and his supposed mandate to carry out legal reform. Mantel writes, "The conclusion is unavoidable that Ezra was not authorized by Artaxerxes to change the constitution of Judea, religiously or otherwise"—p. 62. "We propose, therefore, that Ezra's mission was not concerned either with Persian governmental affairs or with official, cultic religion of Judah. It was concerned with the Community of the Exile...which was within the Judaean state, the autonomous community of the Jews who had returned from Babylonian exile"—p. 63. The Sons of Golah group had become lax in religious practice because they lacked leadership, according to Mantel. The high priest did not identify with this group. Mantel then goes on to describe the nature of the disagreements with those who maintained a strict adherence to the Law. This division has continued throughout Jewish history, he thinks. "The high priest and his followers became known as Sadducees and Boethuseans. The community of Godah became first the Hasidim of the Maccabean era and then the Pharisees"—p. 84.

C86. Moehring, Horst R. "Persecution of the Jews and the Adherents of the Isis Cult at Rome A.D. 19." *Novum Testamentum* 3 (1959): 293-304.

The worship of the Egyptian goddess Isis was widespread around the Mediterranean world, being promulgated by sailors and merchants. The followers of Isis were persecuted in Rome around the years 59 and 48 BCE. Tacitus mentions in his writings that the cult was also suppressed in 19 CE by the Emperor Tiberius. Scholars have written that this suppression was ordered on moral grounds and also affected the Jews. Josephus on the other hand offers two varying accounts of these events, stating that the Jews were not associated with the suppression of the Isis cult. Moehring analyzes both accounts and points out that "It is exactly this inability, or unwillingness, of the Roman authorities to differentiate between 'the other' Oriental cults and Judaism which forces Josephus to introduce and emphasize this distinction in his own narrative"—p. 303. Moering compares the "novelistic" elements in the accounts by Josephus with that in Livy's discussion of the suppression of the Bacchic cult, and asks if the events in Josephus are really based on history.

C87. Neusner, Jacob. "Comparing Judaisms." *History of Religions* 18 (November, 1978): 177-191.

This article is a review of E. P. Sanders' *Paul and Palestinian Judaism*. Sanders uses three bodies of literature to describe Palestinian Judaism; namely, Tannaitic literature, the Dead Sea Scrolls, and Apocrypha and Pseudepigrapha. Neusner deals specifically with Sanders' use of Tannaitic literature. He finds Sanders' work flawed, because he defines ancient ideas in contemporary theological terms. To compare a system, Neusner thinks, you must understand the exegesis and interpretation of the documents that are central to that system. Nesusner writes, "But Sanders does not describe Rabbinic Judaism through the systematic categories yielded by its principle documents"—p. 180. Neusner thinks that Sanders seeks to answer questions which come from Pauline theology and not from the Tannaitic documents. He writes of Sanders, "He has not even asked whether these sayings form the center and core of the Rabbinic system or even of a given Rabbinic document"—p. 187.

C88. Neusner, Jacob. "The History of Earlier Rabbinic Judaism: Some New Approaches." *History of Religions* 16 (February, 1977): 216-236.

"The formative history of rabbinic Judaism, that mode of Judaism which claims that a dual Torah, one in writing, the other transmitted orally, was revealed to Moses at Sinai and in its ramifications is now contained in the rabbinic literature, is concluded by the publication of Mishnah-Tosefta, circa, A.D. 200"—p. 216. "The first problem is insufficient attention to the orginally sectarian character of rabbinic Judaism, the fact that in its formative century, it in no way achieved the normative status later on accorded to it"—p. 217. The second problem is that the "...generality of books on talmudic or rabbinic Judaism is organized in categories drawn from nineteenth- and twentieth-century histories of Christian, particularly Protestant, theology; the intellectual agendum is shaped within Christian theological faculties and not within the Judaic literature which supposedly comes under analysis and description"—p. 220. The huge size of the corpus of rabbinic material, and the fact that it is not approaced in a historical-critical fashion are other signficant problems. "The investigation of the history of the religious and legal ideas of a tractate of Mishnah-Tosefta must begin with a fresh exegesis of the tractate"—p. 226. Neusner then shows in detail how this should be done.

C89. Neusner, Jacob. "Idea of Purity in Ancient Judaism." *Journal of the American Academy of Religion* 43 (March, 1975): 15-26.

Though Neusner mentions Mary Douglas' *Purity and Danger*, he says he does not want to argue with her ideas, but rather wants "...to construct an agendum out of anthropological thought for the interpretation of the various expressions of the idea of purity in ancient Judaism"—p. 15. "Certainly without a notion of the meaning of purity, one cannot understand either the Dead Sea yahad ('commune') or the Pharisaic havurah ('fellowship'). Purity serves to differentiate one sect from another"—p. 15. Neusner analyzes the development of the idea of purity both before and after the destruction of the Temple. "The concern for purity did continue, particularly in Talmudic Judaism, and for many centuries purity-laws were studied and greatly developed. This seems to me decisive testimony against the priestly view that purity ever was primarily a cultic concern"—p. 26.

C90. Neusner, Jacob. "Judaism After Moore: A Programmatic Statement." *Journal of Jewish Studies* 31 (Autumn, 1980): 141-156.

In 1927 George Foot Moore's *Judaism in the First Centuries of the Christian Era: The Age of Tannaim* was published. Most of the reviews were favorable, except for the one by F. C. Porter. Though Neusner respects Moore's work, he thinks Porter's criticisms were largely valid, and they have been ignored rather than dealt with by scholars. Porter criticized Moore's failure to take into account halakhic evidence in his definition of norms and his conception of what evidence enters into a description of "Judaism"—p. 142. Neusner says there is no clear social foundation for a construct called "Judaism" in that time, and therefore there is no self-evident boundary as to what evidence should be admitted. Neusner reopens the study of the topic with a new definition of what is under study. He shows why Moore should be succeeded rather than repeated, and what should be done to advance to the next stage of study.

C91. Neusner, Jacob. "Judaism in Late Antiquity." *Judaism* 15 (Spring, 1966): 230-240.

In this review essay, Neusner writes about some of the ideas of Saul Lieberman, Morton Smith, E. E. Urbach, Joseph Bonsirven, and others who have written on Judaism in late antiquity. Given the state of scholarship at the time he is writing, Neusner says he awaits a new synthesis on the subject.

C92. Neusner, Jacob. "Pharisaic-Rabbinic Judaism: A Clarification." *History of Religions* 12 (February, 1973): 250-270.

Neusner examines how pre-70 Pharisaism became post-70 rabbinic Judaism. He studies two persons: namely, Yohanan b. Zakkai, founder of the institution at Yavneh, and Eliezer b. Hyrcanus, the first important master of the Yavnean period. Having presented some important points about their writings, Neusner writes, "To be sure, we are scarcely able to claim that rabbinism begins with Yohanan or that Pharisaism ends with Eliezer. But Yohanan's tradition certainly reveals the main themes of later rabbinism.... And

Eliezer's laws and theological sayings are strikingly silent about what later on would be the primary concern of the rabbinic authorities, the oral Torah...."—p. 264. Neusner believes that the symbolic component of rabbinism comes from the scribes, whom he describes as a profession and not a sect.

C93.   Neusner, Jacob. "Studies in Judaism; Modes and Contexts." *Journal of the American Academy of Religion* 37 (June, 1969): 131-140.

Neusner offers a definition of the subject of what is included in Jewish studies, and a distinction about the settings in which Jewish studies are pursued. In his definition Neusner lists several items, including Torah, and says that we must also define what we mean by terms like Jew or Jewish or Judaism or Judaic. He then writes about how the study of Jewish history would fit with the study of general history in a university setting. He continues by writing about the relationship of Jewish studies within a university, as opposed to studying it in a Jewish school. Neusner asserts, "In my view, any cultural or religious tradition has the right to be taken seriously in its own terms, and especially by those to whom it addresses itself. It is not enough to study the traditions and lore of the Jews as aspects of 'humanity'..."—p. 137. He continues, "I argue, therefore, that certain kinds of Jewish studies belong within the university curriculum, others belong only within Jewish institutions of higher learning..."—p. 138.

C94.   Neusner, Jacob. "The Use of the Mishnah for the History of Judaism Prior to the Time of the Mishnah: A Methodological Note." *Journal for the Study of Judaism in the Persian, Hellenistic and Roman Period* 11 (December, 1980): 177-185.

"The history of Judaism should tell us the story of how various groups or classes formed diverse modes of life and appealed to diverse views of the world in order to make sense of their own situation. For the history of religious ideas abstracted from the social realities of the people who held those ideas explains nothing"—p. 177. Neusner points out that we cannot prove that what is attributed to early authorities in the Mishnah was really true in the time they lived. He thinks the literary and redactional traits of the Mishnah do not permit differentiation among layers because "...the governing literary traits of Mishnah are imposed within the processes of redaction, penultimate and ultimate"—p. 179. Neusner says we must ignore the temporal sequence in which sayings are said, although " ...named authorities come together in groups...." He lists five qualifications for the proposition that we can know something of the time before the Mishnah by using the Mishnah as a basis for that knowledge. He says that facts he has discovered have led him to think that a different picture could be drawn of the history of the ideas in the Mishnah than what he presented "...in my Histories of the law"—p. 184.

C95. Nolland, John. "Uncircumcised Proselytes." *Journal for the Study of Judaism in the Persian, Hellenistic and Roman Period* 12 (December, 1981): 173-194.

Neil J. McEleney had written an article in which he maintained that there was a current of Jewish thought in the early first century that permitted converts to Judaism to observe the Law and customs, and be considered a Jew without being circumcised. Nolland reexamines the evidence cited by McEleney and comes to a different conclusion. Concerning the cited Philo material, Nolland thinks circumcision is not really the question Philo poses, and so the cited passage will not yield an answer on this topic. The passage shows that he assumed proselytes were in fact circumcised. Nolland then examines the difficulties with interpreting Epictetus on this issue, because Nolland thinks Epictetus' choice of ablution language is a "literary decision"—p. 182. Concerning Talmudic material, Nolland thinks McEleney has not properly followed the thread of the argument in the passages. "We must conclude therefore that none of the texts brought forward stand scrutiny as firm evidence for a first-century Jewish openness to the possibility of accepting as a Jewish brother a convert to Judaism who felt unable to undergo circumcision"—p. 194.

C96. "Publications of David Daube." *Journal of Jewish Studies* 25 (February, 1974): 7-15.

This bibliography records publications issued by a major scholar in the field from 1932 through the year 1973. An expert in ancient law, Daube brought his expertise to bear on certain New Testament passages and the relation of first-century Judaism to the New Testament.

C97. **Pusey, Karen.** "Jewish Proselyte Baptism." *Expository Times* 95 (February, 1984): 141-145.

Pusey looks at the possible relation of Jewish proselyte baptism to Christian baptism. She thinks that we cannot prove beyond the shadow of a doubt from the sources that Jewish proselyte baptism was observed in the first century CE—but that it looks probable. She shows that the lustrations were part of a ceremony which involved circumcision for men and a sacrificial offering, and says that we need to keep in mind that the Rabbinic statements for the most part refer to the entire initiation rite. She writes, "Is there any meaning attributed to proselyte initiation that would more likely have influenced the Christian rite? The nearest is the use of death as a symbol of separation from the gentile past"—p. 144. She thinks it possible that John the Baptist used the Jewish rite as his pattern. In closing she writes, "We may be confident that baptism provides the Christian with a firm link with Judaism and that a theology of baptism which does not take account of the parent rite will be seriously deficient"—p. 145.

C98. **Stewart, Roy A.** "Judicial Procedure in New Testament Times." *Evangelical Quarterly* 47 (April-June, 1975): 94-109.

Stewart uses the Mishnah and Talmud to highlight Jewish legal procedure, with a special emphasis on penal aspects. He also consults the *Digest of Justinian* for aspects of Roman law. He first covers the Jewish judicial system in general, and then looks at Talmudic and relevant New Testament material related to what he calls "excommunication" from the synagogue. In his next section he covers corporal chastisement, and then moves to Jewish capital punishment, as well as material related to the death of Jesus. He concludes with a look at the crucifixion of Jesus, and the judicial element in the concept of the Paraclete.

C99. **Stone, Michael E.** "Judaism at the Time of Christ." *Scientific American* 228 (January, 1973): 80-87.

Stone reviews the discoveries that have led to the idea that Judaism between 200 BCE and 100 CE was remarkably diverse, with some beliefs even called "pagan" by Stone. "Perhaps the first indication of the variety of Jewish religious expression in the period between 200

B.C. and A.D. 100 came with the translation into European languages of Jewish books that had been preserved only by the Ethiopian church and other Eastern Christian churches. Chief among these were the Book of Enoch and the Book of Jubilees..."—p. 80. Stone reviews some of the contents of these volumes, and then turns to the Nag Hammadi library discoveries, and their implications for understanding the Judaisms of the time. He goes on to talk about the mystical elements in rabbinic Judaism, the papyri found at Elephantini, and the presence of Jewish sacrafical cults outside of Jerusalem. Finally, he examines Jewish painting and manuscript illumination in the late Hellenistic and Roman periods.

C100. Vermes, Geza. "Hanina Ben Dosa: A Controversial Galilean Saint from the First Century of the Christian Era." *Journal of Jewish Studies* 23 (Spring, 1972): 28-50.

Vermes looks at the passages in the Mishnah which mention this saint, and from them derives three subjects under which Ben Dosa is discussed: namely, Healer, Miracle-worker, and Teacher. He looks at various Mishnaic and Talmudic passages, and discusses their construction, meaning, and what may be considered late additions to the passages. In this manner, Vermes seeks to construct a reliable picture of Hanina Ben Dosa.

C101. Vidal-Naquet, Pierre, translated by M. Jolas. "Interpreting Revolutionary Change: Political Divisions and Ideological Diversity in the Jewish World of the First Century A.D." *Yale French Studies* No. 59 (1980): 86-105.

Vidal-Naquet uses sociological theory to examine accounts such as those in Josephus in order to analyze the meaning of revolutionary activity by the Jews in the first century. He looks at the nature of the conflicts and the class struggle involved. He also examines the Maccabeean revolt and some comments of Philo on these situations. "The supreme characteristic of these insurrections," Vidal-Naquet says, "is that they concern, and can only concern Jews alone, but that, in addition, each group had its own conception of what it meant to be Jewish and would not budge from it"—p. 103.

C102. Zeitlin, Solomon. "A Life of Yohanan Ben Zakkai." *Jewish Quarterly Review* 62 (January, 1972): 145-155.

Zeitlin notes that you must separate legend and history when writing a life such as he proposes here, and then he criticizes the recent book by Jacob Neusner on Yohanan Ben Zakkai. He says that Neusner "...did not utilize proper Rabbinical literature"—p. 146. Zeitlin then looks at the Babylonian Talmudic material on Zakkai, and carries on a running argument with the presentation Neusner had made. He writes of Neusner's efforts, "The book is replete of inaccuracies and faulty renderings of rabbinic texts." "Before venturing to write on the sages of the Talmud a thorough knowledge of the Talmud is indispensible"—p. 155.

C103. Zeitlin, Solomon. "Masada and the Sicarii." *Jewish Quarterly Review* 55 (April, 1965): 299-317.

A history of the fortress at Masada is given according to the presentation in Josephus. Zeitlin relates the various battles at Masada and the reactions and actions of the Sicarii. He then reviews the work of archaeologist Yadin at Masada, which he says has not yet overturned any previous knowledge. Zeitlin thinks Josephus' information on Masada is reliable. He challenges some of Yadin's conclusions, and then reviews Yadin's writings about the calendar. Somewhat amazingly, Zeitlin argues that the Dead Sea Scrolls are not from the Second Commonwealth period, but derive from the Middle Ages. He says an archaeologist involved in work on the Second Temple Period must know the vast literature which is a part of that period.

C104. Zeitlin, Solomon. "Sicarii and Masada." *Jewish Quarterly Review* 57 (April, 1967): 251-270.

Zeitlin says Josephus is the only source of information about the Sicarii, and that he thought they were responsible for the great catastrophe which befell the Jews. Zeitlin gives special attention the the speech of Eleazar at Masada, and the topic of the suicide of those at Masada. "The Sicarii were fanatics, endeavoring by the use of terror to force their ideas on their fellow Judaeans. In so doing they destroyed even the visage of the Judaean State. Masada did not fall to the Romans. The Sicarii did not counterattack to protect Masada, they offered no resistance. They committed suicide and by this act they simply delivered Masada to the Romans"—p. 262. Zeitlin then turns to various criticisms of the work of Yigael Yadin, who had led a group of archaeologists in a dig of Masada.

JEWISH LITERATURE

C105. Avery-Peck, Alan J. "Mishnah's System of Santification." *Society of Biblical Literature Seminar Papers* No 21 (1982): 1-7.

Avery-Peck examines Tractate Terumot in the Mishnah to deal with the question of how Israel was to be sanctified when the Temple and land had been lost after 70 CE. He argues that although Rabbinical insights were foreign to the scriptural basis of the agricultural laws, the heave offering became the foundational answer to the question of sanctification. Holiness then depended on the action of the people who separated the heave offering from all other agricultural products.

C106. Bampfylde, Gillian. "The Similitudes of Enoch: Historical Allusions." *Journal for the Study of Judaism in the Persian, Hellenistic and Roman Period* 15 (1984): 9-31.

Bampfylde examines scholarly opinions of the origin of the Similitudes of Enoch and historical references within the book. He believes that the Parthian invasion of Roman territory in 51-50 BCE forms the background of 1 Enoch 56.

C107. Basser, Herbert W. "Allusions to Christian and Gnostic Practices in Talmudic Tradition." *Journal for the Study of Judaism in the Persian, Hellenistic and Roman Period* 12 (July, 1981): 87-105.

References to the animosity of early Christianity and Judaism as shown in the Talmudic tradition are reviewed. Basser cites such items as references to Christian fasts on Wednesday and Friday, and to bishops as "angels of destruction." Using information from Mircea Eliade's *The Sacred and the Profane*, he investigates a Tannaitic text which relates to the sacred space of the synagogue. He closes with a discussion of Gnostic dualism and the "polemical device of folk-etymology"—p. 99.

C108. Baumgarten, Albert I. "Miracles and Halakah in Rabbinic Judaism." *Jewish Quarterly Review* 73 (January, 1983): 238-253.

The use of miracles to prove specific halakic positions is investigated in Rabbinic writings, especially those of Rabbi Eliezer ben Hyrkanos. After analyzing a set of miracle stories told in support of opposing halakic positions, Baumgarten concludes that those Rabbis not in power tried to influence the course of events by the use of miracle stories.

C109. Birnbaum, Ruth. "The Polemic on Miracles." *Judaism* 33 (Fall, 184): 439-447.

Birnbaum examines texts from the classical Talmudic age and the eighteenth century (the time of the rise of Hasidism) to see the relation of the conception of miracle to "normative" Judaism. The question of which takes precedence, faith or miracle, is examined along with God's work in nature as miracle. The subtleties of the Hasidim in their conceptions of the working of miracles by their leaders is also reviewed. Birnbaum finds that halakhah and not miracle eventually becomes the basis for authority.

C110. Goldenberg, David. "Once More: Jesus in the Talmud." *Jewish Quarterly Review* 73 (July, 1982): 78-86.

Goldenberg reviews a new book on this subject by Johann Maier, author of *Jesus von Naazareth in der talmudischen Uberlieferung*. In the last thirty years, he says, new manuscripts and fragments have been uncovered and "major strides have been made in the various text-critical methodologies of Rabbinic literature." However, Goldenberg says this that this new work errs in two ways. First, conclusions must be based on the correct version of the text and on the entire literary phenomenon, and he thinks Maier fails in this regard. He offers ten examples of texts which he thinks Maier has either misinterpreted or ignored. He also offers ten examples of faulty methodology, one of them being the idea that centuries separate the original text from our earliest manuscripts, in one example used by Maier. Goldenberg writes, "With this type of reasoning one might as well say nothing at all about the original text!"—p. 81.

C111. Green, William Scott. "Reading the Writing of Rabbinism: Toward an Interpretation of Rabbinic Literature." *Journal of the American Academy of Religion* 51 (June, 1983): 191-206.

Green challenges the ways in which modern scholarship has sought to understand rabbinic documents and uses the Mishnah as a test case. If we try to understand the Mishnah historically there is a problem: "Because rabbinic documents constitute the only direct testimony about the ancient rabbis, the mere attempt to understand them historically encloses us in a hermeneutical circle"—p. 192. Another difficulty is that because part of the Mishnah pertains to the Temple at a time when the Temple no longer existed, Green says it must be treated as its own fictional world. We cannot use a political approach to understand it, or a sociological approach either, because the relations of literature and society are complex, and a document does not provide enough information to arrive at the kind of "thick description" which would be necessary to use a sociological approach. We must look at what world the text has created. In the instance of the Mishnah, Green says the following. "The Mishnah clearly exemplifies the list genre. Its tractates and subtractates comprise series of independent units that are paratactically arranged but demonstrate formal and thematic coherence"—p. 200. "From this perspective, the Mishnah may be envisioned as a kind of primal list, mastery of which determined competence and credibility in rabbinic society"—p. 202. "This preliminary account at least raises the possibility that genres, the generative devices of literature, have a cognitive dimension as well as an aesthetic one, and that this feature merits serious attention in any attempt to understand and interpret rabbinic texts and to explain how rabbinic Judaism adapted and persisted over the course of time"—p. 203.

C112. Halperin, David J. "Crucifixion, the Nahum Pesher, and the Rabbinic Penalty of Strangulation." *Journal of Jewish Studies* 32 (Spring, 1981): 32-46.

Halperin points out the argument among scholars as to whether the Jews practised crucifixion or saw it as alien and loathsome. He then examines the commentary (peser) on Nahum found in the fourth cave at Qumran. Halperin thinks the commentator was thinking of the rebellion against Alexander Jannaeus when he had 800 rebels crucified before him. The words "strangles prey for his lionesses" is evidently understood by the Qumran commentator to refer to crucifixion, Halperin believes—p. 33-34. Halperin now examines other Tannaitic sources, and concludes, "Our observations on the Nahum Pesher permit a better explanation of the relation of selibat quesa to heneq. Jews borrowed the practice of crucifixion from the

Romans, and, as we shall see, 'naturalized' it into Jewish law by invoking Deuteronomy 21:22-23, which prescribes the 'suspension' of criminals. Crucifixion was perceived as a prolonged and agonizing form of strangulation, heneq, and was at some point drastically modified into the quick and relatively humane form of strangulation prescribed by the Mishnah"—p. 40. "We have here, I propose," Halperin writes, "the origin of the principle—repeated as a tradition long after its grounds had been forgtten—that 'any death penalty prescribed by the Torah without specification is necessarily strangulation'"—p. 43. Halperin thinks the Rabbinic rejection of crucifixion occured at Yavneh in 70 CE. "We can only guess at the rabbis' motives for rejecting crucifixion and reinterpreting Deuteronomy 21:22-23. Humanitarian considerations may have been at work; or, possibily, a growing hatred of everything Roman"—p. 46.

C113. Hayward, Robert. "The Present State of Research into the Targumic Account of the Sacrifice of Isaac." *Journal of Jewish Studies* 32 (Autumn, 1981): 127-150.

Hayward examines the Targumic versions of the Abraham and Isaac story from Genesis 22. He concentrates on the Aquedah or Binding of Isaac in the Targums, and criticizes the views of P. R. Davies and B. C. Chilton on this subject. He quotes their view when he writes, "The Jewish doctrine of the Aquedah (=binding) regards the Offering of Isaac...as an actually accomplished sacrifice in which blood was shed, constituting a definitvely expiatory or redemptive act for all Israel." Then he says, "We may say at once that the Targums to the Penteteuch do not support such a narrow definition"—p. 129. Much of his attention is given to the Targum Ps-Jon, and he emphasizes the importance of the Temple mount in comments such as: "All Targums agree that Isaac was bound on the mountain in Jerusalem where the Temple was to be built" (p. 132); or "This stress on the visual appearance of God's presence is not accidental, since it will become very clear soon that the Targums have used Aqedah to prove the sole legitmacy of Jerusalem and its Temple as the place of sacrifice"—p. 133. As he examines the theological significance of the Aqedah, he says, "This idea is strikingly similar to the Targumic notion that the two went to the sacrifice 'with a perfect heart,' and it is very difficult to see how Davies and Chilton can possibly describe Philo's Isaac as an ignorant and passive victim"—p. 135. Examining Abraham's prayer in the Palestinian Targums, he notes the stress placed on Abraham's obedience, which is another way of talking about the meaning of doing this act with an undivided and whole heart. Among his closing conclusions, Hayward writes, "The Targums to the Pentateuch, speaking of the Aqdah, convey the idea that Isaac, a grown man, in total agreement with Abraham, willingly consented to be bound in sacrifice upon an altar on the Temple mount. They present Isaac as a perfect victim, and strongly emphasize that he is an archetypal martyr"—p. 148.

C114. Hayward, Robert. "Some Notes on Scribes and Priests in the Targum of the Prophets." *Journal of Jewish Studies* 36 (Autumn, 1985): 210-221.

In examining the Targum of the Prophets, Hayward finds that "...the evidence of the Targums suggests that 'spr,' even when it translates Hebrew 'nby,' means just what it always means, namely, scribe"—p. 211. Also, "If we survey all the available evidence for the translation of Hebrew 'nby' in the Targums, we discover first of all that 'spr' occurs as a rendering of this word only in the Targum of the Prophets, never in the Targums of the Pentateuch or Writings"—p. 211. Noting the close relationship of the priests and scribes in the Gospels, and that this relationship never occurs in the Mishhah, Hayward concludes, "Given the tendency of post-70 Judaism to play down the power of the priests and to assert the authority of scribe and sage, we may reasonably argue that those verses of the Targum of the Latter Prophets which link scribes and priests in tandem may well derive ultimately from the first century AD or earlier"—p. 213. Among his conclusions are the ideas that when the Targum of the Prophets translate the Hebrew "nby" they refer to a scribe and not a false or professional prophet. Both the prophets and scribes are seen as teachers of the Torah in the Targum. The scribes are seen as an important body of men in the organization and administration of the Jewish Community—p. 220-21.

C115. Heinemann, Joseph. "Early Halakhah in the Palestine Targumim." *Journal of Jewish Studies* 25 (February, 1974): 114-122.

Heinemann investigates the amount of early material, perhaps as far back as the Second Temple period, embedded in the Palestinian Targumim, and how it can be identified. Scholarship gives an early date for the traditions embedded in this Targum. Because interpretations of Scripture are preserved that disagree with Halakhah as laid down by the Tannaim and Amoraim, some have said it represents pre-Tannatic halackhic traditions. But Heinemann concludes we cannot assume the antiquity of certain aggadic traditions soley because they are in one of these Targumim.

C116. Kirschner, Robert. "Apocalyptic and Rabbinic Responses to the Destruction of 70." *Harvard Theological Review* 78 (January-April, 1985): 27-46.

Kirschner uses 2 Baruch and 4 Ezra to look at the apocalyptic response to the events of the year 70 CE, and Lamentations Rabbah to look at rabbinic response. He says these three books are linked by their Palestinian provenace, and by the fact that they address the national calamity of the destruction of the Temple. He recognizes that four centuries separate Lam. Rab. from the other two books, and that they have a conceptual distance as well; yet he thinks that the differences in the types of literature they represent has been overly emphasized. While both 2 Barauch and 4 Ezra "...insist that God himself decreed and executed the destruction of the Temple" (p. 34), God is not held responsible because of the defect in human nature which apocalyptic writers held, says Kirschner. "Thus God is absolved of guilt for the catastrophe not only on account of Israel's culpability but because of his own ulterior motive. The destruction of Jerusalem is a divine dispensation to pave the way for the climax of human history"—p. 37. In Lam. Rab., however, God is distressed and weeps at the destruction of the Temple. "Among the varieties of Judaism in late antiquity, two basic theodicies emerged from the catastrophe of 70: divine transcendence and divine identification"—p. 44.

C117. Lachs, Samuel T. "Rabbinic Sources for New Testament Studies—Use and Misuse." *Jewish Quarterly Review* 74 (October, 1983): 159-173.

Lachs believes that New Testament scholars should be grounded in and understand rabbinic literature, and that a joint effort of Greek contextual specialists and rabbinic scholars is needed. Jewish scholars should know New Testament scholarship, and New Testament scholars need to know more of the Hebrew roots which may be behind many New Testament expressions.

C118. Le Deaut, Roger. "Targumic Literature and New Testament Interpretation." *Biblical Theology Bulletin* 4 (October, 1974): 243-289.

Having offered a long list of examples of the way in which Targumic literature can offer relevant material for understanding the New Testament, Le Deaut illustrates ancient exegetical techniques. He closes with an overview of the importance of the Old Testament for the New Testament, and comments on the fact that the New Testament writers not only inhereted a translated Bible, the Septuagint, but one interpreted by a lengthy tradition. He also points out the importance of the intertestamental period for the development of later Judaism.

C119. Lieberman, Saul. "Light on the Cave Scrolls from Rabbinic Sources." *American Academy for Jewish Research: Proceedings* 20 (1951): 395-404.

The light Lieberman thinks is shed on the Scrolls has to do with the term "heterodoxy." He quotes three times when this term is used in the Tosefta. Each instance has to do with ways in which what Lieberman calls "ultra-pious extremists," as Jews try to be more strict than the rabbis. One area has to do with benedictions to the sun, and Lieberman writes, "The only pious Jews of whom we know that they were accused of addressing some invocations to the sun were the Essenes"—p. 398. He concludes that it was only when these extremists took on the character of sects that the Rabbis characterized their opinion as heterodoxy, a somewhat milder term than heresy.

C120. Lightstone, Jack N. "Problems and New Perspectives in the Study of Early Rabbinic Ethics." *Journal of Religious Ethics* 9 (Fall, 1981): 199-209.

Lightstone thinks that the categories of Protestant systematic theology have often been used when studying Judaic ethics, and that this is a mistake, because the materials have been lifted out of their literary and systematic contexts. This approach also ignores the significant variance of thought within the documents. Therefore, studies of early rabbinic ethics must analyze the individual documents, and only then may ethical data be "abstracted and viewed against their systematic contexts"—p. 199. "Simply weaving isolated Mishnaic and Talmudic passages into a fabric of a discussion of rabbinic ethics may, as it does in the above instance, not only skew but also miss entirely the points made in the documents themselves. To be sure, a commitment to the systemic analysis of individual documents entails holding at bay one's interest in specifically ethical issues, at least until one has stored out the document's larger structures of thought"—p. 207.

C121. "The Mishnah: Methods of Interpretation." (A symposium.) *Midstream* 32 (October, 1986): 38-42.

Five scholars present brief points of view on Jacob Neusner's interpretation of the Mishnah. Two of them had written reviews of Neusner's *Judaism: The Evidence of the Mishnah*; these scholars comment about Neusner's responses to their reviews. The article closes with brief comments by Neusner in reaction to this article. The scholars are Meir Bar-Ilan, Shaye J.D. Cohen, William Scott Green, Samson H. Levey, Hyam Maccoby, and, of course, Neusner himself.

C122. Neusner, Jacob. "Exegesis and the Written Law." *Journal for the Study of Judaism in the Persian, Hellenistic, and Roman Period* 5 (December,1974): 176-178.

Responding to an article by Joseph Baumgarten entitled, "Form Criticism and the Oral Law" (appearing in the *Journal for the Study of Judaism in the Persian, Hellenistic, and Roman Period* 5 [1974]: 34-40), Neusner writes, "The primary question, to which Mr. Baumgarten does not yet supply his answer, is, what criteria will serve to show, when met, that we have an originally oral pericope, that is a pericope which has been formulated orally and transmitted orally?"—p. 177. Neusner thinks Baumgarten does not analyze the actual sources carefully enough, but depends on "external sayings"—p. 178.

C123. Neusner, Jacob. "Form and Meaning in Mishnah." *Journal of the American Academy of Religion* 45 (March, 1977): 27-54.

Neusner analyzes the lingusitic character of Mishnah-Tosefta with special reference to the Order of Purities. He finds that those who redacted the Mishnah proposed that it be transmitted by memorization rather than through writing. Also, the "system of grammar and syntax" which was distinctive to the Mishnah was intelligible to the members of the particular community, namely, the rabbis. Neusner then writes about the ways and meaning of memorizing Mishnah, which he says were based on recurrent syntactical patterns. It is the pattern of the way things are said that led to the creation of its own world for memorization. Mishnaic rhetoric has a perception of order and balance and a conviction of the mind's centrality in constructing order and balance.

C124. Neusner, Jacob. "History and Purity in First-Century Judaism." *History of Religions* 18 (August) 1978): 1-17.

Neusner thinks the Mishnah's system of uncleanness was in place by the turn of the first century CE, and he describes its three components. He argues that it rests on "eternally recurrent natural forces" which are above history—p. 1-2. "The argument, that at the core of the system is the conviction that what is normal is clean and what is abnormal or disruptive is unclean, is powerfully supported by the convictions of the Priestly Code on why Israel should keep clean and normally is clean. It is because the opposite of unclean is holy"—p. 4. Neusner examines in detail the system of cleanness of the Essenes, and compares and contrasts it with the system of the Mishnah. He argues that changes in the system were not due to historical events such as the destruction of the Temple, but to tensions and questions within the system itself.

C125. Neusner, Jacob. "History and Structure: The Case of Mishnah." *Journal of the American Academy of Religion* 45 (June, 1977): 161-192.

Neusner examines why the Mishnah ends when it does, and whether there is something within the development of the Order of Purities which led to the cessation of the development of the laws. He examines the Mishnah's internal stucture, and whether the ideas themselves were fully exhausted, leading to a cessation of development. He then examines any possible influence of the events of the time. He thinks that with the loss of the hope of the rebuilding of the Temple, there was a loss of interest in the development of the matter of purity.

C126. Neusner, Jacob. "Innovation Through Repetition: The Role of Scripture in the Mishnah's Division of Appointed Times." *History of Religions* 21 (August, 1981): 48-76.

Neusner thinks that finding out what Scripture a particular kind of Judaism seeks to view as important—and what it ignores—tells us much about the structure of its system. However, you must also look at the context in which those choices are made. "The Mishnaic division of appointed times forms a system in which the advent of a holy day, like the Sabbath of creation, sanctifies the life of the Israelite village through imposing on the village rules in the model of those of the Temple"—p. 50. Neusner looks at these times and the role of Scripture in them. You cannot make sense of the Mishnaic tractates "...without constant attention to the unfolding of its topic in one of the Mosaic codes"—p. 57. He then shows how this works in several tractates: "...what is important in the Mishnah is not the relationship to Scripture—however literal—but the autonomy from Scripture imparted to the Mishnah by the people who stand behind both its language and its inner character, that is to say, the sages of the mid-second century and their disciples. Theirs is the message, and to their own day did they deliver it"—p. 68-69.

C127. Neusner, Jacob. "Map Without Territory: Mishnah's System of Sacrifice and Sanctuary." *History of Religions* 19 (November, 1979): 103-127.

Neusner says that to compare religions, you must first compare whole systems in their historical context. In this article he describes the subsystem of sacrifice and sanctuary in the Mishnah, and then turns to the question of "...how Mishnah in this topic addresses itself to the world of the late first and second centuries A.D. in which the document as a whole comes into being"—p. 103-04. Finally, he locates Mishnah "...its world view and intellectual structure, in the larger context both of Judaism and of the history of religions of late antiquity"—p. 104. Since the Temple was already in ruins when this Mishnaic subsystem was created, Neusner says, "It describes, with remarkable precision and concrete detail, a perfect fantasy"—p. 110. The important question then becomes, says Neusner, not what the Mishnah says here, but why we have the document at all. "...so far as they wish to say something about sacrifice in the abstract, its meaning and significance in the life of Israel here and in the heavens, it is not only that Scripture's message remains valid but also that it is exhaustive: all said there is right, and all that is right is said there"—p. 114. Neusner describes a mistake made by most New Testament Christian scholars, who think of the destruction of the Temple as the end of Old Testament Judaism. Writing about some of the work of S. G. F. Brandon, Neusner says, "Brandon's judgment of the world framed by the Mishnah to begin with hardly exhibits understanding (or even knowledge) of those ways in which the destruction of the Temple turned out to inaugurate not a time of decay and dissolution, but a remarkable age of reconstruction and creativity in the history of Judaism"—p. 118. The rabbis of the Mishnah write like scribes, and present a mediating document between the old and the new. "By including in Mishnah a division on sacrifice and sanctuary, the sage addresses Israelite society with the message that cosmic order is now to be replicated"—p. 126.

C128. Neusner, Jacob. "The Teaching of the Rabbis: Approaches Old and New." *Journal of Jewish Studies* 27 (Spring, 1976): 23-35.

This is a review article of the book by Ephraim E. Urbach, *The Sages: Their Concepts and Beliefs.* Though Neusner praises the book, his criticisms include the following: "Urbach's selection of sources for analysis is both narrowly canonical and somewhat confusing"—p. 25. Neusner doesn't think that the world view of the Talmudic sages emerges in a way that they would have recognized, because Urbach ignores too much of the halakhah. He also has reservations about the methodological issues involved in the study of such historical and literary texts. In terms of the problem of selection from such a vast corpus, Neusner writes, "But should we not devise means for the filtering downward of some fundamental, widely and well attested opinions, out of the mass of evidence, rather than capriciously selecting what we like and find interesting"—p. 27. "The major problem is to derive, from arcane and trivial details of laws of various sorts, the world-view which forms the foundations of, and is expressed by, these detailed rules"—p. 35.

C129. Neusner, Jacob. "Toward the Natural History of a Religion: The Case of the Palestinian Talmud." *Religion* 13 (January, 1983): 19-36.

A new translation into English of the Palestinian Talmud, the *Yerushalmi*, has prompted Neusner to write. He first examines why he considers it important to translate this document into English, and then "conduct a set of taxonomical studies centered upon that document itself"—p. 20. He reviews the historical setting of this

Talmud, the system it involves, the character of the evidence, how a natural history of its religion should proceed, and the principles which should be followed for such a study. "...a more sophisticated grasp of how the document came into being and the relationship between what people really said and did and what the Talmud's framers claim they said and did will open many paths of inquiry and interpretation"—p. 35.

C130. Neusner, Jacob. "The Written Tradition in the Pre-Rabbinic Period." *Journal for the Study of Judaism in the Persian, Hellenistic and Rabbinic Period* 4 (July, 1973): 56-65.

In speaking of glosses to the tradition, Neusner writes, "It would therefore seem plausible, according to present theories as to the formulation and transmission of 'oral' traditions, that the presence of glosses and their acceptance into the traditions may signify the glossed words existed in some written form, though, admittedly, this is by no means certain"—p. 56. Neusner points out that there is no evidence before 70 CE as to "how Pharisaic authorities formulated and transmitted their materials"—p. 57. He continues by looking at passages of the Mishnah which seem to indicate that "...before 70 some sort of traditions, later handed on to Yavnean masters and glossed by them, did exist"—p. 58. He then turns to the entire tractate of Berakhot to look for fundamental stratum. At the end of the article Neusner acknowledges the tentativeness of what he has written, and adds, "...what we cannot show, we do not know..."—p. 65.

C131. Rowland, Christopher. "The Visions of God in Apocalyptic Literature." *Journal for the Study of Judaism in the Persian, Hellenistic and Roman Period* 10 (December, 1979): 137-154.

Rowland thinks the study of apocalyptic literature is wrongly dominated by an interest in its eschatological element. Much of what is contained, he points out, is simply "glimpses of things which are normally hidden from human perception"—p. 139. The documents often speak of things as they actually are in the heavenly world. The subjects of interest to the mystic are often the subject matter of apocalyptic. He compares and contrasts the vision of God in Ezekiel and Revelation 4 with the vision of God in 1 Enoch. For example, he writes, "Another development as compared with Ez. 1, and one which becomes a distinctive feature of several of the apocalyptic visions of God is the inclusion of the rivers of fire (14,19) which flow from under God's throne"—p. 142. Rowland also says, "In the New Testament the best example of a vision of God and his heavenly court is to be found in Rev. 4. This chapter itself shows no evidence whatsoever of Christian influence, and, treated in isolation, it is quite clear that it is entirely Jewish in its inspiration"—p. 145. After discussing the vision of God in the Apocalypse of Abraham 17-19, Rowland draws a number of conclusions including this interesting statement. "Apocalyptic must be recognised as an important, indeed invaluable, source for the reconstruction of the origins of Jewish mysticism, even if at present we are not in a position to ascertain whether it is the parent of the kind of meditation which was practiced among the rabbis and, for that matter, the predecessors of the rabbis who flourished before the fall of Jerusalem"—p. 154.

C132. Sauders, James A., ed. "Jacob Neusner Issue." *Biblical Theology Bulletin* 14 (July, 1984): 81-125.

Neusner is one of the most prolific and creative writers of our time on the Mishnah, Talmud, and other Jewish topics in the first and second centuries CE. This issue contains the following articles: "Presenting the Issue: Jacob Neusner—Expositor of the Rabbinic Canon," by James Sanders; "From Text to Context: Building Bridges in the Study of Humanity," by Jacob Neusner; "Judaism and Scripture: The Case of Leviticus Rabbah," by Jacob Neusner; "Methodology in Talmudic History," by Jacob Neusner; "One Theme, Two Settings: The Messiah in the Literature of the Synagogue and in the Rabbis' Canon of Late Antiquity," by Jacob Neusner. The issue concludes with a list of the "Major Scholarly Works of Jacob Neusner," plus a list of books received.

C133. Sanders, James A. "Palestinian Manuscripts, 1947-1972." *Journal of Jewish Studies* 24 (Spring, 1973): 74-83.

"The spring of 1972 marked the twenty-fifth anniversary of the discovery of the Qumran manuscripts. 1947 was the beginning of a period of more than twenty years during which ancient manuscript materials have been recovered along the west littoral of the Jordan Fault as far north as the Wadi-ed-Daliyeh and as far south as Masada"—p. 74. Sanders publishes a list of "...where the photographs and responsible transcriptions have been published..."—p. 74. He includes both book and periodical material, and concludes with a helpful list of study aids.

C134. Schafer, Peter. "Merkavah Mysticism and Rabbinic Judaism." *Journal of the American Oriental Society* 104 (July-Sept., 1984): 537-541.

Schafer covers three items in this review article: namely, Ithamar Gruenwald's *Apocalyptic and Merkavah Mysticism*, David J. Halperin's *The Merkabah in Rabbinic Literature*, and Ira Chernus' *Mysticism in Rabbinic Judaism*. Schafer questions the use of the idea of "esotericism" in the Gruenwald volume, and the lack of a distinction between Hekhalot literature and other literatures of ancient Judaism. He writes about the need to understand the exegetical content of some of the ecstatic mysticism Halperin writes about, plus the lack of a real link between Merkavah mysticism and midrash as presented in the Chernus volume. Schafer's main approach seems to be to question the methodological approaches of each volume.

C135. Schafer, Peter. "Research Into Rabbinic Literature: An Attempt to Define the *Status Quaestionis*." *Journal of Jewish Studies* 37 (Autumn, 1986): 139-152.

Rather than summarizing an immense field, Schafer says he will "...present the most important approaches in research on the basis of which rabbinic literature has been and is being studied"—p. 139. He lists five approaches: 1) the traditional-halakhic approach, in which all literature is subsumed under Halakhah; 2) the exploitative-apologetic, an approach used by Christians; 3) the thematic approach, in which theological topics are selected from Rabbinic literature; 4) the biographical approach, in which great rabbis of the past are studied; and 5) the study of rabbinic literature as a whole, and its nature as literature. A second approach in this area is exemplified by Jacob Neusner in which the focus in on interpretation "...immanent in the work"—p. 146.

C136. Schiffman, Lawrence H. "Legislation Concerning Relations with Non-Jews in the Zadokite Fragments and in Tannaitic Literature." *Revue de Qumran* 11 (December, 1983): 379-389.

"The Damascus Document XII, 6-11 contains a series of regulations dealing with relations with non-Jews. These prescriptions form a serekh, (1) a list of laws compiled even before the editor of the Zadokite Fragments redacted this text from its disparate parts. (2) Most of these regulations closely parallel similar prescriptions found in tannaitic literature. This study will examine the sectarian passage and compare it to its Rabbinic parallels"—p. 379. Schiffman then reviews the prohibitions agains killing Gentiles, against plundering Gentiles, against the sale of Kosher animals to Gentiles, against the sale of untithed produce to Gentiles, and against the sale of "Canaanite" servants to Gentiles. The Zadokite Fragments "...augment biblical law, discussing only matters not explicitly mentioned in the Bible"—p. 389. When the two bodies of literature are compared on the issue of Gentiles, there are striking parallels. This is not usually the case. "Indeed, we can probably assume that in this respect the Qumran sect and the Pharisees of the Second Commonwealth period would have been in full accord." "This study reminds us that in the rush to differentiate the Judaisms of the Second Temple period, the common elements must not be ignored"—p. 389.

C137. Segal, Alan. "Covenant in Rabbinic Writings." *Studies in Religion/Sciences Religieuses* 14:1 (1985): 53-62.

Segal begins by discussing early studies, which formed a series of arguments between Christians and Jews about whether the Christian church had become the community for whom the covenants were now valid—plus a discussion of the nature of covenant itself. Special emphasis is given to the work of E. P. Sanders, and the nature of the idea of covenant in rabbinic writings. Segal then examines liturgy and ritual as an untapped source of information for the rabbinic view of convenant. He looks especially at circumcision, the daily service, the Sabbath service, and the Shema and Tefillin (putting the Law as a sign on the hand and a frontlet between the eyes). In a final section, he discusses the Shema and the Ten Commandments.

C138. Towner, W. Sibley. "Halakhic Literary Patterns: Types, History, and Affinities with New Testament Literature." *Jewish Quarterly Review* 74 (July, 1983): 46-60.

Towner begins by pointing out the differences in the forms used in halakhic passages by the Tannaim, and the types of forms identified for other portions of scripture by the critics. He offers examples of exegetical patterns, enumeration patterns, and nonexegetical patterns. He next focuses on the history of these patterns, and closes by comparing the patterns with New Testament literature. In his last section, he highlights the difficulties of the comparisons, and discusses a few ideas for a methodology to engage in such a comparison. The starting point is to recognize that "...both early Christian and first-century Rabbinic circles transmitted tradition, whether orally or in written form, through the medium of stereotyped literary patterns is the starting point"—p. 59. Though there are significant differences here, Towner says they should not be overstated, because "...the New Testament writers too were concerned both with the application of the law and the interpretation of Scripture"—p. 60.

C139. Towner, W. Sibley. "Hermeneutical Systems of Hillel and Tannaim: A Fresh Look." *Hebrew Union College Annual* 53 (1982) 101-135.

Towner lists six historical factors which led Rabbinic Judaism to an elaboration of a hermeneutic. They were: the canon of Scripture was fixed; a body of authoritative Torah not part of that canon had to be kept in relationship to it; the institutions of Bet-Kenesset and Bet-Midrash emerged as settings suitable for carrying on the hermeneutical task; sectarian competition increased the urgency for an explicit hermeneutic; Hellenistic culture offered models from its own interpretive tradition; and the normative role of the Temple in religion ceased. Towner then reviews the seven hermeneutical rules attributed to Hillel, and the thirteen attributed to R. Ishamel, and offers a literary, logical analysis of each one. He closes with a comparison of these results with the hermeneutical devices found in the Old and New Testaments and the larger Hellenistic milieu.

C140. Vermes, Geza. "Jewish Literature and New Testament Exegesis: Reflections on Methodology." *Journal of Jewish Studies* 33 (Spring-Autumn, 1982): 361-376.

Jewish documents such as the Mishnah are used as external background material to help understand the New Testament. Vermes points out several shortcomings of this approach, including the fact that the written materials are later than the New Testament, though they are probably based on teachings which are older than their written form. He also argues with J. A. Fitzmyer's use of Aramaic texts to the exclusion of all else. Vermes thinks we should see the New Testament as part of a continuum of Jewish teachings which inludes the Mishnah, Targums, Talmud, and other Jewish writings. He concludes, "Positively, what is required is an effort to examine the movement of Jewish religious-theological thought as a whole, and while so doing, to determine the place, significance and distinctiveness of its constituent parts. In other words, instead of looking at the New Testament as an independent unit set against a background of Judaism, we have to see it as part of a larger environment of Jewish religious and cultural history"—p. 374-75.

C141. Vermes, Geza. "Methodology in the Study of Jewish Literature in the Graeco-Roman Period." *Journal of Jewish Studies* 36 (Autumn, 1985): 145-158.

"...methodology often precedes, pre-conditions and occasionally interferes with the analytical study of a text, the essential spade-work in every kind of literary research"—p. 145. Vermes seeks to answer the question, "How should a late twentieth century student approach Jewish literature of the inter-Testamental age, and how does his *modus operandi* differ—if at all—from that of his predecessors?"—p. 145. Vermes explains the other goals of the article in the following quotation. "In this paper I propose first to outline the changes that have occurred say, between 1880 and 1980; second, to describe, with the help of concrete examples, how the growth of information has influenced our understanding of Jewish literature in the Graeco-Roman period; and third, to conclude with a few general remarks on methodology in the light of a century of discoveries, trials and errors"—p. 146. He writes of the Qumran Scroll, the contribution of Ethiopic studies, and the tremendous advances since the discovery of various ancient documents. Since Vermes was engaged with Fergus Millar and Martin Goodman in the revision of Emil Schurer's *The History of the Jewish People in the Time of Jesus Christ,* he relates much of the research to changes of opinion on various topics since the time of Schurer. He closes with a lighthearted counsel on methodology: "Take care in gathering the evidence, and make sure that you have understood it. Be pragmatic and not dogmatic. When nothing seems to make sense, keep cool. He who perseveres will muddle through"—p. 158.

C142. York, Anthony. "The Targum in the Synagogue and in the School." *Journal for the Study of Judaism in the Persian, Hellenistic and Roman Period* 10 (July, 1979): 74-86.

"My intention in this paper is to study some of the rabbinic texts bearing on this problem and to direct attention to the implications of these texts relative to the subject expressed in the title of this study, *i.e.*, the Targum in the Synagogue and School"—p. 75. He begins with a study of Megillah 4,1 from the Talmud Jerushalmi. York finds that there was a written Targum in use in the synagogue in the fourth century. After further examination of other passages, he writes, "Therefore, on the one hand tradition, historical and literary research and the results of modern archaeology, all agree that there were written Targumim in the Tannaitic and post-Tannaitic period, and probably in the pre-Tannaitic period as well. On the other hand, the passage before us specifically prohibits written Targumim"—p. 79. York works on a solution to this. "When therefore R. Samuel includes the Targum among the tradition of the Oral Law, he is stating precisely the same opinion as in the first two sayings attributed to him in its passage, namely, the Targum is to be accorded the same status as the Hebrew text"—p. 80. He explores the identity of R. Samuel, and finds him to be a school teacher; and it is the school teachers who read the Targum in the synagogue. "Here it should be emphasized that there was not a sharp distinction between the school system and the synagogue, at least in the Tannaitic period in Palestine"—p. 83. "Thus it seems to me that the Targum which had such an important role in the synagogue services was also employed within the school system *per se*"—p. 83. "Perhaps also in discussing the origin and purpose of the Targum we should widen our horizon to include the school as well as the synagogue as the *raison d'être* for the Targum"—p. 86.

C143. Zeitlin, Solomon. "Dreams and Their Interpretation from the Biblical Period to the Tannaitic Time: An Historical Study." *Jewish Quarterly Review* 66 (July, 1975): 1-18.

Zeitlin says he does not want to deal with dreams from a psychological point of view, but he asks the following question: "Were they considered as an act of divination endowed with the power of efficacy, or were they regarded as worthless and disturbing?"—p. 1. He then reviews dreams in the Bible. "There can be no question that during the Biblical period prior to the

Restoration dreams were regarded as acts of divination possessing the power of efficacy"—p. 1. He examines the dreams of Joseph, Daniel, Mordecai, and others. Dreams are mostly given to kings and royalty, but in the Talmud they are given to the common people. "In the Palestinian Talmud it is stated that dreams are neither advantageous nor disadvantageous; certainly they are not acts of divination and the dreamer should not be very concerned about them"—p. 15.

JOHN THE BAPTIST

C144. Davies, Stevan L. "John the Baptist and Essene Kashruth." *New Testament Studies* 29 (October, 1983): 569-571.

Davies thinks John the Baptist's choice of food and drink may not have been that of an ascetic, but of someone concerned with food purity as outlined in the Essene laws of Kasruth. The Essenes also ate locusts and honey. Davies examines this fact, and the idea that John the Baptist might have associated with the Essenes.

C145. Rivkin, Ellis. "Locating John the Baptizer in Palestinian Judaism: The Political Dimension." *Society of Biblical Literature Seminar Papers* No. 22 (1983): 79-85.

Rivkin begins with Josephus' account of John the Baptist in Book XVIII: 116-119 of the *Antiquities*, which shows him as a righteous man whose message was so eloquent that he was feared by Herod even though he was not advocating a revolt against Rome. Rivkin then focuses on the several political problems Herod had at the time, issues that would have made him more sensitive to John; specifically, he mentions the hacking down of the golden eagle that Herod had erected at the Temple as a symbol of loyalty to Rome. The protestors were burned alive, and the anger this act engendered among the Jews led to violence. When Emperer Augustus decided to assign a Roman administrator to Judea, he ushered in an era of permanent revolution. The idea of the two realms, one political and the other religious, meant that as long as the Romans did not invade the religious realm, "...the religious leaders would not intrude into the realm of Caesar"—p. 81. "The decision of Augustus to bring Judea directly under Roman rule thus cracked the mosaic of Judaism and erased the marker separating the realm of Caesar from the realm of God." "When, therefore, John the Baptist echoed the prophets by calling on the people to repent and live lives of righteousness, justice and piety, he was, by implication holding out the hope that if the repentance was sincere and if enough of the people abandoned their sinful ways, God would usher in the glorious end of days envisioned by the grand prophets who had spoken in his name. Herod the Tetrarch thus had good reason to fear the political implications of John's religious teachings once it became evident that he was attracting crowds who might in a surge of religious exaltation and zeal act out on the political implications of John's call for repentance and let loose a torrent of revolutionary violence"—p. 83-84. "The tragic fate of John the Baptist thus lays bare the larger tragedy of the Jewish people held tightly in the grip of Rome. From the moment Herod died until the last defendant of Masada had breathed his last, there was virtually no day without its demonstration, no week without its disturbance, no month without its riots, and no year without its rebellion"—p. 85.

JOSEPHUS

C146. Baumgarten, Albert I. "Josephus and Hippolytus on the Pharisees." *Hebrew Union College Annual* 55 (1984): 1-25.

Baumgarten believes Hippolytus used a copy of Josephus' writings which had been revised by an author who was more pro-Pharisee than Josephus. After doing a comparative textual analysis of appropriate sections of Hippolytus and Josephus, Baumgarten explores scholarly opinion concerning the two authors. Special note is made of the passages in both authors that focus on the Pharisees.

C147. Amaru, Betsy H. "Land Theology in Josephus' *Jewish Antiquities*." *Jewish Quarterly Review* 71 (April, 1981): 201-229.

Comparing and contrasting the land theology of the Bible with that of Josephus' *Jewish Antiquities*, Amaru describes the land theology of the Bible as a "covenantal triad of God-People-Land." She writes: "...in every instance of covenant-making not only is land mentioned but the specific territory of land promised is denoted as God's gift." Amaru believes that Josephus downplays the acquisition of land from gift to providential assistance.

C148. Armenti, Joseph R. "On the Use of the Term 'Galileans' in the Writings of Josephus Flavius." *Jewish Quarterly Review* 72 (July, 1981): 45-49.

Armanti challenges the view of Solomon Zeitlin that in his *Vita*, Josephus refers to the Galileans as a political rather than a geographical group.

C149. Blosser, Don. "The Sabbath Year Cycle in Josephus." *Hebrew Union College Annual* 52 (1981): 129-139.

Examining Josephus' idea of the Sabbath year, Blosser argues that Josephus sometimes referred to the seventh year, when he should have referred to the eighth year (the first year of the cycle). Taking into account and identifying specific dates, such as the destruction of the Second Temple, Blosser finds Josephus more accurate on this issue than most scholars had thought.

C150. Broshi, Magen. "The Credibility of Josephus." *Journal of Jewish Studies* 33 (Spring-Autumn, 1982): 379-384.

Broshi suggests checking Josephus' accuracy by looking at archaeological data. He finds Josephus accurate even when describing things Josephus could not have seen, such as the walls at Masada. He also suggests checking geographic descriptions and numbers of people. Broshi believes Josephus used Roman imperial commentaries as part of his sources. He recognizes Josephus' inaccuracies as well which he says range from "vagueness to blatant exaggeration," but he also says in many instances Josephus' data are entirely or largely accurate.

C151. Byatt, Anthony. "Josephus and Population Numbers in First Century Palestine." *Palestine Exploration Quarterly* 105 (January-June, 1973): 51-60.

Byatt shows the dimensions of the problem in a chart of scholars' "speculative guesses" concerning the population of Palestine in the first century CE. He then turns to a discussion of the terms "village" and "town," and shows the confusing way these terms are used in Josephus and the New Testament. Byatt argues that, although Josephus often did not stick to strictly technical definitions because he was more impressed with the size of a place, Josephus is generally consistent.

C152. Feldman, Louis H. "Josephus as a Biblical Interpreter: The Aqedah." *Jewish Quarterly Review* 75 (January, 1985): 212-252.

Josephus' account of the Aqedah, the binding of Isaac in preparation for sacrifice by Abraham, is hellenized in Feldman's view, because Josephus adds clarity and uniform illumination while omitting those Biblical details that create suspense. In Feldman's view, Josephus seeks to build up Abraham and Isaac while ignoring theology and theodicy.

C153. Feldman, Louis, *et al.* "The Meaning of Josephus." [a symposium]. *Midstream* 32 (May) 1986): 26-32.

Moses Aberbach had written an article on Josephus and his critics, and had challenged some of the ideas of Yitzhak Baer. This symposium of disinguished faculty responded to some of Aberbach's ideas, and attempted to assess the works of Josephus in terms of reliability. The participants included: Louis Feldman, David Flusser, David Ladouceur, Tessa Rajak, and Samuel Schwartz. The participants reached a number of conclusions: at some points Josephus can seem amazingly accurate in his pronouncements, but closer inspection often raises questions; it is questionable that Josephus followed the Halakhic principles of the Pharisees; Josephus wanted to realize his ideals, and these changed over time; "Josephus' account has a high degree of internal coherence, and that, while not an automatic guarantee of truth, does lend credibility"—p. 28. The article ends with Aberbach's responses to the participants' criticisms.

C154. Freyne, Sean. "The Galileans in the Light of Josephus' *Vita*." *New Testament Studies* 26 (April, 1980): 397-413.

Freyne believes that a "failure" to differentiate the terminology of Josephus in his various works has tended to identify the Galileans as revolutionaries—p. 397. He indicates that in Josephus' *Vita*, "the Galileans are the country people, as distinct from the inhabitants of the major towns, and they are Josephus' loyal supporters, military nationalists, but not essentially revolutionary or subversive"—p. 412.

C155. Goldenberg, David. "The Halakha in Josephus and in Tannaitic Literature." *Jewish Qrarterly Review* 67 (July, 1976): 30-43.

Goldenberg looks at four halakot as presented in Josephus and in the Tannaitic literature. He compares and contrasts them with the evolution of halakha. The law of returning a lost object and of assisting a fallen animal are two of the halakot examined.

C156. Malinowski, Francis X. "Torah Tendencies in Galilean Judaism According to Flavius Josephus: With Gospel Comparisons." *Biblical Theology Bulletin* 10 (January, 1980): 30-36.

Malinowski covers four areas, namely: (1) erroneous views of Galilean Judaism; (2) distinctive ways of practicing Judaism; (3) Josephus' portrait of Galilean Judaism; and (4) Gospel similarities to Josephus' Galilean Jew. Though he acknowledges Josephus' description of the four "sects" within Judaism at that time, Malinowski says Josephus presented a "monolithic" picture of Judaism to reassure the Romans that there was nothing to fear from the Jews. He presents Josephus' view of Galilean Judaism as having three fundamentals: first, admiration for the expert in Jewish law; second, respect for priests; and third, the centrality of the holy city of Jersualem. Among the Gospel similarities Malinowski cites are: Jesus' absolute regard for God's Lordship and Jesus' desire for obedience to the Law as God's word (in spite of the complex question of Jesus annulling various Mosaic laws).

C157. Shutt, R. J. "The Concept of God in the Works of Flavius Josephus." *Journal of Jewish Studies* 31 (Autumn, 1980): 171-189.

Shutt takes another look at a theme which had been treated in some of the writings of A. Schlatter. Shutt begins with the fact of Josephus' religiousness and his involvement in two cultures, Jewish and Gentile. He first examines Josephus' use of Greek words for God in their various contexts in his writings. Next comes a review of the titles and characteristics of God in Josephus' work. He finishes with a look at the ways in which Hellenistic culture may have influenced Josephus' views, especially the notions of "fate" and "fortune." Though he thinks Josephus' opinions were consistent with Jewish Scripture, he also points out, "As a result of his contact with the Gentile cultures, and partly also because he sought to express his Judaism in terms of that Greek culture, he used expressions and language which are neither Jewish nor Scriptural, in order to convey his meaning...."—p. 186.

C158. Vermes, Geza. "A Summary of the Law by Flavius Josephus." *Novum Testamentum* 24 (October, 1982): 289-303.

Vermes says that Josephus' interest in the Law was not "...in detailing what was licit or illicit but in providing a religious explanation and moral justification of the Jewish way of life"—p. 290. Vermes acknowledges that Josephus enriches his re-telling of the Law with material from halakhah and haggadah current in his time, but notes Josephus thought he was not changing the sense of the Law. He then reviews several places where Josephus says he is summarizing the Torah. Vermes especially notes Josephus' lack of concern with purity law, and his statement that there was Torah reading on the sabbath. Vermes summarizes the main themes Josephus deals with, and shows how he handles the Law in those sections of his writing.

C159. Zeitlin, Solomon. "Who Were the Galileans? New Light on Josephus' Activities in Galilee." *Jewish Quarterly Review* 64 (January, 1974): 189-203.

Zeitlin notes that in his *Vita* Josephus mentions the Galileans as a distinct group thirty-four times. Zeitlin begins to examine who the Galileans were by giving a brief account of the political structure of Galilee. He uses material from Josephus and Maccabees for this reconstruction. "I venture to say that the term 'Galileans' in *Vita* does not have a geographical connotation, but is an appellative name given to the revolutionaries against Rome and the rulers of Judaea who were appointed by Rome"—p. 193. Zeitlin then goes on to look at this idea in detail in relation to the other references to the Galileans in Josephus. "Looking retrospectively at the history of the last days of Jerusalem, we may say that the Zealots, Sicarii and Galileans, who were all hardliners of the hawks, were greatly responsible for the destruction of the state"—p. 203.

JUDAISM AND CHRISTIANITY

C160. Alexander, Philip S. "Rabbinic Judaism and the New Testament." *Zeitschrift für die Neutestamentliche Wissenschaft und die Kunde der Alteren Kirche* 74 (1983): 237-246.

Having commented on the use of the Mishnah, Talmud, and Midrash in New Testament studies, Alexander reviews the weakness of many New Testament scholars in handling Rabbinic texts. He encourages scholars to get beyond Ralshi's interpretations of the Talmud, and establish the meaning it had at the time of the writing. He concludes by urging New Testament scholars to exercise the same care with the study of Rabbinic texts that they do with New Testament passages.

C161. Barr, James. "The Question of Religious Influence: The Case of Zoroastrianism, Judaism, and Christianity." *Journal of the American Academy of Religion* 53 (June, 1985): 201-235.

Having examined the use of words like resurrection or fire in both Zoroastrianism and Judaism, Barr finds no evidence that Iranian religion influenced Judaism. In one example of his conclusions, he writes: "...if the resurrection idea was taken over from Iranian religion, it can have been taken over only on the basis of inner-Jewish reasonings and movitations...."—p. 224.

C162. Beckwith, Roger T. "The Daily and Weekly Worship of the Primitive Church in Relation to Its Jewish Antecedents." *Evangelical Quarterly* (Part I) 56 (April, 1984): 65-80; (Part II) 56 (July, 1984): 139-158.

Using the New Testament, Philo, Josephus, Didache, Old Testament, intertestamental writings, and early Rabbinic writings as background, Beckwith reviews issues such as worship in the Temple, synagogue, and Jewish home. He also examines the use of the Shema and Tephillah (eighteen benedictions), and the use of scripture in the home and synagogue. He then turns to the transition to Christian worship, with its stress on the Lord's Supper, which had the Passover meal as background. Finally, he reviews the Christian use of scripture and forms of prayer.

C163. Brandon, S. G. F. "Primitive Church and Judaism." *Modern Churchman* 41 (September, 1951): 156-168.

Brandon reviews Paul's writings, especially II Corinthians, plus studies of early Judaism, and concludes that the Jerusalem church did not see a soteriological significance in Jesus' death. He believes the teaching of the Jerusalem church was hostile to the idea of Jesus' divinity and the soteriological role proposed by Paul. Still, the fact that Paul's view prevailed must be explained. Brandon says what brought this about was the fall of Jerusalem in 70 CE. He also says the Gospel of Mark blends an emphasis on the historical Jesus with the theology of Paul.

C164. "Christians Among Jews and Gentiles: Essays in Honor of Krister Stendahl on His Sixty-Fifth Birthday." *Harvard Theological Review* 79 (January, April, July, 1986): entire issue (320 p.).

In addition to including a 16-page bibliography of Stendahl's writings, this special issue of the *HTR* includes several articles of special interest to this bibliography: "Jewish Women's History in the Roman Period," by Bernadette Brooten; "Jews, Gentiles and Synagogues in the Book of Acts," by John Gager; "Death Scenes and Farewell Stories: An Aspect of Master-Disciple Relationship in Mark and Some Talmudic Tales," by Jacob Neusner; and "Christians and Jews in First Century Alexandria," by Birger Pearson.

C165. Donaldson, Terry L. "Levitical Messianology in Late Judaism Origins, Development and Decline." *Journal of the Evangelical Theological Society* 24 (September, 1981): 193-207.

Donaldson believes that in addition to the the expectation of a Davidic Messiah, there was at one time an expectation of a Messiah from the line of Levi. What brought this about were the following events: 1) the victories of Judas Maccabeus led to an eschatological belief that a new heaven and a new earth would eventually come; 2) the Hasmonaean dynasty was given a legitimacy by reference to the Melchizedekan precedent of having a priest and king in one person; 3) the peace and prosperity of the reigns of Simon and John Hyrcanus led to the idea that a messianic age was being realized; 4) the seed of Levi and the Hasmonaean line were being spoken of in messianic terms; 5) during the decline of the Hasmonean rule, anti-

Levitical sentiment developed, and the Pharisees revived Davidic messianology; 6) Qumran also developed this Levitical messianology, but in a parallel fashion to the other developments. Donaldson examines a number of apocryphal texts in support of his contention.

C166. Dunn, James D. "Was Christianity a Monotheistic Faith from the Beginning?" *Scottish Journal of Theology* 35 (August, 1982): 303-336.

Dunn's answer to the question which forms his title is given in his last paragraph: "...Christianity had to redefine its monotheism. But because it was the one God of Jewish faith whom those first Christians recognized in and through this Jesus it was a redefinition and not an abandoning of that monotheism. It is thus a fundamental insight and assertion of Christianity that the Christian doctrine of the Trinity is but a restatement of Jewish monotheism"—p. 336. The author begins his article with an examination of the Gnostic redeemer myth, which spoke of a divine being coming down from heaven to redeem mankind from their bodies. He asks if this was a pre-Christian myth, and if so, was it used as an explanation of who Christ was? This potentially created a problem for monotheism, because it saw this divine being as separate from God. Dunn finds the evidence for the myth to be post-Christian, and determines that the Christian church used mostly the Sophia (Wisdom) and Logos (Word) conceptions to explain the meaning of Jesus. Dunn also explores the ideas of glorified heros such as Elijah, angels, the Son of Man concept, first and last Adam, and Sophia-Logos as conceptions used to explain the meaning of Jesus. In all of these, he thinks the conception of the one God, of monotheism, was carefully guarded by Christians as they used available conceptions and modified them to explain Jesus.

C167. Grant, Robert M. "Dietary Laws Among Pythagoreans, Jews, and Christians." *Harvard Theological Review* 73 (January-April, 1980): 299-310.

Grant begins with a consideration of Pythagorean symbola as presented in Aristotle's *On the Pythagoreans*. He shows how allegory was used to deal with the abstentions involved. Grant reviews the work of Aristoxenus and the Neoplatonists in this regard, as well as Philo. In dealing with views of Jewish dietary laws, Grant looks at Plutarch, the Epistle of Aristeas, and 4

Maccabees, which Grant says "finds the work of reason expressed not in finding reasons for defending the law but in producing the self-control that overcomes desire for fish, birds, and animals forbidden by the law"—p. 303. In looking at the Christian teachings, he first examines the apostolic decree of Acts 15:20 and 29, and then the Didache and the fourth-century *Apostolic Constitutions*. He shows the use of allegory again from the Epistle of Barnabas, and closes his article with a look at related teachings in the Synoptic Gospels, and how this was handled by some of the early Church Fathers.

C168. Katz, Steven T. "Issues in the Separation of Judaism and Christianity After 70 C.E.: A Reconsideration." *Journal of Biblical Literature* 103 (March, 1984): 43-76.

Katz examines and questions the prevailing scholarly consensus concerning the attitude and actions of the Yavnean sages and their immediate heirs toward Christians. Katz finds the evidence supposedly supporting four interpretations to be too slim. These are: 1) the circulation of official anti-Christian "letters"; 2) the issuing of a "ban" against Jewish Christians; 3) the issuing of a prohibition against the "reading" of "heretical books"; and 4) the promulgation of Birkat ha-minim (the blessing against heretics). Katz states that, if the material on which these four theories are based turns out not to have a legitimate basis, then the case for the obverse conclusion is strengthened. That is, "there was no official anti-Christian policy at Yavneh, or elsewhere before the Bar Kochba revolt and no total separation between Jews and Christians before (if immediately after?) the Bar Kochba revolt"—p. 76.

C169. Koenig, John. "Occasions of Grace in Paul, Luke, and First Century Judaism." *Anglican Theological Review* 64 (October, 1982): 562-576.

Koening examines Jewish documents to show terms which communicated the notion of grace. He does not find a "linguistic centrality" of grace in Judaism—p. 563. He does see in Paul the idea of grace as "outcroppings" of God's work in Christ as he extends his reign worldwide. He also believes that the Dead Sea Scrolls show that the Qumran community understood itself as chosen by God—an act of grace.

C170. Maccoby, Hyam. "Christianity's Break With Judaism."
Commentary 38 (August, 1984): 38-42.

Maccoby reviews James Charlesworth's *The Old Testament
Pseudepigrapha,* and finds that Charlesworth has a "much more
respectful assessment of rabbinic Judaism" (p. 38) than R. H.
Charles. Maccoby thinks that the inclusion of the Third Book of
Enoch in this collection shows the interest of Pharisees in mysticism
as well as legal matters. Though this is a fifth-century CE book, it is
an example of a genre which is pre-Christian. Christianity can now
be seen as just another Jewish sect, and the New Testament as
Jewish literature of the time. However, Maccoby believes that
Paul's emphasis on salvation through the death of Jesus separates
the New Testament from other Jewish literature. He asks, "Where in
Jewish literature is the concept of the death of God to be found? The
answer is simple: nowhere..."—p. 39. Maccoby closes his review
by showing that rabbinic Judaism did not despair concerning this
world, while the pseudepigrapha do.

C171. Moe, D. L. "Cross and the Menorah." *Archaeology* 30 (May,
1977): 148-157.

In an archaeological dig in 1975 a menorah etched into a plater wall
and a cross-shaped stone were discovered at Stobi in Southern
Yugoslavia. These two items helped unravel some problems related
to the excavated buildings in the same area. Moe reviews the
"historical context and previous archaeological work at Roman
Stobi"—p. 148. Stobi is the largest and best preserved of the
classical sites in what had been ancient Macedonia. Settled in the
third-century BCE, it began to thrive when the Romans established
law and order after 168 BCE. Archaeologists had found a Cenral
Basilica, a hall below it, and what was called a House of Psalms in
almost the same area. Two synagogues, one on top of the other,
were also discovered there. "By virtue of the menorah graffito, we
now know that the public hall itself indisputably had been a
synagogue with an earlier synagogue identified by the inscriptions
of Polycharmus below it"—p. 156. The discovery of the cross also
proved that the Basilica was later rebuilt as a Christian church. The
Basilica was constructed around the end of the fourth-century CE.

C172. Moore, George Foot. "Christian Writers on Judaism."
Harvard Theological Review 14 (July, 1921): 197-254.

This article is a watershed in the history of a Christian writing on Judaism. Moore took a more appreciative stance toward Judaism, and tried to show the way in which earlier writing toward Judaism had been polemic in intent. Though there is difference of opinion about the extent of his success, scholars have often cited Moore's work in their own essays. Moore begins by surveying early church history through the eighteenth century. He writes, "Christian interest in Jewish literature has always been apologetic or polemic rather than historical"—p. 197. "The volume of anti-Judaic apology still extant or known to us through titles and quotations is considerable"—p. 198. After a lengthy review showing how scholars had sought to engage in a polemic against the Jews with their work, Moore turns to the period covering the nineteenth century to the present. Moore finds the beginning of the modern study of Judaism by Christians to be in the work of August Friedrich Gfrörer. "Where the subject of investigation is the relation of primitive Christianity to its contemporary Judaism, whether the motive be a historical understanding of nascent Christianity or an apologetic exhibition of the superiority of the religion of Jesus to that of the Scribes and Pharisees, the critical ordering and evaluation of the Jewish sources is of much greater importance than when a general comparison of Judaism and Christianity is proposed..."—p. 253. Moore points out that Christians writing on this subject only know the names of the Jewish sources, and not their content.

C173. Parkes, James. "Jewish Background of the Incarnation." *Modern Churchman* n.s. 4 (October, 1960): 33-44.

Parkes tries to understand the implication of the phrase "fullness of time" in the passage from Galatians 4:4 where Paul writes, "when the fullness of time came, God sent forth his Son, born of a woman, born under the Law"—p. 33. Parkes notes, "...it was possible to travel from Jerusalem to the Atlantic by both the northern and the southern shores of the Mediterranean, and to penetrate to the North and Black Seas, with one language and currency, along a road more passable in winter and summer, and more efficiently policed, than was to be the case for fifteen hundred years after the Roman empire fell"—p. 35. Parkes talks of the importance of the Jewish villages and coherence of a single religion as important for the spread of the Christian message. He is trying to make a case for the idea that these situations were in the plan of God, and that it was the "right and best" time for Jesus to come. He shows that the idea of a messianic age was also important, in order that Jesus could be understood. "From a Jewish point of view the person of a messiah was always secondary to the conception of a messianic age"—p. 44.

C174. Roth, Cecil. "Messianic Symbols in Palestinian Archaeology." *Palestine Exploration Quarterly* 87 (May-October, 1955): 151-164.

Roth looks at symbols on Jewish monuments from the first centuries of the Christian era to the disintegration of the Roman empire. He concludes that they did mean something, and were not simply used for ornamental purposes; thus, they must be considered independently and "...they should be interpreted where necessary in the light of medieval Jewish ritual art, as well as of contemporary documentation"—p. 151. "The guiding principle in the Jewish symbolism of the early centuries which I venture to propose is the Messianic Idea, or rather, the hope for Redemption in its wider sense. It must be born in mind that this was the very basis of Jewish life. The destruction of the Temple in the year 70 did not diminish it"—p. 151. Roth begins by looking at what he says was the most common group of symbols, "...the seven-branched Temple Candelabrum (the Menorah), flanked on the one side by the curved ram's horn (sophar) and on the other by the palm-branch (lulab)"—p. 152. He thinks all three in a unity represented a Messianic symbol. He then examines these symbols on gravestones and on synagogues. Roth also reviews Jewish coins. In this way he offers his own interpretation of the meaning of these symbols.

C175. Sanders, E. P. "Judaism and the Grand 'Christian' Abstractions: Love, Mercy and Grace." *Interpretation* 39 (October, 1985): 357-372.

Sanders thinks that the body of Rabbinic material which has been used to support the idea that Pharisaism was legalistic points instead to confidence in God's grace, and obedience as the appropriate response to this grace. He reviews the material which has been used for this purpose, and points out that they all derived from those who were enemies of a mainstream Judaism. He continues by looking at various groups such as the Priests, the Pharisees (regarded negatively in the New Testament), and the common people (viewed negatively by Rabbinic literature). Sanders then shows the positive views of the same persons as presented by Josephus. He closes by reviewing all three groups and the ways they might be evaluated with what he calls "fair generalizations"—p. 367. He recognizes the bias in all the sources, and tries by taking that into account while finding a more balanced view. He finishes by writing, "Not every Jew was observant, and not everyone correctly understood the great principles of the faith. Yet Judaism in the time of Jesus and Paul was a noble religion, based on belief in God's mercy and grace, and inculcating in its members virtuous action and consideration to others. Mercy, in Judaism as in Christianity, begets mercy"—p. 372.

C176. Sandmel, Samuel. "Palestinian and Hellenistic Judaism and Christianity: The Question of the Comfortable Theory." *Hebrew Union College Annual* 50 (1979): 137-148.

Sandmel thinks the idea of a clearly delineated Palestinian or Hellenistic Judaism or Christianity is simply a comfortable theory, *i.e.,* "one which satisfies the needs of the interpreter, whether theological or only personal, when the evidence can seem to point in one of two opposite directions"—p. 139. He says the proper way to study this issue is through a comparative study of texts such as Micah or Job in the Septuagint. Since the Hebrew of these books is in some parts almost unintelligible, the translator's choice of words shows something of the Judaism of that time and place. Comparing the Bible's treatment of Adam, Noah, and Abraham with their treatment in Philo would be another possibility. Since in Christianity the New Testament is all in Greek, Sandmel says we must look for clues on this issue in the writings of Paul. Sandmel even speaks of the influence of Paulinism in the Gospel of Mark.

C177. Sigal, Phillip. "Early Christian and Rabbinic Liturgical Affinities: Exploring Liturgical Acculturation." *New Testament Studies* 30 (January, 1984): 63-90.

Sigal thinks that all of the New Testament, including the Gospel of Luke, was written by Judaic authors. He believes that research into the targumic and Aramaic foundations of the NT will have an even greater influence in the future. "New Testament material was designed for congregations including both persons of Judaic faith, who accepted a form of Christology but remained observant of more or less Judaism, and of persons who came into the new movement called 'The Way' from the pagan world"—p. 63. "This also helps explain why the early liturgy would be quite Judaic in both structure and content although now and then re-constituted in a hellenistic-christological manner"—p. 63. Sigal first discusses the parallels between the evolving forms of liturgy in the rabbinic synagogue and the Christian church. "At this juncture I wish to be more specific and posit the hypothesis that we have in this early church liturgy more fully presented in The Apostolic Constitutions a selection of church poietes, that is, a Christian adaptation of a prayer form present in the Judaic matrix of the early church"—p. 69. Sigal then looks at the form of the Lord's Prayer, the liturgical passage of Philippians 2: 10-11, and the kedushah which is rooted in Isaiah 6:3. He concludes, "The foregoing shows that Judaic worship materials were acculturated to Christian need and through the traditional methods of midrash expressed in piyyutim the early church christianized older Jewish prayers"—p. 83.

C178. Sloyan, Gerard S. "Jewish Ritual of the 1st Century CE and Christian Sacramental Behavior." *Biblical Theology Bulletin* 15 (July, 1985): 98-103.

Sloyan begins by looking at various prayers which come from Mishnaic tractates in the Siddur, or prayer book. He compares Jewish ritual with Christian to show that the idea that they were incompatible cannot be sustained. He looks at the meaning of sacrament in the Christian understanding, especially through the writings of Bultmann. In terms of the care with which Jewish ritual is observed, he notes, "...the 'primitivism' or 'legalism' that is looked at askance by some Christians is rooted in the conviction that the rites have been divinely authorized. In the Jewish outlook, everything must be done just as prescribed because the injunctions are the LORD's"—p. 99. He closes with a look at the way the term "sacramental" would need to be understood in Judaism and Christianity: "...while Judaism has no sacramentalism in the systematic sense developed by Christianity, a sacramental idea is to be found germinally in both the Bible and the Mishnaic epoch"—p. 101.

C179. Smith, Gail. "Jewish, Christian and Pagan Views of Miracle Under the Flavian Emporers." *Society of Biblical Literature: Seminar Papers* No. 20 (1981): 341-348.

Smith begins with a look at Plutarch's views on miracles. She then begins a comparison of Jesus in the Gospel of Mark as related to miracle, with Josephus and more on Plutarch. She concludes that though Mark, Josephus and Plutarch would have agreed that miracle is the result of "...divine power originating in God...," Plutarch would not have agreed with the other two that God was omnipotent—p. 347.

C180. Smith, Morton. "A Comparison of Early Christianity and Early Rabbinic Traditions." *Journal of Biblical Literature* 82 (June, 1963): 169-176.

Smith criticizes conclusions B. Gerhardsson' *Memory and Manuscript*, which he says distorts both rabbinic and Christian tradition. Gerhardsson had argued that Judaism had developed a method for transmitting the unwritten Torah. However, Gerhardsson had used rabbinic materials from the third century to develop his idea of this methodology, and then tried to argue that the New Testament materials were transmitted in the same manner. Smith says that to try to read these materials back into the situation before 70 CE represents a distortion. Smith says Gerhardsson neglects "...the enormous difference which separated the small, exclusive, sectarian Pharisaic party of the temple period from the rabbinic organization of the third century, as by Roman law established, with authority over all Roman Judaism"—p. 171. Smith questions the idea that Jesus taught as a rabbi, and points out that the parallels in the New Testament show a freer divergence than parallels in rabbinic writings. "Second: The gospel material is predominantly narrative, the rabbinic material predominantly expository"—p. 173. After highlighting a number of other problems with Gerhardsson's theories, Smith writes, "...traces of rabbinic technique as are to be found in the gospels are suspect because of the well-known increase of Pharisaic and of Essene influence on the church in Jerusalem during the period prior to 70"—p. 175. Writing about the Gospel's concern with the important Jewish topic of the Law, Smith writes, "How a careful, rabbinic tradition should have produced, about this central rabbinic concern, the mess of contradictory scraps of evidence which the gospels preserve, it is impossible to conceive"—p. 176.

C181. Stylianopoulos, Theodore G. "New Testament Issues in Jewish-Christian Relations." *Journal of Ecumenical Studies* 13 (Fall, 1976): 70-79.

Stylianopoulos looks at what the New Testament has to say about Jewish-Christian relations. The historical issues he finds are: 1) the idea that the Christians were but one community within a very diverse Judaism; 2) the ministry of Jesus was accomplished within Judaism; 3) the claims of the early church distinguished it from wider Judaism; 40 tensions resulted from the Jews' non-acceptance of the gospel, and from the success of the mission to the Gentiles; and 5) the growth of the number of Gentiles in the Church led to its final separation from Judaism. The theological issues he highlights are: 1) the Messianic claims made about Jesus; and 2) the identification of the true Israel. "Jewish-Christian dialogue might well center on the nature and implications of the claim of the church to be an eschatological step beyond the faith community centered on the Mosaic law; such a dialogue might well be self-purifying to the church"—p. 70.

THE LAW

C182. Barbour, R. S. "Loyalty and Law in New Testament Times." *Scottish Journal of Theology* 11 (December, 1958): 337-351.

The loyalty of the Jew to the Jewish people and to the land is examined against the background of loyalty to state and religion of the Greeks. Jesus' understanding of the Law and the Temple is then explored.

C183. Basser, Herbert W. "The Development of the Pharisaic Idea of Law as a Sacred Cosmos." *Journal for the Study of Judaism in the Persia, Hellenistic and Roman Period* 16 (June, 1985): 104-116.

The Talmud, the writings of Josephus, the Qumran Scrolls, as well as the insights of medieval rabbis, provide the sources for Basser's study. He writes, "For the Rabbis, practice (of the law) was the way to enter the spiritual cosmos. An act was only valid in so far as it was accomplished by spiritual intention"—p. 107. The Pharisees attacked the roots of Hellenistic culture by retarding the growth of religious literature, limiting public discussion to law and ethics, while keeping metaphysics a private matter. The Pharisees' desire for a single offical text of the Torah is also explored.

C184. Baumgarten, Joseph M. "Form Criticism and the Oral Law." *Journal for the Study of Judaism in the Persian, Hellenistic and Roman Period* 5 (June, 1974): 34-40.

Baumgarten believes that there was an avoidence of written halakha before Yavneh, and he argues against the view of Jacob Neusner that there was a written Pharisaic tradition before Yavneh. Baumgarten uses form criticism, which he finds useful if there is "patience with details of law and concern with internal evidence"—p. 40.

C185. Baumgarten, Joseph M. "The Un-Written Law in the Pre-Rabbinic Period." *Journal for the Study of Judaism in the Persian, Hellenist and Roman Period* 3 (October, 1972): 7-29.

In considering whether there was a ban on writing halakhot in the pre-rabbinic period, Baumgarten studies Josephus, Philo, and rabbinic sources. He argues that the existence of the Qumran writings is evidence that "the ban on writing halakhot was totally non-existent in the pre-rabbinic period." He does recognize the diversity of Jewish groups in the first century, but acknowledges the possibility that some groups may have had such a ban.

C186. Carlston, Charles. "Things that Defile (Mark 7:14) and the Law in Matthew and Mark." *New Testament Studies* 15 (October, 1968): 75-96.

Mark's passage sets aside the Jewish dietary laws. This relates to the broader questions of the Law and primitive Christianity. Carlston says that the argument of his paper is "...that four or five separate strata can be discerned in the two accounts of the parable: a pre-Markan and a Markan form which reject food laws, a pre-Matthean stratum that insists on a literal keeping of the Law, including the dietary regulations, and a Matthean stratum that is sympathetic to the more rigorous view even while moving in the direction of an ethical transmutation of the Law's demands"—p. 75. In analyzing the differences in the Markan and Matthean passages, Carlston shows how in Matthew it is Jesus who affirms the law, but it is Jesus' teaching which is the key to the will of the Father. While Matthew does not insist on keeping all of the food laws, Carlston thinks Matthew doesn't set them aside as irrelevant—as Mark clearly does.

C187. Dunn, James D. "Mark 2.1-3,6: A Bridge Between Jesus and Paul on the Question of the Law." *New Testament Studies* 30 (July, 1984): 395-415.

Dunn first inquires about which Jesus we are dealing with when it comes to the Law. Is it the Jesus of Mark 7, who denies that anything outside a man can defile him, or is it the Jesus of Matthew 5, who thinks even the least of the commandments is important? When it comes to Paul, Dunn points out that, since E. P. Sanders' work, "...the stereotype of earning salvation by the merit of good works simply does not fit first century Judaism..."—p. 396. Dunn's conclusion is that Paul was not objecting to the law *per se*, but to the idea of the law as "...proof and badge of Israel's election..."—p. 396. Paul did not want the concept of the law to in effect confine the grace of God to Israel, just because the Jews had the law. Dunn then examines Mark 5 to see if a bridge can be found between Jesus and Paul on this issue.

THE MACCABEES

C188. Davies, Philip R. "Hasidim in the Maccabean Period." *Journal of Jewish Studies* 28 (Autumn, 1977): 127-140.

Davies reviews several theories about the nature of the Hasidim, who are mentioned in I and II Maccabees. He then reviews a recent and detailed theory which "...accords to the Hasidim an extremely important role in not only the history of second-century Judaism, but the religion of post-exilic Judaism as a whole, and especially the later stages"—p. 127. Davies thinks there are two primary weaknesses with this theory. First, he says the theory is held together by "...an interlocking web of assumptions" (p. 128), and there is not much explicit evidence to support extensive discussion about the Hasidim. Since any theory must be grounded in reality, he points out that "...there is nothing in the explicit evidence—by which I mean the references in I and II Maccabees—to justify any of the main suppositions of the hypothesis"—p. 128. Davies is commenting mostly on the work of Martin Hengel, who thinks the Hasidim are a clearly defined Jewish party in I Macc. 2:42. Davies examines I Macc. 2:42, I Macc. 7:12f, and II Macc.14:6, and demonstrates that these three texts do not support the conclusions which have been drawn about the Hasidim from them. Further, "...the very existence of an Hasidic sect is an assumption which the texts do not justify"—p. 133.

C189. Millar, Fergus. "Background to the Maccabean Revolution: Reflections on Martin Hengel's 'Judaism and Hellenism'." *Journal of Jewish Studies* 29 (Spring, 1978): 1-21.

In 1974, Martin Hengel's *Judaism and Hellenism: Studies in Their Encounter in Palestine During the Early Hellenistic Period* was published. Millar indicates this is a very important work, but expresses some reservations about the idea of a "...Hellenistic reform movement on the part of a group within the Jewish community..."—p. 1. Having reviewed Hengel's interpretation, Millar suggests other ways of looking at the same evidence from the 160s BCE. He looks at the Jewish community in the early Hellenistic period and the relation of Antiochus Epiphanes to Judaism. He closes with a section on the Temple Cult and Hellenism from 167-4 BCE. Millar writes, "I would argue, firstly, that the evidence shows how un-Greek in structure, customs, observance, literary culture, language and historical outlook the Jewish community had remained down the earlier second century, and how basic to it the rules reimposed by Ezra and Nehemiah had remained"—p. 20. "...there was a reform movement, initiated from within the community, but confined to the High Priesthood of Jason..."—p. 21.

THE MESSIAH

C190. Horsley, Richard A. "Popular Messianic Movements Around the Time of Jesus." *Catholic Biblical Quarterly* 46 (July, 1984): 471-495.

Horsley thinks that recent scholarship has shown that contemporary Jewish messianology is a weak foundation from which to explain early Christian christology. He also believes that the domination of a literary approach needs to be changed, and social phenomena need to be examined. Therefore, he analyzes the participants in popular "messianic" movements, and examines the traditions out of which they responded to their situations. Since the idea of Zealots has been shown to be merely a scholarly construct, he focuses on the Israelite-Jewish tradition of popular "anointed" kings as the source of movements which found agents of redemption in their "kings." Horsley shows how these kings were distinguished from the bandits described in Josephus. He finds three basic characteristics in these popular movements which included a "king": "...Kingship was constituted by popular election or anointing; it was conditional on the king's maintenance of a certain social policy; and the anointing of a new king was generally a revolutionary action"—p. 477. "The kings and their movements mentioned by Josephus occurred at two particular points during the early period of Roman domination: during the massive popular uprising following the death of Herod, and during the first great Revolt against Rome, A.D. 66-70"—p. 480. "...the prophetic movements looked to the divine inititative in signs and wonders like those of the exodus from Egypt or the Battle of Jericho of old, whereas the messianic movements took direct political and military action"—p. 495. Horsley finds the movements which had a "king" sought to liberate the Jewish peasantry. This is a more convincing background for understanding Jesus than the literary conceptions used previously.

C191. Klein, Ralph W. "Aspects of Intertestamental Messianism." *Concordia Theological Monthly* 43 (September, 1972): 507- 517.

Klein examines apocrypha, pseudepigrapha, and Qumran scroll passages about a Messiah. He thinks intertestamental believers did not distinguish between earthly and heavenly hopes, and that a Messiah was thought necessary in order to correct the entire situation. Jesus' message was tied to first-century Palestinian culture. While he finds continuity between Jewish Messianic thought and the New Testament, Klein believes that Old Testament and intertestamental expectations "shattered and refracted" in Jesus—p. 517.

C192. Liver, J. "The Doctrine of the Two Messiahs in Sectarian Literature in the Time of the Second Commonwealth." *Harvard Theological Review* 52 (July, 1959): 149-185.

Liver looks at some of the texts discovered in Qumran Cave I and Cave 4, as well as certain Pseudepigrapha concerning the idea of two Messiahs. He finds a long-term development within eschatological writings concerning the Messiah. "The striving for redemption of the Dead Sea Sect, the fact that for hundreds of years it had been customary to see in the high priest the only ruler and leader of the people, and the central position of the sons of Zadok in the Sect brought about the formation of a doctrine which placed at the head of the congregation of Israel in future times a high priest—

the anointed of Aaron. But the unlimited authority of the Bible, which the Sect shared with the rest of the people of Israel required the appearance of a Davidic Messiah in any eschatological system where redemption is brought by earthly persons. And so, when they formed this image of an eschatological priest, they could not disregard the prophecies on the house of David in the Bible; and they placed at the side of the anointed of Aaron the anointed of Israel, that is, the king who would arise from the house of David"— p. 182. Liver says there is no evidence for a doctrine of two Messiahs outside the Dead Sea Sect and its related circles. He thinks the doctrine of the two Messiahs in the Book of the Testaments of the Twelve Patriarchs is identical to that found in the writings of the Dead Sea Sect—p. 183.

C193. Neusner, Jacob. "Messianic Themes in Formative Judaism." *Journal of the American Academy of Religion* 52 (June, 1984): 357-374.

"...just as, for antiquity, we cannot speak of a single 'Judaism' but only of 'Judaisms,' so we cannot imagine there was a '(the) Messianic idea of Judaism' everywhere present, always authoritative"—p. 357. What does exists is a theme, Neusner says, worked out in distinctive ways by each group within Judaism. Neusner mentions a number of views existing in the Bible and the Old Testament Apocrypha and Pseudepigrapha on the Messiah. He then looks at what he calls facts about the Messiah in the canon of Rabbinic Judaism. He offers a chronological table of documents, beginning with the Mishnah, and continuing with the Tosefta, Abot, and Abot de R. Nathan, Siddur or prayerbook, Targum Onquelos, and others. In the table he displays the concept of the Messiah presented in each document. He also looks at greater length at the Messiah in the Mishnah and Talmud, and then compares them. In a concluding section he writes, "We find in the rabbinic canon no such thing as the Messianic idea. The sources reveal no such harmonious, encompassing construct"—p. 370. "Klausner and Scholem provide portraits of a composite that, in fact, never existed in any one book, time, or place, or in the imagination of any one social group..."—p. 370-71. "So, to state the argument briefly, just as established conventions of the Messiah-myth served the Church merely to classify Jesus at the outset, but later on other taxa came into play, so the Messiah-myth found no consequential place in the rabbinical canon at the outset, that is, in the Mishnah, but later on that same myth became the moving force, the principle mode of teleological thought, in the Talmudic sector"—p. 372. "What the canon set forth at the end, in its rich eschatological-messianic myth and symbolism, states precisely what the Mishnah at the outset had defined as its teleology, but in the idiom of life and death, nature and super-nature. The rabbinical canon in its ultimate form delivered the message of sanctification, garbed in the language of salvation"—p. 374.

C194. Neusner, Jacob. "Mishnah and Messiah." *Biblical Theology Bulletin* 14 (January, 1984): 3-11.

When the Temple fell to the Babylonians in 586 BCE, Israeli thinkers turned to writing history to understand what had happened. Their theology became eschatology, and in this framework a Messiah was a natural component of a system which turned its attention to salvation. Though we would expect Judaism to become a deeply Messianic religion, the writing of the Mishnah altered that: "...a vast and influential document presented a kind of Judaism in which history and did not define the main framework in which the issue of teleology took a form other than the familiar, eschatological one, and, in consequence, in which historical events were absorbed, through their trivialization in taxonomic structures, into a non-historical system"—p. 3. Neusner then surveys the discussion of the Messiah in the Mishnah: "...the figure of a Messiah at the end of time, coming to save Israel from whatever Israel needs to be saved from, plays a negligible role in the Mishnah's discourse"—p. 7. "When in analyzing the foundations of Judaism, we move from species, eschatology, upward to genus, teleology, we find ourselves addressing head-on the motives and goals of the mishnaic system"—p. 8. The interest of the Mishnah was a system of sanctification for Israel; the Messiah myth would return to the Talmud, but only within the framework already set out by the Mishnah. "We find in the Mishnaic sector of the rabbinic canon no such things as 'the Messianic idea,' and the rabbinic sources as a whole reveal no such harmonious, encompassing construct"—p. 9.

THE NEW TESTAMENT

C195. Barrett, C. K. "New Testament Eschatology." *Scottish Journal of Theology* 6 (June, 1953): 136-155; and (September, 1953): 225-243.

Using Mark 9:1 as a crucial text, Barrett examines whether the idea of a future "day of the Son of Man" (p. 228) goes back to Jesus—or just the early church. He considers Synoptic eschatology as an "ellipse with two foci"—p. 231. There is the "eschatological crisis precipitated within the ministry of Jesus" (p. 231), and the eschatological consumation in the future. Late Jewish apocalyptic ideas are also reviewed to understand how they contributed to eschatological conceptions.

C196. Barth, Markus. "Traditions in Ephesians." *New Testament Studies* 30 (January, 1984): 3-25.

Barth studies the way Old Testament texts are quoted and interpreted in intertestamental Judaism. In this context, he studies the "Scripture hermenutics" (p. 6) of the author of Ephesians. In addition, Jewish and Christian forms of worship, as well as Gentile and pagan beliefs, are reviewed as background for several expressions in Ephesians.

C197. Brown, John P. "Techniques of Imperial Control: The Background of the Gospel Event." *Radical Religion* 2 (1975): 73-83.

Brown believes the Christian movement developed among the poor people of rural areas who were on the fringe of the Roman Empire, and then among poor persons of the cities who were at the heart of the Empire. He thinks Jesus and the Gospels embodied the alienation and hope of the poor. In Brown's view, Paul wrote for the urban poor. Brown sketches the history of Galilee and Jerusalem, and then applies a linguistic study to show the political realities of Jesus' time. He shows the Gospel writers focusing on the poverty and suffering of the people, and emphasizes the control of Rome as shown in the Passion narratives.

C198. Charlesworth, James W. "A Prolegomenon to a New Study of the Jewish Background of the Hymns and Prayers in the New Testament." *Journal of Jewish Studies* 33 (Spring-Autumn, 1982): 265-285.

Charlesworth focuses on the Jewish background of Christian hymns and prayers. He believes Jesus and his followers used fixed prayers developed during the intertestamental period, although their emphasis may have been on personal, spontaneous prayer. Christianity borrowed, "in a refined manner," Jewish hymns and prayers, and this continued until the Council of Nicea. He points out literary and theological parallels, as well as a continuum of expressed needs in Jewish and Christian prayers.

C199. Clark, Kenneth W. "The Gentile Bias in Matthew." *Journal of Biblical Literature* 66 (June, 1947): 165-172.

Clark says it is commonly held that the Gospel of Matthew was written by a converted Jew. He argues for Gentile authorship, and turns many of the arguments for Jewish authorship on their head. For example, in terms of the genealogy, he says Luke also has such a genealogy, and even the pagan Epictetus was interested in such material. He thinks the idea that God has renounced Israel because of the refusal of the gift of Jesus was only possible in the mind of a Gentile, and that the Gentile bias of the Gospel of Matthew is the main point of the book.

C200. Cook, Michael J. "Interpreting 'Pro-Jewish' Passages in Matthew." *Hebrew Union College Annual* 54 (1983): 135-146.

Cook believes four passages in Matthew, often cited as pro-Jewish (*i.e.* Matthew 5:17; 10:5-6; 15:24 and 23:2) are actually consistent with Matthew's anti-Jewish stance. They reflect the editorial activity of a redactor, and not the historical Jesus, and thus should not be used to establish Jesus' loyalty to the Jewish people. He questions scholarly opinion on these passages, because in his view they are all used to set up a denegration of Judaism in the passages immediately following.

C201. Crockett, L. "Luke iv. 16-30 and the Jewish Lectionary Cycle: A Word of Caution." *Journal of Jewish Studies* 17:1/2 (1966): 13-46.

Crockett examines assertions made in Aileen Guilding's book, *The Fourth Gospel and Jewish Worship*. His article attempts an "...objective summary of the evidence for and against the existence in New Testament times of a lectionary for both the law and the prophets." He also sees the need for a "... brief and clear summary of the sources of our knowledge of the lectionary cycle and the evidence for it in the first century C.E.—especially in regard to the prophets." He does all this by listing the sources of knowledge for the triennial lectionary, and then presenting the "important arguments for evidence that such a cycle was in use in the first century C.E." Finally, he evaluates the "use of the lectionary cycle in the interpretation of Luke iv. 16-30."

C202. Donaldson, James. "The Title Rabbi in the Gospels—Some Reflections on the Evidence of the Synoptics." *Jewish Quarterly Review* 63 (April, 1973):287-291.

In the Gospel of Mark the common form of address for Jesus is "teacher." In Matthew, however, this term is not a from of address by the disciples of Jesus, but is "restricted to those who do not recognize Jesus as Kurios"—p. 288. He concludes, "It is my opinion that the Synoptic Gospels themselves can offer no evidence for or against the argument on whether the title rabbi in the gospels is anachronistic or not"—p. 290. He also says of this title of address to Jesus: "Ordination cannot be implied from the mode of address"—p. 290.

C203. Enslin, Morton S. "New Apocalyptic." *Religion in Life* 44 (Spring, 1975): 105-110.

Enslin finds the evidence for the idea that the Gospel of Mark preserves the teaching of Peter to be inadequate. He then proposes that the author of Mark wrote to present a new apocalyptic that was not based on hideous beasts and suddenly appearing angels, but upon the idea that Jesus was going to reappear at any moment. The gospel was a call to preparation for that event.

C204. Lachs, Samuel T. "Studies in the Semitic Background to the Gospel of Matthew." *Jewish Quarterly Review* 67 (April, 1977): 195-217.

Lachs speculates about the Hebrew or Aramaic texts which may have been behind the Greek texts of certain New Testament passages. He offers examples of how easy it would be to misread certain Hebrew letters and choose the wrong word for translation. His first example concerns the use of "betrothed" of Mary rather than "husband" of Mary. In another example he speaks of the idea of a "city" set on a hill in relation to the image of light, and suggests that the term "fire" would make more sense. He shows how the Hebrew for the words "city" and "fire" are very similar.

C205. Montefiore, Claude G. "The Religious Teaching of the Synoptic Gospels in Its Relation to Judaism." *Hibbert Journal* 20 (April, 1922): 435-446.

Montefiore first asks what we mean by Judaism, and shows the difficulty of confusing modern Judaism with the Judaism of the time of Jesus. He writes, "...it is improper to make violent contrasts between the religious teachings of the Gospel and that of Judaism (to the discredit of the latter), if it can be shown that, along its own lines and by its own development, Judaism arrived at much the same teaching?..."—p. 436. He thinks that other than the disagreement about Jesus himself and his authority, and the disagreement about the Law, the teachings of Jesus and the teachings of the Judaism of his time were very compatible, as shown in the teachings about the nature of God and his mercy. Turning from the Law and the external to the internal or moral, Montefiore says we find more compatibility between Judaism and Jesus: "Jesus was a Jew who never dreamed of founding a new religion; he only wanted to reform and purify the religion of his fathers"—p. 439. "There are, therefore, many passages in the Gospels which seem to be, and indeed assuredly are, intensely characteristic of the Gospels and the teaching of Jesus, and which yet are perfectly 'Judaic'"—p. 440. "Judaism to-day, and more especially Liberal Judaism, is universalistic, and, like Jesus, and perhaps even more trenchantly, we Liberal Jews have 'fulfilled,' or are 'fulfilling,' the Law"—p. 446.

C206. Nickelsburg, George W. "Reading the Hebrew Scriptures in the First Century: Christian Interpretations in Their Jewish Context." *Word World* 3 (Summer, 1983): 238-250.

Nickelsburg says that most Christians think that the authors of the New Testament understood and interpreted the Old Testament in the categories of promise and fulfillment. While he thinks there is some truth to this, he also believes there were other categories which were important. He surveys some of these categories, and within each one discusses the Jewish methods of interpretation, and looks at relevant material in the New Testament. Categories discussed include: fulfillment of promises and prophecies, servant of the Lord, Torah and Wisdom, and the patriarchs as paradigms. While Nickelsburg finds deep roots of Christian interpretation of Scripture in Judaism, he recognizes that "Characteristic of these interpretations are unique blends of eschatological beliefs and radical claims about the Torah, which would have been far from self-evident to many first century Jews"—p. 250

C207. Vermes, Geza. "Jewish Studies and New Testament Interpretation." *Journal of Jewish Studies* 31 (Spring, 1980): 1-17.

Vermes points out that most New Testament scholars are not familiar with the languages and literature which form the Jewish background of the New Testament. Therefore he says, "...I will have to devote a good deal of this paper to a historical survey of the attitude of New Testament interpreters to Jewish religious literature written between 200 B.C. and A.D. 400 thought capable of throwing light on the text of the Gospels and on other documents of the Christian canon"—p. 1. Such research began with the idea that Jesus was the opponent of Judaism. Vermes works his way to the nineteenth century, where he gives attention to Srack and Billerbeck's work and Kittel's *Theological Dictionary.* He then points to the Holocaust and the discovery of the Dead Sea Scrolls as two reasons for the reassessment of early Judaism by Christian writers. Of of the changes in attitude that must still take place, Vermes feels, is a re-evaluation of the place of the New Testament, so that all other documents are not always subservient to it. In fact, Vermes says we should do away with the distinction between the New Testament and other Jewish documents, and understand that the New Testament "...is historically part of the greater body of first-century Jewish literature"—p. 14. "We shall not get the revival of scholarship that we look for until interpreters of the Christian Gospels learn to immerse themselves in the native religion of Jesus the Jew, and in the general climate of thought of the world and age in which he lived"—p. 17.

C208. Williamson, Clark M. "The New Testament Reconsidered: Recent Post-Holocaust Scholarship." *Quarterly Review* (United Methodist) 4 (Winter, 1984): 37-51.

"...there are strongly negative images of Jews and Judaism in the New Testament and that what we may fairly call 'anti-Judaism' has long constituted a frame of reference in terms of which these images and the larger New Testament have been interpreted. It is this interpretive scheme which is being decisively challenged by several recent scholars"—p. 37. Williamson reviews the anti-Judaism model by commenting on two recent scholars: "Jeremias is or is thought to be by some a counterweight to Rudolf Bultmann in New Testament scholarship. Both share a common failing, however: neither knew Second Temple Judaism from its own sources and each was quite capable of caricaturing it"—p. 39. He then turns to two of the major areas where Christian scholarship has changed its point of view on Judaism: namely, the Pharisees and Paul. Though he cites the fact of Luther's writings against Jews, Williamson thinks we need to look at the core of Luther's theology, which would show the following: "The justification of Gentile Christians is by the sheer grace of God and not by some spurious 'work' of overcoming Judaism"—p. 49.

C209. Winter, Paul. "The Cultural Background of the Narratives in Luke I and II." *Jewish Quarterly Review* 45 (October, 1954): 160-167.

Winter wants to show that these two introductory chapters of Luke could not have been written by "...anyone but a person, or persons, rooted in Jewish social traditions, religious custom, and general folklore, and acquainted with the topographic features of the surroundings in which the story is set"—p. 160. He then looks at the ideas of Zekharyah as a priest of the course of Abiyah, and the drawing of lots for liturgical assignments, and shows why these items support his conclusion.

THE OLD TESTAMENT

C210. Davies, William D. "Reflections About the Use of the Old Testament in the New in Its Historical Context." *Jewish Quarterly Review* 74 (October, 1983): 105-136.

Davies examines the use of sacred texts in Greek culture to see if it proves a clue to understanding the use of the Old Testament in the New Testament. While he finds some parallels, such as the divine origin of ancient oracles, he also finds significant differences. Greek texts were not copied with as much care, they did not form the same kind of foundation for the people, and historical events such as the Exodus were absent. He finds the Oral Law and Jewish exegetical-interpretive traditions as the context appropriate for understanding this problem.

C211. Lightstone, Jack N. "The Formation of the Biblical Canon in Judaism of Late Antiquity." *Studies in Religion/Sciences Religieuses* 8:2 (1979): 135-142.

Lightstone sounds a note of caution for all who wish to look at post-biblical Judaism. "Naive positivism, apologetics, polemic, arbitrary pronouncement, and gross speculation have been, and in many cases continue to be, the rule in books and articles treating post-biblical Jewish history"—p. 136. He questions several of the customary scholarly assumptions in regard to the shape and fixing of the Jewish canon. The "linear model" of the development of the canon, for example, seems too simplistic "...in the light of what we know (or at least suspect) regarding the editorial processes which produced the Pentateuch and Former Prophets..."—p. 137. Also, the assumption of a normative Judaism in the first century has been shown to be most questionable, and yet this assumption was important in viewing the development of the canon. Lightstone also shows the inaccuracy of G. F. Moore's assumptions in his *Judaism in the First Centuries of the Christian Era*. "...without recourse to Moore's conviction regarding a normative, institutionalized religion in Judaism of late antiquity, one may not assume that books known and respected in one circle will have soon come even to the attention of other groups—let alone to be revered"—p. 140-41. Finally, the events at Jamnia are questioned. Lightstone thinks a "Christian" model of councils has been superimposed on this event, and he questions whether the rabbis of the late first century sought to fix the limits of the canon.

C212. Miller, Merrill. "Targum, Midrash and the Use of the Old Testament in the New Testament." *Journal for the Study of Judaism in the Persian, Hellenistic and Roman Period* 2 (October, 1971): 29-82.

The increasing sense by scholars of the usefulness of Targums for New Testament study can be understood most clearly when the omission of such materials from works like Schurer's, G. F. Moore's, and others are noted. Items covered in this article include the factors contributing to a re-evaluation of both language and date of Targum, issues emerging from the new study of Targum, and the Jewish exegetical tradition, especially its structures, forms, and methods. Some of the topics within Jewish exegetical tradition include the definition, origin, and evolution of Midrash, hermeneutical rules and terms, and the interpretation of the Bible at Qumran. Miller then turns to a review of recent studies of the Old Testament in the New Testament, including the work of such scholars as C. H. Dodd, Barnabas Lindars, and K. Stendahl. He concludes with a section of bibliographical references to other areas relevant to study of Jewish and Christian exegetical traditions.

PALESTINE

C213. Bowersock, G. W. "Old and New in the History of Judaea" [review article]. *Journal of Roman Studies* 65 (1975): 180-185.

Bowersock reviews Vol. 1 of Vermes and Millar's revision of Schurer's *The History of the Jewish People in the Age of Jesus Christ*. He praises their work, but questions trying to revise within Schurer's framework rather than attempting a new work, especially in light of the Qumran and other archaeological discoveries. He then makes suggestions for additions to the bibliographies, and reviews the strengths and weaknesses of the revisions relating to historical items such as the "revised register of the governors of Syria"—p. 182. He also thinks a revision of Schurer's view of Herod the Great would have been in order.

C214. Fitzgerald, G. M. "Palestine in the Roman Period, 63 B.C.-A.D. 324." *Palestine Exploration Quarterly* 88 (January-April, 1956): 38-48.

Having listed and commented on the political rulers of the period, Fitzgerald discusses important archaeological remains of the period, with an emphasis on some of the important synagogues.

C215. Fitzmyer, Joseph A. "The Languages of Palestine in the First Century A.D." *Catholic Biblical Quarterly* 32 (October, 1970): 501-531.

Fitzmyer notes that, with the deportation of Palestinian Jews to Babylonia in the early sixth century BCE, a shift in the language habits of the people of Palestine occurred. The classical Hebrew of the pre-exilic period gave way to a more Aramaicized form. He continues with an examination of the extent to which other languages were used in Palestine and when they were employed. He lists Latin, Greek, Aramaic, and Hebrew. He examines inscriptions on buildings of the time, and literary evidence, including the Dead Sea Scrolls. Although Aramaic was the most common language used at the time of Jesus of Nazareth in Palestine, he points out that Hebrew and Greek were also spoken. He examines how these issues can affect our understanding of certain New Testament passages.

C216. Meshorer, Y. "Beginning of the Hasmonean Coinage." *Israel Exploration Journal* 24:1 (1974): 59-61.

Though many scholars had assigned the first Hasmonean coinage to John Hyrcanus I, Meshorer argued that Alexander Jannaeus was the first Hasmonean ruler who minted coins. With the discovery of a new piece, some additional light had been shed on the problem. If his original theory is confirmed, "...one may assume that Jannaeus' first coins were those tiny and rare coins (Pl.9:H-I) which were struck in Jerusalem toward the very end of the second century B.C. or the beginning of the first century B.C. (after the death of Anltiochus VIII?)"—p. 61.

C217. Meyers, Eric. "Galilean Regionalism As a Factor in Historical Reconstruction." *American Schools of Oriental Research: Bulletin* No. 221 (February, 1976): 93-101.

Meyers shows how scholars such as Geza Vermes have seen Galilee as a place where Jesus was influenced to have a kind of Judaism which was out of touch with mainstream first-century Judaism. What Meyers wants to do in this essay is to "...suggest a new and collateral way to address this problem. To continue speaking about Galilean Judaism without reference to current or past studies in the archaeologically-related disciplines of historical geography and epigraphy, not to mention the study of the material culture itself, is—in this author's view—to ignore great amounts of evidence and to speak *in vacuo*"—p. 93. Meyers writes about Josephus on Galilee, as he covers the geographical and topographical factors influencing Galilean history and culture. He then turns to the regionalism of Galilee as reflected in material culture, and discusses language, ceramics, and architecture, especially of synagogues. "A study of the topography and material culture of Galilee in late antiquity provides an opportunity for reconsidering Galilean social and religious conditions in the first centuries of the Common Era"—p. 100. "It may not yet be possible to relate these elements to specific statements in the New Testament of rabbinic corpora; but sooner or later literary historians will have to confront the growing array of materials, like the all important data from Beth-She'arim, that seems to be clustering by regions well known from literary records"—p. 101.

C218. Meyers, Eric. "Recent Literature of the Archaeology of Eretz Israel." *Jewish Book Annual* 36 (1978): 88-96.

Meyers seeks to review some of the then-recent publications in the field to show "...the nonspecialist how one goes about finding his/her way in this field"—p. 88. He mentions the *Bulletin of the American Schools of Oriental Research* and *Biblical Archaeologist* as two journals through which one can keep up with American research on the subject. Meyers goes on to discuss the Gezer Project of Hebrew Union College's Nelson Glueck School of Biblical Archaeology, and some associated publications. He also mentions the *Israel Exploration Journal* and the *Encyclopedia of Archaeological Excavations*. In a final section on "Useful Guides," he lists A. Negev's *Archaeological Encyclopedia of the Holy Land*, and Brian Fagan's *In the Beginning: An Introduction to Archaeology*, as well as a number of other sources.

C219. Rajak, Tessa. "Contrasting Worlds in First-Century Palestine" [review article]. *Journal of Roman Studies* 72 (1982): 170-174.

Rajak reviews two books, the revision of Vol. 2 of E. Schurer's *The History of the Jewish People in the Age of Jesus Christ*, and P. Vidal-Naquet's *Il Buon Uso del Tradimento: Flavio Giuseppe e la Guerra Giudaica*. The introduction to Josephus' *Jewish War* by Vidal-Naquet is a much smaller work, covering (among other things) the great diversity within Judaism of the first century, which was not as clear to Schurer when he wrote his book.

C220. Vogel, Eleanor K. "Bibliography of Holy Land Sites." *Hebrew Union College Annual* 42 (1971): 1-96.

Vogel lists the Holy Land sites alphabetically, and under each enumerates the persons and organization responsible for archaeological digs, and the years the excavations have continued. She also offers a chronological list of publications dealing with the results of the digs.

C221. Vogel, Eleanor K., and Brooks Holtzclaw. "Bibliography of Holy Land Sites: Part II." *Hebrew Union College Annual* 52 (1981): 1-92.

This sequel to C220 uses the same format as before, iteming publications since 1970 and a few omissions from the previous work.

PASSOVER

C222. Davies, Philip R. "Passover and the Dating of the Aqedah." *Journal of Jewish Studies* 30 (Spring, 1979): 59-67.

Davies begins, "The Jewish doctrine of the Aqedah (=binding) regards the Offering of Isaac, narrated in Gen.22, as an actually accomplished sacrifice in which blood was shed, constituting a definitively expiatory or redemptive act for all Israel"—p. 59. He then examines evidence for whether the idea of Aqedah or the Christian idea of the atonement of Christ came first, thereby influencing the development of the other conception. He concludes: "...we have every ground for believing that the Christian Atonement doctrine together with the emergence in the second century CE of a Christian Isaac-Jesus typology is responsible for the linking of the Aqedah with Passover—as it was, indeed, influential in the development of the Aqedah as a whole"—p. 67.

PAUL THE APOSTLE

C223. Best, Thomas F. "The Apostle Paul and E P Sanders: The Significance of Paul and Palestinian Judaism." *Restoration Quarterly* 25:2 (1982): 65-74.

In his examination of E. P. Sanders's work, Best lists the following items: 1) Sanders views Christianity and Judaism as religions of salvation; 2) Sanders wishes to do away with the thinking of Judaism as a "works-righteousness" religion; 3) Sanders believes the covenant is the presupposition of Rabbinic literature, which Sanders views as practical rather than theoretical.

C224. Bronson, David B. "Paul and Apocalyptic Judaism." *Journal of Biblical Literature* 83 (September, 1964): 287-292.

Bronson argues for the ideas that before his conversion, Paul was an apocalyptic Jew and that he discovered "salvation history." He credits D. Rossler's *Gesetz und Geschichte* (1957) for the idea, since Rossler described the difference between apocalyptic and Rabbinic Judaism. Bronson also notes apocalyptic elements in Paul's theology, such as the importance of the resurrection and exaltation, a cosmic perspective, and the idea of Israel rather than Rome as "the agent of God's healing and restoring purpose in history"—p. 290.

C225. Callan, Terrance. "Pauline Midrash: The Exegetical Background of Gal 3:19b." *Journal of Biblical Literature* 99 (December, 1980): 549-567.

Paul twice uses the setting of the giving of the Law as an argument as to why Gentiles need not obey it—and this is one of those passages. In Galations 3:19b, Paul says the law was ordained by angels but given through a mediator. Following the lead of N. A. Dahl, Callan says that midrashic interpretation of scripture stands behind Paul's comments on the Galations passage, and he places those comments in the context of interpretations of scripture at that time. Since angels are not mentioned in the scriptural account of the giving of the Law, Callan thinks Midrash is the logical background for Paul's remarks.

C226. Cohn-Sherbok, Dan. "Paul and Rabbinic Exegesis." *Scottish Journal of Theology* 35 (April, 1982): 117-132.

Some scholars have asserted that St. Paul employs tools of Rabbinic exegesis to interpret Old Testament passages, and further that he used many of Hillel's seven hermeneutical rules. Cohn-Sherbok says no one has yet undertaken a detailed comparison of Paul's hermeneutics and that of the rabbis, and that is what he does in this article. By examining both direct and indirect exegesis in Paul and the rabbis, he concludes that Paul incorporated a wide variety of traditional modes of Scriptural exegesis. Cohn-Sherbok defines direct and indirect exegesis in this way: "...(1) Direct and explicit exegesis where the Biblical text is commented upon or accompanied by a remark; (2) Indirect exegesis is where a text is cited to support an assertion."

C227. Davies, William D. "Paul and the People of Israel." *New Testament Studies* 24 (October, 1977): 4-39.

Since Paul thinks that faith in the Messiah, rather than observance of the traditional norms or the Law, is the essential mark of belonging to the people of God, Davies wonders what this redefinition does to the Jews as an ethnic identity. In order to answer this, Davies covers the idea of Israel in 1 Thessalonians, Galatians, II Corinthians, and Romans. Paul believes the Jews still have a place in the plan of God, and that their refusal of the Messiah is temporary. Thus, Davies thinks Paul believes the Jews will be saved at the end of history. He writes, "For him, there is no 'solution' to the Jewish question until we are at the very limit of history and at the threshold of the age to come, when God will be all in all and the distinctions of this world even between Jew and Gentile are transcended and even Christ himself is made subordinate to the Father"—p. 34. Further describing Paul's thought, he writes, "For him the particularity of Christ is bound up with the particularity of Abraham and the choseness of his descendants, because it was the same God who was active in them all"—p. 35.

C228. Enslin, Morton S. "Paul and Gamaliel." *Journal of Religion* 7 (July, 1927): 360-375.

The evidence for the idea that Paul studied under Gamaliel in Jerusalem is suspect in Enslin's view, as is the idea, presented from Paul's letters, that Paul had received rabbinical training. Paul's language does not show this kind of instruction, according to Enslin.

C229. Gauenta, Beverly. "Comparing Paul and Judaism: Rethinking Our Methods." *Biblical Theology Bulletin* 10 (January, 1980): 37-44.

A survey of methods previously used to compare Paul and Judaism is followed by an examination of E. P. Sanders's method as presented in his *Paul and Palestinian Judaism*. After offering criticisms of Sanders, Gauenta indicates the need to study these issues deductively—that is, exegetically. She thinks that each of Paul's letters should be examined to see if it individually displays a pattern. Only then could we speak of an overall pattern. She concludes by speaking of one pattern of Paul's religion: namely, that Christians belong exclusively to Christ.

C230. Gundry, Robert H. "Grace, Works and Staying Saved in Paul: (Reply to E. P. Sanders, *Paul and Palestinian Judaism*; *Paul, the Law and Jewish People*)." *Biblica* 66:1 (1985): 1-38.

Gundry takes exception to E. P. Sanders' views of Paul's theology as represented in Sander's books, *Paul and Palestinian Judaism* and *Paul, the Law and the Jewish People.* Though he begins with several pages of grateful acknowledgment of the work Sanders has done, he quickly moves to a more traditional understanding of Paul's thought. For example, "Outside Galatians and Romans, too, Paul repeatedly identifies faith and rejects works as the principle of continuance in salvation...," Gundry writes—p. 9. Gundry refers to the experience of salvation and faithfulness as getting in and staying in respectively. Gundry's main attack on Sanders comes from Gundry's belief that Sanders ignored those elements in first-century Judaism which have been refered to as "works righteousness." He writes, "Since Paul's own righteousness had included works accomplished as well as status granted, we must say that his opposing the works of the law to faith in Christ includes an attack on self-dependence as well as an indication of dispensational shift"—p. 15. Gundry states: "We conclude, then, that Paul is not criticizing the Jew's unbelief in Christ instead of their attempt to perform the law, but that he is criticizing their unbelief as caused by an attempt to perform the law"—p. 19.

C231. Neusner, Jacob. "Sanders' 'Paul and the Jewish People'" [book review]. *Jewish Quarterly Review* 74 (April, 1984): 416-423.

In this reveiw of E. P. Sanders' *Paul, the Law, and the Jewish People,* Neusner says conceptual and epistemological questions he had about Sanders' earlier work have not been answered by this book. Neusner thinks we need to know the historical setting of a saying attributed to a rabbi before we can rightly interpret it. He faults Sanders for several assumptions. "First, it is simply taken for granted that whatever is said by any Rabbi or other authority within the corpus chosen as 'Judaism' testifies to the nature of the 'Judaism' characteristic of most Jews in the 1st century. Second, it is assumed that if a saying is attributed to a Rabbi or a story is told about him, that saying or story tell us about things really said and done, not only at the time of the Rabbi in question, but also in the 1st century. Finally, every difficulty in harmonizing the diverse rabbinic documents is ignored"—p. 416-17. Neusner says this renders everything said about Judaism useless. Neusner then shows how these assumptions operate in the book itself. The essential problem this causes, according to Neusner, is that even though the book talks about many things other than Judaism, the picture of Judaism drawn by Sanders provides the foundation for all the other discussions.

C232. Sanders, E. P. "Patterns of Religion in Paul and Rabbinic Judaism: A Holistic Method of Comparison." *Harvard Theological Review* 66 (October, 1973): 455-478.

Sanders begins by pointing to two ways that Paul and Judaism have been understood. Paul is said to support justification by faith, while Judaism is said to support works righteousness. Sanders points out the oversimplification of these views. The other approach is to concentrate not on generalized essences, but on individual motifs. He then says we need to compare the whole with the whole, but a problem exists in comparing an individual (Paul) with a group (Judaism). Sanders chooses to compare Paul "with one significant variety of Palestinian Judaism, Rabbinic Judaism"—p. 457. He notes the pattern of each religion, though sketchily, he admits. He also says the purpose is not genealogical, in the sense of trying to show Paul derived this or that concept from Judaism. He then describes the Tannaitic pattern, looking at the ideas of election and Temple sacrifice. Along the way he points out problems with the Strack-Billerbeck commentary on the Talmud and Midrash. He then examines the idea of righteousness in Paul's writings. Essentially, Sanders finds a different religious pattern in Paul from that of Judaism. "The religion of the Tannaitic literature revolves around the following concepts: covenant, commandment, obedience, disobedience, guilt, repentance, atonement, and forgiveness. While many of the concepts—though not all, guilt and forgiveness being notably absent—appear here and there in Paul's letters, they are not determinative for Paul's view of the relation between God and man. His thought revolves rather around the polarities death/life; slavery/freedom; in the Flesh/in the Spirit. This is more than a theological dispute among Jews as to whether or not Jesus was the Messiah. This is a totally different religious pattern"—p. 476.

THE PHARISEES

C233. Baumgarten, Albert I. "The Name of the Pharisees." *Journal of Biblical Literature* 102 (September, 1983): 411-428.

Baumgarten examines the use of the word "akribeia" by Josephus, the New Testament, and Nicolaus. He believes the term came from the Pharisees themselves, since it means "scrupulous exactness," and was used to support the Pharisees "claim to excellence." Having compared related terms, he concludes that the term may have meant "the specifiers"—p. 420. He also believes the word "separatist" in a derogatory sense was used in reference to the Pharisees.

C234. Baumgarten, Albert I. "The Pharisaic Paradosis." *Harvard Theological Review* 80 (January, 1987): 63-77.

Baumgarten examines various sources such as Josephus to find how the word "Paradosis" or tradition is used in them in relation to the Pharisees. Since the word appears in independent sources but is used in much the same sense, he proposes that the way the term is used goes back to the Pharisees themselves. The term is a technical one, referring to "regulations observed by the Pharisees but not written in the law of Moses"—p. 66. Baumgarten reviews the debate between the Sadducees and Pharisees on this issue. He also shows how other groups such as the Christians dealt with the issue, and by an examination of the sources, tries to construct what he thinks was the Pharisaic response to the arguments against them.

C235. Cohen, Shaye J. "The Significance of Yavneh: Pharisees, Rabbis and the End of Jewish Sectarianism." *Hebrew Union College Annual* 55 (1984): 27-53.

After 70 CE, the rabbis gathered at Yavneh to launch the "program" which resulted in the Mishnah 100 years later. Cohen says that though the rabbis were probably Pharisees, he thinks there is no evidence that they were motivated by Pharisaic self-consciousness or an "exclusivistic ethic." On the contrary, Cohen thinks the rabbis' goal was to stop sectarianism and create a society where vigorous debate was encouraged. The Mishnah shows conflicting legal opinions, but all contained within the community. In short, Cohen understands Yavneh not as a witch-hunt to exclude others, but as a grand coalition of different groups within the Judaisms of the time.

C236. Cook, Michael J. "Jesus and the Pharisees—The Problem as It Stands Today." *Journal of Ecumenical Studies* 15 (Summer, 1978): 441-460.

Using the New Testament, Josephus, and Rabbinic literature, Cook finds these sources internally contradictory on Jesus' relation to the Pharisees. He examines the problems occasioned by these contradictions, obstacles to defining who the Pharisees were in Jesus' day, and the traditions about conflicts between Jesus and the Pharisees. Cook believes that scholars should strive for expertise in both Rabbinic and New Testament materials, and that there are too many variables to solve the problem of Jesus and the Pharisees, at least at the time when this essay was written.

C237. Ellenson, David. "Ellis Rivkin and the Problems of Pharisaic History: A Study in Historiography." *Journal of the American Academy of Religion* 43 (December, 1975): 787-802.

Analyzing Rivkin's methodological approach and conceptual framework, Ellenson finds that his conceptual model includes four categories: time, structure, process, and causality. Ellenson shows how this model is used to analyze texts, specifically in relation to the origin of the Pharisees.

C238. Geller, Markham J. "Alexander Jannaeus and the Pharisee Rift." *Journal of Jewish Studies* 30 (Autumn, 1979): 202-211.

Geller points out the rift between the Pharisees and the Hasmonean House. He notes that the sources don't agree on which ruler "ostracised" the Pharisees. Josephus says it was Hyrcanus, while bQidd 66a indicates Alexander Jannaeus. Geller cites sources indicating the faithfulness of Hyrcanus to Jewish practice, and upon re-examination of the sources, he concludes the appropriate ruler was actually Jannaeus.

C239. Klijn, A. F. "Scribes, Pharisees, High Priests and Elders in the New Testament." *Novum Testamentum* 3 (1959): 259-267.

Klijn notes differences in parallel Gospel passages which deal with the groups mentioned in his title. He looks at these passages, and traces the next development in the tradition. Among his ideas are that Matthew and Luke hesitate to use the word scribes, preferring to speak of Pharisees. He thinks a distinction must be made between the passion narratives and the other Gospel passages. "It is evident that in the evangelical tradition the significance of the different Jewish groups appears to be unknown. The Pharisees are becoming the most important opponents of Jesus. In certain passages a bringing together of different groups appears to be an attempt to designate the Jewish leaders as a whole"—p. 265.

C240. Marcus, Ralph. "The Pharisees in the Light of Modern Scholarship." *Journal of Religion* 32 (1952): 153-164.

"The English plural form 'Pharisees' comes to us indirectly from the Greek New Testament Pharisaioi, which in turn is based on the Aramaic Perishayya, corresponding to Hebrew Perushim. The Hebrew and Aramaic words mean 'Separatists,' being passive participles of roots meaning 'to separate.' This much is almost certain. What is not so certain is the origin of the name"—p. 153. Marcus goes on to discuss various theories of the origin of the name. He then reviews Jewish history after the Babylonian exile to see if he can discover the origin of the group. Marcus then reviews the writings of Josephus and some literature of the Tannaite period to gain a fuller understanding of the Pharisees. He concludes with a survey of some of the more important scholarly work on the Pharisees, and the relation of Jesus and the Pharisees.

C241. Neusner, Jacob. "From Exegesis to Fable in Rabbinic Traditions About the Pharisees." *Journal of Jewish Studies* 25 (Summer, 1974): 263-269.

Neusner argues for understanding the difference between the Mishnah, which was intended to be transmitted orally, and other documents of the time which may not have independent oral traditions behind them, even where there seem to be two versions of the same story. Neusner takes a clue from redaction criticism of the Gospels, and employs the method to analyze the account of Hillel and the vain prayer. He compares two accounts of this in the Mishnah and writes, "I believe that it is now clear that even within a single pericope we observe the development of an anonymous exegesis into a Hillel-story"—p. 266. He thinks that the story develops from the exegesis, and the story in both versions is secondary and deriviative. "If this be accepted, then I may propose that one version of the Hillel and the prozbul tradition consists of a similar development of exegesis of Deut. 15:3 and Deut. 15:9"—p. 266. He then analyzes how this happened.

C242. Neusner, Jacob. "The Rabbinic Traditions About the Pharisees Before A.D. 70: The Problem of Oral Transmission." *Journal of Jewish Studies* 22:1/4 (1971): 1-18.

"The rabbinic traditions about the Pharisees before A.D. 70 are contained in pericopae of Talmudic and Midrashic literature which mention either those masters who lived before the destruction of the Temple or the Houses of Shammai and Hillel"—p. 1. Neusner says that there are 371 items in 655 passages. He questions the idea of an oral tradition, and begins by pointing out that "...all evidence supporting the oral theory relies on literary data"—p. 4. After reviewing a number of problems with the ideal of an oral tradition (as it has normally been thought of among the scholars), Neusner concludes, "...the traditions before 70 are not said to have been orally formulated and orally transmitted in the manner of the later rabbinical Tannaim. We are, in fact, nowhere told how the Pharisees before A.D. 70 preserved their extra-biblical traditions"—p. 18.

C243. Rivkin, Ellis. "Defining the Pharisees: The Tannaitic Sources." *Hebrew Union College Annual* 40-41 (1969-1970): 205-249.

Though Rivkin recognizes that Josephus, the New Testament, and the tannaitic literature all display a lack of clarity about the Pharisees, he decides to build a definition of the Pharisees from the tannaitic literature using self-validating controls. In the first group of texts he examines, he discovers that the term prusim is always juxtaposed to Sadducees. There are other texts where the use of this term has a non-Pharisee meaning or is ambiguous. There are texts where prusim means ascetics and heretics, and so the use of the term itself is not sufficient. Only those texts which juxtapose prusim to sduqim or Sadducees prove to be useful. Rivkin's definition of the Pharisees has several elements. First, they were "...a scholar class dedicated to the supremacy of the twofold Law, the Written and the Unwritten"—p. 247. They opposed the Sadducees on this point, and even set up the regulations for the burning of the red heifer, insisting that the High Priest follow their lead. "The Pharisees utilized this name, only in controversies with the Sadducees. In all other texts, they appear as the hakamim 'Sages,' as the sofrim 'Scribes,' as the scholar class legislating the anonymous halaka, as individual spokesmen for the class, as the scholars who sit in the bet din 'Legislature'"—p. 247. The term prusim actually has the definition of heretic at some points, and so Rivkin thinks it was used by the Sadducees to challenge the authority of the Pharisees and make the word "Pharisee" an undesirable term. "The scrupulous avoidance of the name prusim by the hakamim-sofrim thus accounts for the paradox that the very literature that would be expected to give us the most information about the Pharisees hardly ever mentions them by this name at all." "The Pharisees once liberated from the limited, circumscribed, and rare usage of prusim and identified as the hakamim-sofrim can reclaim their identity as that scholar class that created the concept of the twofold Law, carried it to triumphant victory over the Sadducees, and made it operative in society"—p. 248.

C244. Rivkin, Ellis. "Pharisaism and the Crisis of the Individual in the Greco-Roman World." *Jewish Quarterly Review* 61 (July, 1970): 27-53.

Rivkin wonders "...not only of how monotheism vanquished polytheism, but of how the Pentateuchal Judaism of a relatively undeveloped agricultural-priestly society could grip the hearts and minds of individuals nurtured in polytheism and acculturated to urbanization"—p. 28. He also wonders where Christianity found those elements which made it unique, particularly in its concern for the individual. He finds it in "...a revolutionary form of Judaism that emerged at a time when the Hellenistic monarchies were giving clear signs of disintegration and that transmuted a hierocratic, cultic, agriculturally-oriented Pentateuchal Judaism into a Judaism centered in the aspirations of the individual for eternal individuation, solace, comfort, inner security and reassurance, and in a God sovereign over multiplicity and frightening novelty. This revolutionary form was Pharisaism, and the raw materials from which it emerged were Pentateuchal monotheism, polis institutions, Hellenistic modes of thought and analysis, and creative innovation"—p. 29.

C245. Rivkin, Ellis. "Scribes, Pharisees, Lawyers, Hypocrites: A Study in Synonymity." *Hebrew Union College Annual* 49 (1978): 135-142.

Rivkin looks at the way the scribes and Pharisees seem to be spoken of as one and the same group in Matthew 23 and in other portions of Matthew. He says the solution to this problem is to understand that the Hebrew word "sofer" was used by Ben Sira, while the originally equivalent Greek word "grammateus" did not undergo such a change. Jesus would have used the term "soferim" to refer to the Pharisees, and not "perushim," the term used by the Sadducees. However, when the Greek term "grammateus" was used to translate this word, the term "Pharisee" was added to clarify Greek understanding.

C246. Roth, Cecil. "The Pharisees in the Jewish Revolution of 66-73." *Journal of Semitic Studies* 7 (Spring, 1962): 63-80.

Roth characterizes the Pharisees as being interested in personal conduct but not in politics. "The Pharisees hence played no part qua Pharisees in the great Revolt against Rome in the autumn of 66, although doubtless the crowds that thronged the streets and were the backbone of the insurrection were largely or even predominantly Pharisee in complexion"—p. 63. Roth then reviews the activities of the leader of the Revolt, R. Simon (Simeon) ben Gamaliel, using some Talmudic material and Josephus for some of the survey, and employs a chronological approach for the events. He concludes by briefly covering some of the other rabbis of the period and their relation to the Revolt. He thinks the Pharisees were neutral or even opposed to the Revolt at the beginning, but that once it happened they accepted it. Several prominent Pharisees were appointed to various government posts.

C247. Schwartz, Daniel R. "Josephus and Nicolaus on the Pharisees." *Journal for the Study of Judaism in the Persian, Hellenistic and Roman Period* 14 (December, 1983): 157-171.

"In this study, I propose to examine Josephus' statements regarding the Pharisees, in order to determine to what extent they are his own original compositions or rather taken over from the writings of Nicolaus of Damascus"—p. 157. Schwartz finds hostility towards the Pharisees in Josephus steming from a conviction that they were the ones who incited the masses against the rulers. Schwartz explains the differences of view on the Pharisees in the *Antiquities* and the *Vita* from the view in Jewish Wars as stemming from the fact that they were written at different times. The non-political view of the Pharisees was taken when the rebellion against Rome was closer to the time of writing. "...we must note that in BJ, but not in AJ, Josephus suppressed Nicolaus' claim that the oath which the Pharisees refused expressed loyalty not only to Herod, but also to Augustus"—p. 161. Schwartz argues that Josephus used accounts by Nicolaus, but that he altered them at crucial points.

C248. Wild, Robert A. "The Encounter Between Pharisaic and Christian Judaism: Some Early Gospel Evidence." *Novum Testamentum* 27 (April, 1985):105-124.

Wild examines pre-70 CE traditions in the Gospels concerning whether Jesus' early followers, perhaps even Jesus himself, were Pharisees. He begins by examining Neusner's view that the Pharisees were not always dominant. He then moves to Gospel passages, and argues that Matthew 23:23, for example, shows a Pharisaic approach on the part of Jesus to tithing. Wild concludes, "...yet while such a theory holds some attraction for me, I must nonetheless stress the absence of clearly probative evidence for it"—p. 124.

C249. Zeitlin, Solomon. "The Origin of the Pharisees Re-affirmed." *Jewish Quarterly Review* 59 (April, 1969): 255-267.

Zeitlin says many scholars argue that the Pharisees began at the time of Jonathan the Hasmonean. He argues that they originated in the latter part of the fifth century BCE, and not during the second century BCE. "It was at the time of the canonization of the Pentateuch that there arose a difference of views in regard to the unwritten laws"—p. 257. Zeitlin then reviews the arguments with Dr. Louis Finkelstein, and offers his own interpretation of the evidence: "Dr. Finkelstein, who has retracted from his former position and advances the theory that the Pharisees came into being in the early part of the fourth century BCE, does not explain the forces which brought about their origin"—p. 266. Zeitlin ends by reaffirming his original opinion that the Pharisees originate in the fifth century BCE.

C250. Zeitlin, Solomon. "Pharisees: A Historical Study." *Jewish Quarterly Review* 52 (October, 1961): 97-129.

Zeitlin writes that the general view that the Pharisees or Perushim were called that because they separated themselves from those who were unclean, and that the Perushim and Haberim were identical, are views which are historically inaccurate. "No reference is made in the entire tannaitic literature of antgonism between the Perushim and the Ame ha'aretz. ...in the early tannaitic literature the term Ame ha'aretz has the connotation of farmers. It has also been held that the Pharisees separated themselves from the Essenes. This view likewise is untenable since there is no reference in the entire tannaitic literature to any discussion between the Essenes and the Pharisees"—p. 98. Zeitlin then makes a case for the idea that the opponents of the Pharisees were the Zadokites or Sadducees, and he investigates the sources to determine when this conflict came about between the two groups. "It was at the time of the canonization of the Pentateuch that there arose a difference of views, ideology, in regard to the Halakot"—p. 102. "The clash of different views on the binding of the oral law on man could not have arisen during the Hasmonean period when the Judaean community had been in existence for many centuries. It could come only after the Pentateuch was canonized"—p. 104-05. Zeitlin examines evidence in Josephus and the Talmud for his viewpoint. "We have the right to maintain that some controversies between the Pharisees and Jesus and his disciples could not have occurred during their lifetime"—p. 121. He concludes with this interesting remark: "In the hearts of the Jews, Eretz Israel, was always considered the Holy Land, the Land of Israel, the land that always belonged to them. They never abandoned the hope that a new state would be established in the land of Israel"—p. 129.

C251. Zeitlin, Solomon. "Spurious Interpretations of Rabbinic Sources in the Studies of the Pharisees and Pharisaism." *Jewish Quarterly Review* 65 (October, 1974): 122-135.

Zeitlin says the Talmud speaks of two different goups of Perushim or separatists. The group which separated themselves from mundane life are attacked in the Talmud, but the group identified as perushim by the Sadducees are not attacked. The lack of distinguishing these two groups leads John Bowker to misunderstand the Talmud, Zeitlin asserts. He also shows that the term "rebellious elder" arose after the destruction of the Temple, and was used of a member of the Sanhedrin who revolted against the decisions of his colleagues. Thus, Bowker's claim that Jesus was tried as a rebellious elder is said to be untrue. Zeitlin also says that Jacob Neusner does not properly distinguish tannaitic, amoriaic, and rabbinic sources, and that he does not understand or comprehend Talmudic sources, offering several examples to support his assertion.

THE SABBATH

C252. Hoenig, Sidney. "The Designated Number of Kinds of Labor Prohibited on the Sabbath." *Jewish Quarterly Review* 68 (April, 1978): 193-208.

"Mishnah Shabbat lists the major acts forbidden on the Sabbath and gives their number as 'forty less one'"—p. 193. "Even though the association of the prohibited kinds of labor on the Sabbath with the Tabernacle performances was recognized by the Tannaim, the reason for the numerical designation of 39 was still sought by later Sages"—p. 195. "To sum up, the Tabernacle association became the basic key adopted by the Rabbis, and the specification of the 39 kinds of work was but an attempt to define and stress the precise meaning of melakhah in the general and all-inclusive phrase 'Ye shall not do any manner of work'"—p. 198. Hoenig then points out that the Book of Jubilees lists 22 kinds of work: "I would suggest that the popular number 22 (an ancient figure for totality of fullness) for the acts of creation and Sabbatical prohibitions preceded the Rabbinic enumeration of 39 kinds of labor prohibited on the Sabbath"—p. 202. "While the affinity of the Sabbatical kinds of labor to the Tabernacle may have been an early tradition stemming from Ezra's period, the actual implementation of the relationship took place in the time of Rabbi 'Akiba, who in his methodology and hermeneutics regarded all basic laws as derived from the period of the Exodus and the Sinaitic Revelation"—p. 205.

C253. Hoenig, Sidney. "An Interdict Against Socializing on the Sabbath." *Jewish Quarterly Review* 62 (October, 1971): 77-83.

Hoenig takes exception to various translations and interpretations of the Zadokite fragment text XI, line 4. Rather than referring to fasting or competition or pooling property as forbidden activities on the Sabbath, he thinks that we must look at the word "voluntarily" as the key to the passage. The exact meaning of the text can only be ascertained "by probing the basic source of this Zadokite rule of 'not mingling on the Sabbath'"—p. 81. Hoenig finds this source in the text of Sahl ben Masliah, a tenth-century Karaite who argued against free social mingling on the Sabbath. "Both the Essenes and Zealots, whether ascetic or belligerent, did not frown on Sabbath mingling. Only the Karaites mentioned and maintained such conduct"—p. 83.

C254. Wacholder, Ben Z. "The Calendar of Sabbatical Cycles During the Second Temple and the Early Rabbinic Period." *Hebrew Union College Annual* 44 (1973): 153-196.

The observance of the Sabbatical year is also known as Release or Shemitah. Wacholder dicusses the pledge to keep Shemitah, the exemption of the Jews from taxation duriing the Shemitah by Alexander, the ascription of the defeat of Judah Maccabee's defeat at Beth-Zur to the Shemitah, whether the Temple was destroyed during a Sabbatical or post-Sabbatical year, and several other topics. The article ends with a lengthy "Calendar of Sabbatical Cycles From 519/18 Before the Christian Era to 440/41 of the Christian Era." This calendar includes a list of the rulers during the various periods.

THE SADDUCEES

C255. Isenberg, Sheldon R. "An Anti-Sadducee Polemic in the Palestinian Targum Tradition." *Harvard Theological Review* 63 (July, 1970): 433-444.

Isenberg examines the massoretic text and various Targums of Genesis 4:3-16. A section of haggadah in the Targums commenting on Vol. 8 of the Genesis 4 passage could be an anti-Sadducee polemic, Isenberg believes, because the Sadduceean position is put in the mouth of the "primal murderer and heretic," Cain.

THE SAMARITANS

C256. Brindle, Wayne A. "The Origin and History of the Samaritans." *Grace Theological Journal* 5 (Spring, 1984): 47-75.

Brindle thinks the formation of Samaritanism was a process rather than a single event, and he lists the following items as a part of the process which also led to animosity between the Samaritans and the Jews: 1) division of the kingdom into north and south (c.931 BCE); 2) the conquest of Israel by Assyria and the importation of foreign peoples and religions; 3) the rejection of the Samaritans by Ezra and Nehemiah; 4) the building of a temple on Mt. Gerizim; 5) the reconstruction of Shechem as the capital of the Samaritans; 6) political and religious "opportunism" by the Samaritans during the persecutions of Antiochus IV; 7) the destruction of the Samaritan temple and Shechem by John Hyrcanus—p. 75.

C257. Collins, Marilyn F. "The Hidden Vessels in Samaritan Traditions." *Journal for the Study of Judaism in the Persian, Hellenistic and Roman Period* 3 (December, 1972): 97-116.

Collins begins with a quote from Josephus (*Antiquities* xviii,4,1) in which Josephus describes a Samaritan gathering at Mt. Gerizim, where they would be shown where the sacred vessels were buried. Collins takes Josephus to be an important early witness to the Samaritan belief in the restoration of true worship in the eschatological age. After reviewing apocraphal, Rabbinic, and Samaritan literature, Collins concludes: 1) the Samaritans had developed a tradition about hidden vessels by the time of Josephus; 2) the tradition about the vessels varies in the literature; 3) an eschatological prophet like Moses was expected; and 4) the Moses figure assimilated Elijah and Jeremiah functions.

C258. Schiffman, Lawrence H. "The Samaritans in Tannaitic Halakhah." *Jewish Quarterly Review* 75 (April, 1985): 323-350.

Schiffman says, "...to the Tannaim and their followers, status within or without the Jewish people was determined only by the halakhic definitions of 'Who is a Jew?' outlined in the various Tannaitic texts"—p. 323. "In the present paper we propose to investigate those who were on the borderline of this process. The Samaritans, as we shall see, were neither in nor out. They constituted a class of 'semi-Jews,' whose identity and legal status were repeatedly to perplex the Tannaim. While halakhic concerns affecting the mutual relationship of the two groups had a profound and lasting effect on Rabbinic views of the Samaritans"—p. 323. Schiffman then reviews two views of the origins of the Samaritans. "Tannaitic reactions to this group proceeded from the assumption that the Scriptural account of the schism found in 2 Kings 17 was accurate"—p. 325. He then reviews Tannatic halakhah in relation to the status of the Samaritans, marriage law, sacrificial law, tithing, and signal torches, which were originally used by the Tannaim to "...inform Jewish communities outside of Israel that a new month had been decreed by observation"—p. 345.

C259. Sloyan, Gerard S. "The Samaritans in the New Testament." *Horizons* 10 (Spring, 1983): 7-21.

Sloyan finds a polemical purpose behind the parable of the good Samaritan, since it must have "rankled those Judean, Galilean and diaspora Jews to whose notice it came"—p. 7. He looks at the scholarly conclusions about the relations of the Jews and Samaritans, and brings his own ideas to the table. Beginning with a study of the Bible on Samaritan separatism, he then looks at when the Jews of Samaria became Samaritans, and reviews material in Josephus on the Samaritans. Finally, he examines the New Testament words about the Samaritans, and the idea of Samaria in the Gospel of John and Acts. Sloyan's own theory is that the Christian movement could not have contemplated an outreach beyond the Jews "...had it not had firmly embedded in its historical consciousness the fact of Jesus' insensitivity to old taboos"—p. 21. "I suggest here only that the ancient schism with Samaria struck his Jewish heart as all wrong. The community reminiscences of his teaching and conduct (although not those committed to the first gospel stratum) were of out-reach to this despised people"—p. 21.

SANHEDRIN

C260. Burkill, T. A. "Competence of the Sanhedrin." *Vigiliae Christianae* 10 (1956): 80-96.

Burkhill considers the arguments that the Sanhedrin did not have the power to inflict capital punishment, and finds them unconvincing. He argues with the conclusions of G. D. Kilpatrick's book, *The Trial of Jesus,* and with a paper by Joachim Jeremias about the powers of the Sanhedrin. He then examines passages in Josephus, the New Testament, and the Mishnah. He argues that the Sanhedrin had the power to inflict capital punishment on Jews "convicted of capital offences against the law of their religion"—p. 96.

C261. Zeitlin, Solomon. "The Political Synedrion in the Religious Sanhedrin." *Jewish Quarterly Review* 36 (1945-1946): 109-140.

Zeitlin presents his arguments in support of the idea that at the time of Jesus there were two Sanhedrins, one a state court, and the other a religious Sanhedrin. He first examines the use of the word synedrion in the Greek authors, II Maccabees, Philo, Josephus, and others. He then discusses the development of the judicial system presented in the Bible and during the Maccabeean period, and of the Bet Din in relation to the Sanhedrin. He supports the idea that Jesus was tried before a state synedrion or council. Zeitlin finishes with a word to his critics: "The students of the New Testament should revise their point of view as to actual responsibility for the crucifixion. The Romans with their stooges—the high priests—crucified many Jews who fought for Jewish freedom and the equality of men before God"—p. 140.

THE SERMON ON THE MOUNT

C262. Lachs, Samuel T. "Some Textual Observations on the Sermon on the Mount." *Jewish Quarterly Review* 69 (October, 1978): 98-111.

Lachs says that though much investigation concerning the Semitic sources for Gospel material has been confined to Aramaic, now that the Qumran texts have appeared, Hebrew must be included as well. Semitic and Rabbinic sources should be used to reconstruct the era in which Jesus lived. "Matthew created a sermon on a mountain in order to present a parallel to the theophany at Sinai, while Luke, finding no necessity to relate his material to that event, omits the mountain scene"—p. 99. Lachs points out that even in the first verse about the Sermon, Jesus "sitting" was a common practice for teachers of his time. Lachs goes on to suggest several alternative readings to some of the verses in the Sermon. For example, he suggests that instead of the idea that Jesus condemned sounding a trumpet while giving alms to the poor, the word should be understood to refer to shofar or "...a container shaped in the form of a horn, hence its name, narrow at the top and wide at the bottom, used as a receptacle for monies given for various charitable purposes"—p. 105. Lachs makes several suggestions of Hebrew words which might be behind the Greek text, and which he thinks might clear up confusion regarding some of the sayings.

THE SON OF MAN

C263. Casey, Maurice. "The Use of Term 'Son of Man' in the Similitudes of Enoch." *Journal for the Study of Judaism in the Persian, Hellenistic and Roman Period* 7 (June, 1976): 11-29.

Casey believes that the term "son of man" in the Similitudes is simply an expression for man and not a heavenly redeemer. He explains why he disagrees with T. W. Manson on this point, and says the term is not a title or a corporate designation. He also points to three different ethiopic terms for "son of man" in the Similitudes, which he says are translation variations. He concludes by reviewing specific passages, and arguing that the "son of man" is Enoch.

THE SYNAGOGUE

C264. Berkouits, Eliezer. "From the Temple to Synagogue and Back." *Judaism* 8 (Fall, 1959): 303-311.

In moving from Temple to synagogue, knowledge of Torah became an obligation, and the rabbi, who was now the leader, rather than the priest, had no religious duties which were not binding on all Jews. However, Berkowitz does find some "regression" to the "clericalism" of the Temple.

C265. Ehrhardt, A. "Birth of the Synagogue and R. Abiba." *Studia Theologica* 9:2 (1955): 86-111.

Ehrhardt tries to build a case for the idea that the synogogue is really a "little sister" of the church, and in its essential form did not come into being until after 70 CE. (Recent scholarship has shown that the synagogue was an active place in Exilic times and perhaps before.) He uses Christian sources to build his case. He traces the struggle between Gamaliel and Akiba at Jamnia, and credits Akiba's insistence on the importance of studying the Law with turning mere meeting places into synogogues. "...the method of rabbinical teaching, if we can assess it correctly, was still in an amorphous state. Gamaliel II, as we have seen, centralized the administrative system of the Synagogue but it was the establishment of the Mishnaic principle which caused the specifically Jewish system of education to become the center of Jewish life"—p. 110.

C266. Meyers, Eric. "Ancient Synagogues in Galilee: Their Religious and Cultural Setting." *Biblical Archaeologist* 43 (Spring, 1980): 97-108.

Meyers writes, "The aim of the present study is to show how earlier researches on the subject of ancient Palestinian synagogues created a developmental typology which has led to a somewhat mistaken understanding of various cultural and religious currents in the Talmudic period"—p. 97. He then mentions the work of M. Avi-Yonah, who outlined three synagogue types, and said there was a straight chronological development of the three, one after another. Meyers shows that they often existed simultaneously. Meyers says that it has been established that "the earliest synagouges in ancient Palestine existed in the 1st century C.E."—p. 99. He discusses whether the evidence of recent archaeology supports the idea that the worshipers always faced Jerusalem. He reviews the basilica type synagogue along with the broadhouse and apsidal types. He ends by noting a conservative tendency in representational art that characterized Upper Galilee, and thinks that the data which shows a interest in self-differentiation in terms of site location is evidence for a genuine religious pluralism among the Jews.

THE TEMPLE

C267. Baumgarten, Joseph M. "Exclusions from the Temple: Proselytes and Agrippa I." *Journal of Jewish Studies* 33 (Spring-Autumn, 1982): 215-225.

Baumgarten focuses on whether proselytes were excluded from sacred areas of the Temple. He examines Qumran document 11 Q Temple 40:6, a Temple warning inscription, and an account in Josephus of an incident during the time of Agrippa I. He concludes, "In sum, none of the sources we have considered provides decisive evidence that proselytes were actually excluded from the Jerusalem Temple"—p. 225.

C268. Bilde, Per. "Roman Emperor Gaius (Caligula)'s Attempt to Erect His Statue in the Temple of Jerusalem." *Studia Theologica* 32:1 (1978): 67-93.

Having described the description of Gaius' attempt as presented in Josephus and Philo, Bilde examines the demolition of the imperial altar at Jamnia as an event which he believes is essential to understanding Gaius "project." In order to avoid the idea of contradiction between Josephus and Philo, Bilde argues for "tendency" and "literary form" as part of historical criticism.

C269. Derrett, J. Duncano. "The Zeal of the House and the Cleansing of the Temple." *Downside Review* 95 (April, 1977): 79-94.

Because of comments by D. Daube, Derrett re-examines the theory that Jesus was put to death because of his attack on the Temple. Derrett tries to resolve the image of Jesus as meek with the image of Jesus "cleansing" the Temple. He says Jesus' essential function required "multifaceted activity." He looks in special detail at the account in Mark 11: 15-19, and concludes that the Gospel writers do not present Jesus as starting a revolution, but as a prophet demonstrating the "authority inhering in him"—p. 92.

C270. Horsley, Richard A. "High Priests and the Politics of Roman Palestine." *Journal for the Study of Judaism in the Persian, Hellenistic and Roman Period* 17 (June, 1986): 23-55.

Horsley finds E. Mary Smallwood's assertion that the Jewish High Priests in the first century CE were not as pro-Roman as had been believed, to be misleading and sometimes incorrect, based on a contextual analyis of Josephus. He believes the Jewish aristocracy pursued their own political-economic interests through collaboration with Rome, and concludes that the High Priests followed rather than led popular protests.

C271. Kaufman, Asher S. "A Note on Artistic Representations of the Second Temple of Jerusalem." *Biblical Archaeologist* 47 (December, 1984): 253-254.

Kaufman examines a coin from the Bar Kokhba period which has a representation of the façade of the hekhal of the Second Temple. Noting a wavy line, he uses various passages of the Mishnah and Babylonian Talmud to support his idea that the line represents the "wisp of scarlet pinned to the façade of the hekhal on the Day of Atonement." He points out the importance of supplementing other archaeological finds with the written record of the time.

C272. Levenson, Jon D. "The Temple and the World." *Journal of Religion* 64 (July, 1984): 275-298.

Levenson shows that a generation of scholars, including Bernhard W. Anderson, John Bright, and George E. Mendenhall, all thought the Temple represented an influence of foreign religion right in the heart of Israel's faith. Paul D. Hanson takes a different view in his book, *The Dawn of Apocalyptic.* Hanson sees two parties at work. "At first glance, Hanson's position appears to be the opposite of that of Anderson, Bright and Mendenhall. He sees the Temple as the bailiwick of exclusivisitic reactionaries, whereas they see it as a dangerous innovation that results from excessive openness toward foreign culture. In fact, the contradiction disappears when we recall that they are writing of the early years of the First Temple, whereas Hanson treats the Second Temple period"—p. 277. Levenson says all these scholars prefer the prophets to the religion of the Temple, and this has caused problems in understanding the Temple. This amounts to the use of a canon within the canon to judge the Temple negatively. He then goes on to develop his criticism of this approach, because in his view it "...links up, first, with certain Protestant tendencies and, second, with a kindred bias toward cultural purism, to yield a position which is indefensible"—p. 278. Levenson closes his article with a positive assessment of the Temple: "The world which the Temple incarnates in a tangible way is not the world of history but the world of creation, the world not as it is but as it was meant to be and as it was on the first Sabbath." "The presence of God is not diminished but concentrated. The glory that had filled the world now fills the Tabernacle and its successors, the Temples of Jerusalem. The Temple is the world before the divine contraction, the world in a state of grace and perfection. No wonder temples in the ancient Near East sometimes contained a paradisal garden and no wonder that Zion, the Temple mountain, 'perfect in beauty' (Ps 50:2; Lam. 2:15), was equated with the Garden of Eden"—p. 297.

C273. Mandell, Sara. "Who Paid the Temple Tax When the Jews Were Under Roman Rule?" *Harvard Theological Review* 77 (April, 1984): 223-232.

Mandell describes the theory that has been accepted for some time that every Jewish man over twenty paid the Temple tax because it was pentateuchal law; and that when Jerusalem fell in 70 CE, the Romans imposed the Didrachmon tax to suppor the upkeep of the temple of Juppiter Capitolinus, and that this was paid universally, as had been the Temple tax. However, Mandell says the primary literature does not support this view. She points out that Mek. Exod 19:1 is one rabbinic text which shows that not all Jews paid the Temple tax, and that the other texts normally chosen to show that they did neither support the idea of a universal tax nor identify the taxes spoken of as the Temple tax. "When Josephus states that all who lived as Jews, anywhere, were subject to the Roman tax as they had previously been subject to the Temple Tax (Bell. 7.6.6 par. 218), he shows that the Romans classify as Jews those who follow the paternal customs or live a Jewish life. But as far as we know, the Pharisees and or the Rabbis were the only sects remaining after the revolt who followed paternal customs or lived a Jewish life. Therefore it was the Pharisees and/or the Rabbis who were classified as Jews by the Romans. We do not know if the Romans also defined others of Jewish stock as Jews"—p. 225-26. Mandell also discusses a number of incorrect beliefs about how widespread the Didrachmon tax was in terms of Jewish payment. She concludes, "Since the Didrachmon was imposed upon circumcised Jews who followed the paternal customs and lived a Jewish life, as a substitute for the Temple Tax which they had paid before 70 CE, and since these Jews were collectively treated as part of the Pharisaic-Rabbinic sect, there can be no doubt that the Temple Tax was paid by these same people: the Pharisaic Jews"—p. 232.

C274. Neusner, Jacob. "Judaism in a Time of Crisis: Four Responses to the Destruction of the Second Temple." *Judaism* 21 (Summer, 1972): 313-327.

Neusner thinks the crisis which faced the Jews was primarily social and religious, not political. He looks at the apocalyptic response, as well as the responses of the Dead Sea community, the Christians, and the Pharisees before and after 70 CE. He concludes with a few words about the response of contemporary Jews.

C275. Saldarini, Anthony J. "Varieties of Rabbinic Response to the Destruction of the Temple." *Society of Biblical Literature Seminar Papers*, No. 21 (1982): 437-458.

Saldarini points to a lack of a systematic discussion of the loss of the Temple in the Talmud. "The halakic literature treats problems occasioned by the loss of the Temple as they occur, but does not ordinarily enter into an extended discussion of the destruction itself or a systematic account of adaptations made"—p. 437. Various responses to the loss of the Temple are the Mishnah, the Bar Kochba War, and certain sections of the midrash, especially midrash on Lamentations. Salarini discusses the work, *The Fathers According to Rabbi Nathan*, where in the interpretation of the sayings of Simeon the Righteous there is an extensive discussion of the destruction of the Temple. Both versions, A and B, are discussed. The article then turns to the Babylonian Talmud Tractate Gittin and Mishnaic discussion of the purchase of land within Israel from Gentiles. Tractate Gittin also has a story of Bar Qamsa as the cause for the destruction of Jerusalem. Saldarini closes with a discussion of the historical problems with the sources, and a review of the importance of Johanan ben Zakkai, who is a central figure in several of the sources.

C276. Zeitlin, Solomon. "The Temple and Worship: A Study of the Development of Judaism: A Chapter in the History of the Second Jewish Commonwealth." *Jewish Quarterly Review* 51 (January, 1961): 209-241.

Zeitlin says the Temple was the spiritual center of Jews, even if they lived outside Judea. He uses Biblical and rabbinic literature to describe the importance of the Temple in Jewish life, as well as the architecture of the Temple and its surroundings. He then discusses the services held in the Temple, the functions of the high priest and the other priests, and the nature of the sacrifices performed there.

THE TRIAL OF JESUS

C277. Danby, H. "The Bearing of the Rabbinical Criminal Code on the Jewish Trial Narratives in the Gospels." *Journal of Theological Studies* 21 (October, 1919): 51-76.

Danby focuses on the examination of Jesus before the Jewish authorities. "How far can evidence contained in the Mishna and kindred literature as to the Sanhedrin's procedure in cases of crimes punishable by death be regarded as of value for the criticism and illustration of the Gospel narratives?"—p. 52. He says previous research has rested on two questionable assumptions: first, "that the Gospels combined give us an essentially complete description of a formal process before a Sanhedrin..."; and second, "that what Jewish scholars at the end of the second century thought to be correct law and procedure was necessarily the accepted practice at the beginning of the first."—p. 55-56. Having examined Mark and Luke's accounts and the Tract Sanhedrin, he doubts that Jesus was put on trial in the technical sense, and holds that the authorities were only permitted a preliminary investigation.

C278. Gordis, Robert, ed. "The Trial of Jesus in the Light of History: A Symposium." *Judaism* 20 (Winter, 1971): 6-74.

Presentations include: "Reflections on the Trial of Jesus," by Haim Cohn; "The Temple and the Cross," by Morton S. Enslin; "A Literary Approach to the Trial of Jesus," by David Flusser; "The Trial of Jesus in the Light of History," by Robert M. Grant; "The Trial of Jesus," by S. G. F. Brandon; "The Trial of Jesus in the Light of History," by Josef Blinzler; "The Last Days of Jesus," by Gerard S. Sloyan; and "The Trial of Jesus: Reservations," by Samuel Sandmel. Sandmel shows the frustration of scholars who deal with this subject, and try to separate historical fact from tendentious purpose, when he writes: "The point is not at all that I regard the Gospel material on the trial of Jesus as devoid of all historical basis, and as only a tissue of legend and of Tendenz. The case, rather, is that I simply do not know how, as a historian, I can separate whatever may be the kernel of historical reality from the other material which I am convinced is not historically accurate. In short, I give up on the problem."—p. 71.

THE ZEALOTS

C279. Brandon, S. G. F. "The Zealots: The Jewish Resistance Against Rome A.D. 6-73." *History Today* 15 (September, 1965): 632-641.

Brandon begins with an explanation of why foreign domination was so oppressive for the Jews, and why it was often perceived as a threat to their religon: "From his childhood, the Jew was brought up to believe that he was a member of a nation, chosen specially by God, out of all other peoples, for a peculiar destiny"—p. 632. The Maccabean victory over the Seleucid rulers seemed to confirm that God would give Israel divine aid in their battles. When Rome incorporated Palestine into the empire, the issue of taxes—or as the Jews saw it, "tribute"—to Rome became a source of offense to most of the people, because they believed that God's own nation should not be required to give money to a foreign nation. Indeed, the taxes collected by Rome supported a government whose head of state thought himself divine. When a census was ordered by the Romans, Judas of Galilee rallied his countrymen to revolt, and although the rebels were defeated, many survivors fled to the hills. Brandon believes that this was the beginning of the Zealot movement. He further points out that we are dependent on Josephus alone for much of the history of this time, and he thinks this is a problem. Josephus's own good standing with Rome meant that he stood to gain by not antagonizing potential patrons, and so he often did not raise the issue of the Zealots' activity at points where Brandon thinks it would have been most likely that the Zealots would have rebelled against the Romans. He also believes that Josephus was hostile to the Zealots (whom he often calls brigands or bandits) because he thought that revolt would only mean the ultimate destruction of the Jews. "Josephus does not use the name 'Zealot' until he comes to describe the revolutionary events in Jerusalem during the winter of A.D. 66-67. What he then says of them reveals his own attitude. Referring to the Zealots, he comments, 'For that was the name they went by, as if they were zealous in good undertakings, and were not rather zealous in the worst actions, and extravagant in them beyond the example of others' (*War* IV, 160-1)"—p. 637.

C280. Roth, Cecil. "Zealots in the War of 66-73." *Journal of Semetic Studies* 4 (October, 1959): 332-355.

Roth again depends on Josephus's accounts for his argument, even though he thinks that Josephus opposed the Zealots, because they were his political enemies and because they were more steadfast than he was. "In the present paper, the attempt will be made to describe the part played by the Zealots in the War of 66-73 in a purely historical sense, and on an analogy with the record and experience of similar groups at similar revolutionary periods in other ages"—p. 333. Roth believes the Sicarii and the Zealots are actually the same group, those identified by Josephus as supporting the "fourth philosophy," with both a political and religious agenda: "At the time of the war against Rome, then, there were two wings, and two leaderships, of the Zealot party. The one, referred to consistently by Josephus as the sicarii, had their base on the Dead Sea, controlling not only Masadah but also a fairly considerable territory in that neighbourhood: this was headed as has been said by Eleazar ben Jair. The other was centered in Jerusalem, and its outstanding figure was another Eleazar, Eleazar ben Simon, described by Josephus (*Wars* IV, 225) as 'the most influential man of the sect, from his ability both to conceive appropriate measures and to carry them into effect'"—p. 342. The Jerusalem group seized the Temple area, Roth thinks, because they were afraid the priestly group was about to come to terms with the Romans. Roth then describes the fighting that persisted until the end of the war: "It was during the great war against the Romans of 66-73 that they were an independent force, and in this period that their social, religious, and political ideals received their fullest expression"—p. 355.

C281. Smith, Morton. "Zealots and Sicarii: Their Origins and Relation." *Harvard Theological Review* 64 (January, 1971): 1-19.

Smith begins with a survey of studies that have been done on the founder of the Zealots, and what the relation of the Sicarii was to the Zealots. He surveys some of the most important studies of this issue, pointing out strengths and weakness of those studies along the way. He mentions some of the evidence from Josephus, and in a concluding paragraph writes, "In all this history there is no evidence of any connection of these Sicarii with the Zealots. The latter, as a party, did not come into existence until the winter of 67-68 (more than a year after Menahem had been murdered and his followers driven out)..."—p. 19.

GLOSSARY

AMORAIM—authors of literature included in a compendium put together somewhere between two and three centuries after the completion of the Mishnah. These were the Jewish scholars of the third and fourth centuries CE. Their views are often included in the Talmud.

APOCRYPHA—ancient Jewish and Christian writings which bore some affinity to the Bible, but which did not make it into the Protestant canon.

GEMARA—Together Mishnah and Gemara make up the Talmud. Gemara is the recounting of the discussion and debates of the rabbis concerning the meaning and application of the Mishnah.

HALAKHAH—a kind of common law which took shape beside the written Torah, as a result of rulings of the early rabbis and discussions of Torah scholars. A kind of day-by-day guide of laws, ordinances, and practical rules.

HAGGADAH—Early Rabbinical interpretations of the historical and religious-doctrinal sections of the Bible.

MIDRASH—the interpretations of the rabbis arranged as a commentary on Scripture. It includes both halakhic and haggadic material.

MISHNAH—the collection of the oral tradition of halakhic rulings. The codification in six sections or Orders of the Oral Torah which included the halakhah or law, and the haggadah or the "preaching," which included maxim, parable, and wise counsel.

PERUSHIM—the term means "separated ones," and some scholars think it referred to a group who were the predecessors of the Pharisees.

PSEUDEPIGRAPHA—a term coming from a Greek word meaning "false superscription." The word has come to stand for those Christian and Jewish writings which were falsely ascribed to the apostles or certain Old Testament heroes. It is a second category of apocryphal literature.

TALMUD, BABYLONIAN—a combination of the Mishnah, its exegesis by Babylonian schools, and other discussions of the Babylonian schools which were codified in the fifth and sixth centuries CE. Haggadah is presented more richly here, and though not all the Mishnah is covered, this Talmud has become the primary one, being four times the length of the Jerusalem Talmud.

TALMUD, JERUSALEM (OR PALESTINIAN)—a combination of the Mishnah, its exegesis by Palestinian schools in the third and fourth centuries CE, and the views of the Amoraim, or scholars of the post-Mishnaic period.

TOSEFTA—a collection of law which does not hold the same rank as the Mishnah. The content of this "supplement" belongs to the period of the Tannaites, or scholars of the Mishnaic age.

AUTHOR INDEX

Abrahams, Israel, B272, B297
Ackroyd, Peter, C68
Albert, I., C146
Albright, William, B273, B274
Alexander, Philip, C160
Alon, Gedalia, B84, B85
Amaru, Betsy, C147
Amusin, Joseph, C1
Armenti, Joseph, C148
Aulen, Gustaf, B50
Aune, David, C69
Avery-Peck, Alan, C105
Avigad, Naham, B41
Avi-Yonah, Michael, B86, B87, B275, B276, B277
Ayers, Robert, B211
Baeck, Leo, B212, B298
Bagattiy, Bellarmino, B22
Bammel, Ernst, B51, B244, B323
Bampfylde, Gillian, C106
Banks, Robert, B236
Barbour, R.S., C182
Barnett, Paul, C50
Baron, Salo, B88, B89
Barr, James, C161
Barrett, C.K., B52, B245, C195
Barth, Marcus, C196
Basser, Herbert, C107, C183
Baumgarten, Albert, C108, C233, C234
Baumgarten, Joseph, B1, C2, C184, C267
Beckwith, Roger, B267, C3, C162
Ben-Dou, M., B42
Ben-Sasson, Haim, B90
Berkouits, Eliezer, C264
Best, Thomas, C223
Betz, Hans, B317

Finegan, Jack, B103, B279
Finkel, Asher, B303
Finkelstein, Louis, B104, B304, B305
Fiorenza, Elizabeth, B216
Fischel, Henry, B156
Fitzgerald, G.M., C214
Fitzmyer, Joseph, B9, B157, B253, C9
Flusser, David, B61, C56
Foakes-Jackson, Frederick, B28, B208
Foerster, Werner, B105
Forkman, Goeran B10
Freedman, David, B280
Frend, W. H. C., B29
Freyne, Sean, B106, C154
Friedlander, Gerald, B319
Fujita, Shozo, C36
Fuks, Gideon, C44
Gager, John, B30
Garnet, Paul, B11
Gartner, Bertil, B12
Gaster, Theodor, B13
Gaston, Lloyd, B44
Gauenta, Beverly, C229
Geller, Markham, C57, C238
Gerhardsson, Birger, B217
Ginzberg, Louis, B158
Glatzer, Nahum, B106
Golb, Norman, C10
Goldenberg, David, C110, C155
Goldstein, Morris, B62
Goodenough, Erwin, B281
Goodman, Martin, B282
Goppelt, Leonhard, B254
Goodblatt, David, B159
Gordis, Robert, C278
Goulder, Michael, B255
Grabbe, Lester, C73
Grant, Frederick, B256
Grant, Michael, B107, B108, B109
Grant, Robert, C167
Green, William, B109, C111
Guignebert, Charles, B110

INDEX OF BOOKS

Jewish Liturgy and Its Development, B164
The Jewish People in the First Century, B135
The Jewish Reclamation of Jesus, B63
Jewish Sects at the Time of Jesus, B310
The Jewish Sources of the Sermon on the Mount, B319
Jewish Symbols in the Greco-Roman Period, B281
A Jewish Understanding of the New Testament. Augmented ed,
    B263
The Jewish World in the Time of Jesus, B110
Jewish Writings of the Second Temple Period, B200
Jews and Christians: Graeco-Roman Views, B235
*Jews and Christians in Antioch in the First Four Centuries of the
    Common Era*, B220
*The Jews and Judaism During the Greek Period: The Background of
    Christianity*, B130
The Jews from Alexander to Herod, B134
*Jews, Greeks and Christians: Religious Cultures in Late Antiquity:
    Essays in Honor of William David Davies*, B111
The Jews in the Roman World, B108
Jews in Their Land in the Talmudic Age, 70-640 C.E, B84
*Jews, Judaism and the Classical World: Studies in Jewish History in
    the Times of the Second Temple and Talmud*, B85
The Jews: Their History, Culture and Religion. 4th ed, B104
Jews Under Roman and Byzantine Rule, B86
The Jews Under Roman Rule, B14
John and Qumran, B5
John the Baptist, B205
Josephus and Modern Scholarship, 1937-1980, B207
Josephus and the Jews, B208
Josephus the Man and the Historian, B210
Judaism and Christian Beginnings, B232
Judaism and Christianity, B211
*Judaism and Christianity: Origins, Developments and Recent
    Trends*, B212
*Judaism and Hellenism: Studies in Their Encounter in Palestine
    During the Early Hellenistic Period*, B112
Judaism and Scripture, B181
Judaism in the Beginning of Christianity, B223
*Judaism in the First Centuries of the Christian Era: The Age of
    Tannaim*, B174
Judaism in the Matrix of Christianity, B224
Judaism in the New Testament Period, B113

INDEX OF PERIODICAL AND
SERIAL ARTICLE TITLES

"Comparing Judaisms," C87
"Comparing Paul and Judaism: Rethinking Our Methods," C229
"Competence of the Sanhedrin," C260
"A Comparison of Early Christianity and Early Rabbinic Traditions," C180
"The Concept of God in the Works of Flavius Josephus," C157
"Contrasting Worlds in First Century Palestine," C219
"The Contribution of Qumran Aramaic to the Study of the New Testament," C9
"Covenant in Rabbinic Writings," C137
"The Credibility of Josephus," C150
"Cross and the Menorah," C171
"Crucifixion, the Nahum Pesher, and the Rabbinic Penalty of Strangulation," C112
"The Cultural Background of the Narratives in Luke I and II," C209
"The Daily and Weekly Worship of the Primitive Church in Relation to Its Jewish Antecedents," C162
"Dead Sea Scrolls," C10
"The Dead Sea Sect in Relation to Ancient Judaism," C18
"Defining the Pharisees: The Tannaitic Sources," C243
"Dealing Honestly With Judaism and Jewish History: James Parkes as a Model for the Christian Community," C72
"Death of Herod the Great," C31
"The Designated Number of Kinds of Labor Prohibited on the Sabbath," C252
"The Development of the Pharisaic Idea of Law as a Sacred Cosmos," C183
"The Dichotomy of Judaism During the Second Temple," C85
"Dietary Laws Among Pythagoreans, Jews and Christians," C167
"The Doctrine of the Two Messiahs in Sectarian Literature in the Time of the Second Commonwealth," C192
"Dreams and Their Interpretation from the Biblical Period to the Tannaitic Time: An Historical Study," C143
"Early Christian and Rabbinic Liturgical Affinities: Exploring Liturgical Acculturation," C177
"Early Halakhah in the Palestinian Targumim," C115
"Ellis Rivkin and the Problems of Pharisaic History: A Study in Historiography," C237
"The Encounter Between Pharisaic and Christian Judaism: Some Early Gospel Evidence," C248
"Episode of the Golden Roman Shields at Jerusalem," C45
"The Epistle of Enoch and the Qumran Literature," C16

"The History of Earlier Rabbinic Judaism: Some New Approaches,"
C88

"Idea of Purity in Ancient Judaism," C89

"The Ideology of the Temple in the Damascus Document," C7

"The Impact of the Dead Sea Scrolls on Jewish Studies During the
Last Twenty Five Years," C20

"The Impact of the Dead Sea Scrolls on the Study of the New
Testament," C21

"Innovation Through Repetition: The Role of Scripture in the
Mishnah's Division of Appointed Times," C126

"An Interdict Against Socializing on the Sabbath," C253

"Interpreting 'Pro-Jewish' Passages in Matthew," C200

"Interpreting Revolutionary Change: Political Divisions and
Ideological Diversity in the Jewish World of the First Century
A.D. Translated by M. Jolas," C101

"The Intertestamental Literature," C34

"Intertestamental Period" (bibliography), C40

"Issues in the Separation of Judaism and Christianity After 70 C.E.:
A Reconsideration," C168

"Jacob Neusner Issue," C132

"The Jerusalem Community and Kashrut Shatness," C43

"Jesus and Power," C66

"Jesus and the Food Laws: Reflections on Mark 7:15," C61

"Jesus and the Pharisees—The Problem as It Stands Today," C236

"Jesus and the Remnant of Israel," C60

"Jesus and the World of Judaism" (review essay), C56

"Jesus' Theugic Powers: Parallels in the Talmud and Incantation
Bowls," C57

"Jewish Background of the Incarnation," C173

"Jewish, Christian and Pagan Views of Miracle Under the Flavian
Emporers," C179

"Jewish Funerary Customs During the Second Temple Period: In
Light of the Excavations at the Jericho Necropolis," C74

"'Jewish Gnosis' And Gnostic Origins: A Survey," C27

"Jewish-Greek Conflict In First Century Caesarea," C80

"Jewish Literature and New Testament Exegesis: Reflections on
Methodology," C140

"Jewish Prayers in the Time of Jesus," C52

"Jewish Proselyte Baptism," C97

"Jewish Ritual of the 1st Century C.E. and Christian Sacramental
Behavior," C178

"The Jewish Sign Prophets—A.D.40-70: Their Intentions and Origin," C50

"Jewish Studies and New Testament Interpretation," C207

"John the Baptist and Essene Kashruth," C144

"Josephus and Hippolytus on the Pharisees," C148

"Josephus and Nicolaus on the Pharisees," C247

"Josephus and Population Numbers in First Century Palestine," C151

"Josephus as a Biblical Interpreter: The Aqedah," C152

"Judah the Essene and the Teacher of Righteousness," C14

"Judaism After Moore: A Programmatic Statement," C90

"Judaism and Gnosticism," C26

"Judaism and the Grand 'Christian' Abstractions: Love, Mercy and Grace," C175

"Judaism at the Time of Christ," C99

"Judaism in a Time of Crisis: Four Responses to the Destruction of the Second Temple," C274

"Judaism in Late Antiquity," C91

"Judicial Procedure in New Testament Times," C98

"Land Theology in Josephus' 'Jewish Antiquities,'" C146

"The Languages of Palestine in the First Century A.D," C215

"Legislation Concerning Relations with Non-Jews in the Zadokite Fragments and in Tannaitic Literature," C136

"Levitical Messianology in Late Judaism: Origins, Development and Decline," C165

"A Life of Yohanan Ben Zakkai," C102

"Light on the Cave Scrolls from Rabbinic Sources," C119

"'Like One of the Prophets of Old': Two Types of Popular Prophets at the Time of Jesus," C75

"Locating John the Baptizer in Palestinian Judaism: The Political Dimension," C145

"Lord's Prayer in the First Century," C58

"Loyalty and Law in New Testament Times," C183

"Luke iv. 16-30 and the Jewish Lectionary Cycle: A Word of Caution," C201

"Map Without Territory: Mishnah's System of Sacrifice and Sanctuary," C127

"Mark 2.1-3,6: A Bridge Between Jesus and Paul on the Question of the Law," C187

"The Martyrdom of the Galilean Troglodytes: A Suggested Traditions-geschichte," C82

"Masada: A Consideration of the Literary Evidence," C78

"Masada and the Sicari" C103

"The Meaning of Josephus" (Symposium), C153
"The Measure of Redemption: The Similitudes of Enoch, Nonviolence and National Integrity," C42
"Merkavah Mysticism and Rabbinic Judaism," C134
"The Message of Jesus," C59
"Messianic Symbols in Palestinian Archaeology," C174
"Messianic Themes in Formative Judaism," C193
"Metaphor of Plant in Jewish Literature of the Intertestamental Period," C36
"Methodology in the Study of Jewish Literature in the Graeco-Roman Period," C141
"Miracles and Halakah in Rabbinic Judaism," C108
"Mishnah and Messiah," C194
"The Mishnah: Methods of Interpretation" (Symposium), C121
"Mishnah's System of Santification," C105
"Mythology of Qumran," C8
"The Name of the Pharisees," C233
"New Apocalyptic," C203
"New Testament Eschatology," C196
"New Testament Issues in Jewish-Christian Relations," C181
"The New Testament Reconsidered: Recent Post-Holocaust Scholarship," C208
"A Note on Artistic Representations of the Second Temple of Jerusalem," C271
"Occasions of Grace in Paul, Luke, and First Century Judaism," C169
"Old and New in the History of Judaea" (Review Article), C213
"On the Use of the Term 'Galileans' in the Writings of Josephus Flavius" C147
"On the Value of Intertestamental Jewish Literature for New Testament Theology," C41
"Once More: Jesus in the Talmud," C110
"The Origin and History of the Samaritans," C256
"The Origin and Subsequent History of the Authors of the Dead Sea Scrolls: Four Transitional Phases Among the Qumran Essenes," C5
"The Origin of the Pharisees Re-affirmed," C249
"Origins of Baptism," C24
"Orthodoxy in Judaism of the First Christian Century," C83
"Orthodoxy in First Century Judaism?: A Response to N. J. McEleney," C69

"Orthodoxy in Judaism of the First Christian Century: Replies to D. E. Aune and L. L. Grabbe," C84

"Orthodoxy in First Century Judaism? What are the Issues?" C73

"Palestine in the Roman Period, 63 B.C.-A.D. 324," C214

"Palestinian and Hellenistic Judaism and Christianity: The Question of the Comfortable Theory," C176

"Palestinian Manuscripts, 1947-1972," C133

"Parties and Politics in Pre-Hasmonean Jerusalem: A Closer Look at 2 Maccabees 3:11," C35

"Passover and the Dating of the Aqedah," C222

"Patterns of Religion in Paul and Rabbinic Judaism: A Holistic Method of Comparison," C232

"Paul and Apocalyptic Judaism," C224

"Paul and Gamaliel," C228

"Paul and Rabbinic Exegesis," C226

"Paul and the People of Israel," C227

"Pauline Midrash: The Exegetical Background of Gal 3:19b," C225

"Persecution of the Jews and the Adherents of the Isis Cult at Rome A.D. 19," C86

"The Pharisaic Jesus and His Parables," C53

"'Pharisaic-Rabbinic' Judaism: A Clarification," C92

"The Pharisaic Paradosis," C234

"The Pharisaic-Sadducean Controversies About Purity and the Qumran Texts," C2

"Pharisaism and the Crisis of the Individual in the Greco-Roman World," C244

"Pharisees: A Historical Study," C250

"The Pharisees in the Jewish Revolution of 66-73," C246

"The Pharisees in the Light of Modern Scholarship," C240

"The Polemic on Miracles," C109

"The Political Synedrion in the Religious Sanhedrin," C261

"Popular Messianic Movements Around the Time of Jesus," C190

"The Pre-History and Relationships of the Pharisees, Sadducees and Essenes: A Tentative Reconstruction," C3

"Pre-Mishnaic Jewish Worship and the Phylacteries from the Dead Sea," C22

"The Present State of Research into the Targumic Account of the Sacrifice of Isaac," C113

"The Present State of the 'Son of Man' Debate," C65

"Primitive Church and Judaism," C163

"The Problem of the Two Messiahs in the Qumran Scrolls," C12

"Problems and New Perspectives in the Study of Early Rabbinic Ethics," C120

"A Prolegomenon to a New Study of the Jewish Rackground of the Hymns and Prayers in the New Testament," C198

"Publications of David Daube," C96

"The Question of Religious Influence: The Case of Zoroastrianism, Judaism, and Christianity," Cl61

"Qumran and Jerusalem: Two Jewish Roads to Utopia," C15

"Qumran Scrolls and Early Judaism," C13

"Rabbinic Judaism and the New Testament," C160

"Rabbinic Sources for New Testament Studies—Use and Misuse," C117

"The Rabbinic Traditions About the Pharisees Before A.D. 70: The Problem of Oral Transmission," C242

"Reading the Hebrew Scriptures in the First Century: Christian Interpretations in Their Jewish Context," C206

"Reading the Writing of Rabbinism: Toward an Interpretation of Rabbinic Literature," C111

"Recent Developments in the Study of Judaism 70-200 C.E.," C70

"Recent Literature of the Archaeology of Eretz Israel," C218

"Recent Study of the Sources for the Life of Jesus," C51

"The Reflection of Historical Events of the First Century B.C. in Qumran Commentaries (4Q 161; 4Q 169; 4Q 166)," C1

"Reflections About the Use of the Old Testament in the New in Its Historical Context," C210

"The Religious Background of the Psalms of Solomon (Re-evaluated in the Light of the Qumran Texts)," C17

"The Religious Teaching of the Synoptic Gospels in its Relation to Judaism," C205

"Research into Rabbinic Literature: An Attempt to Define the Status Quaestionis," C135

"Roman Emperor Gaius (Caligula)'s Attempt to Erect His Statue in the Temple of Jerusalem," C268

"The Roman Fortress at Tel Michal and Jewish Piracy Based in Jaffa," C71

"The Sabbath Year Cycle in Josephus," C149

"The Samaritans in Tannaitic Halakhah," C258

"The Samaritans in the New Testament," C259

"Sanders' 'Paul and the Jewish People'" (Book review), C231

"Scribes, Pharisees, Highpriests and Elders in the New Testment," C239

"Scribes, Pharisees, Lawyers, Hypocrites: A Study in Synonymity," C245

"Sicarii: Ancient Jewish 'Terrorists'," C76

"Sicarii and Masada," C104

"The Significance of Yavneh: Pharisees, Rabbis and the End of Jewish Sectarianism," C235

"The Similitudes of Enoch: Historical Allusions," C106

"Social Legislation of Jerusalem During the Latter Part of the Second Temple Period," C48

"Some Aspects of Traditions Received from Moses at Sinai," C79

"Some Notes on Scribes and Priests in the Targum of the Prophets," C114

"Some Textual Observations on the Sermon on the Mount," C262

"Spurious Interpretations of Rabbinic Sources in the Studies of the Pharisees and Pharisaism," C251

"Studies in Judaism: Modes and Contexts," C93

"Studies in the Semitic Background to the Gospel of Matthew," C204

"The Stuttering Servant Between the Testament," C39

"A Summary of the Law by Flavius Josephus," C158

"The Targum in the Synagogue and in the School," C142

"Targum, Midrash and the Use of the Old Testament in the New Testament," C212

"Targumic Literature and New Testament Interpretation," C118

"The Teaching of the Rabbis: Approaches Old and New," C128

"Techniques of Imperial Control: The Background of the Gospel Event," C197

"The Temple and the World," C272

"The Temple and Worship," C276

"Temple Cult and Law in Early Christianity: A Study in the Relationship Between Jews and Christians in the Early Centuries," C25

"Things That Defile (Mark 7:14) and the Law in Matthew and Mark," C186

"The Title Rabbi in the Gospels is Anachronistic," C67

"The Title Rabbi in the Gospels—Some Reflections on the Evidence of the Synoptics," C202

"Torah and Christ," C63

"Torah Tendencies in Galilean Judaism According to Flavius Josephus: With Gospel Comparisons," C156

"Toward the Natural History of a Religion: The Case of the Palestinian Talmud," C129

"Traditions in Ephesians," C195

"The Trial of Jesus in the Light of History: A Symposium," C278

"Uncircumcised Proselytes," C95

"The Un-Written Law in the Pre-Rabbinic Period," C185

INDEX OF PERIODICALS AND SERIALS

www.ingramcontent.com/pod-product-compliance
Lightning Source LLC
Chambersburg PA
CBHW031237090426
42742CB00007B/233